Manuel Palacio, Jörg Türschmann (Eds.)

Transnational Cinema in Europe

Beiträge zur europäischen Theater-, Film- und Medienwissenschaft

herausgegeben von

Verena Berger, Andrea B. Braidt
und Daniel Winkler

Band 4

LIT

Transnational Cinema in Europe

edited by

Manuel Palacio and Jörg Türschmann

LIT

Cover Image: Jörg Türschmann
Typesetting & Layout: Alexandra Paar
Printed with the support of:
Dekanat der Philologisch-Kulturwissenschaftlichen Fakultät
der Universität Wien

universität wien

Philologisch-Kulturwissenschaftliche Fakultät

Proyecto de Investigación I+D+i "El cine y la televisión en la España de la post-transición" (CSO2012-31895), Ministerio de Economía y Competitividad, Gobierno de España; "Las coproducciones cinematográficas españolas: aspectos sociales y de documentación". Comunidad de Madrid-UC3M. Ayuda a la consolidación de grupos de investigación. Ref. 2011/00098/001.

Bibliographic information published by the Deutsche Nationalbibliothek
The Deutsche Nationalbibliothek lists this publication in the Deutsche Nationalbibliografie; detailed bibliographic data are available in the Internet at http://dnb.d-nb.de.

ISBN 978-3-643-90478-2
A catalogue record for this book is available from the British Library

Klosbachstr. 107
CH-8032 Zürich
Tel. +41 (0) 44-251 75 05
Fax +41 (0) 44-251 75 06
E-Mail: zuerich@lit-verlag.ch
http://www.lit-verlag.ch

LIT VERLAG Dr. W. Hopf
Berlin 2013
Fresnostr. 2
D-48159 Münster
Tel. +49 (0) 2 51-62 03 20
Fax +49 (0) 2 51-23 19 72
E-Mail: lit@lit-verlag.de
http://www.lit-verlag.de

Distribution:
In the UK: Global Book Marketing, e-mail: mo@centralbooks.com
In North America: International Specialized Book Services, e-mail: orders@isbs.com
In Germany: LIT Verlag Fresnostr. 2, D-48159 Münster
Tel. +49 (0) 2 51-620 32 22, Fax +49 (0) 2 51-922 60 99, E-mail: vertrieb@lit-verlag.de
In Austria: Medienlogistik Pichler-ÖBZ, e-mail: mlo@medien-logistik.at
e-books are available at www.litwebshop.de

CONTENTS

PREFACE

The attempt to produce films for the international market has led to lively exchange relationships and meeting points between local as well as national identity discourses and global processes of identity formation. Co-productions alone can no longer be seen as an incentive for national cultural production. Rather, it is necessary to regard co-productions as a privileged site for an analysis of the relations between identity, nation and culture. They allow for an understanding of how, in a globalized world, the field between the local and the global, and the own and the foreign, is continually defined anew, and how new parameters of identity are created. The static concepts of national cinema cultures, which have been effective for a long time, are questioned in the case of co-productions, if not reduced to absurdity.

This volume is the result of a collaboration of two research groups in Madrid and Vienna, more specifically between the group TECMERIN ("Televisión y cine: memoria, representación e industria") of the Departamento de Periodismo y Comunicación Audiovisual of the University of Carlos III[1] and the Department of Romance Studies of the University of Vienna. The topic was "Film and television co-productions in the European context. Identities and processes of cultural transgression". The cooperation was funded by the Ministerio de Economía y Competitividad and the Austrian Agency for International Cooperation in Education and Research (Österreichischer Austauschdienst, OeAD), whom the editors wish to first thank at this point.

Transnational Cinema in Europe consists of articles by members of both research groups as well as by several experts who were generously willing to write about co-productions that were not the cooperation's purpose. Thus, also examples of Australia, England, France, Greece, Italy, Canada and the Scandinavian countries are taken into account. The editors are grateful to all those who have already contributed to the cooperation between Madrid and Vienna. These are Sagrario Beceiro, Concepción Cascajosa, Carmen Ciller, Alberto Elena, Juan Carlos Ibáñez in Madrid, and Verena Berger, Monika Bernold, Hanna Hatzmann, Christopher Laferl, Katharina Müller, Julia Wippersberg in Vienna. Particular thanks are due to Verena Berger, for her indefatigable dedication, her ideas and contacts all over the world. Additionally, the editors would like to thank Matthias Hausmann for the precise and careful corrections, Anahita Abrahamian for the ever punctual and thorough revision as well as the translations into English, and Alexandra Paar for her help concerning the layout.

The editors, Madrid and Vienna, October 2013

---

1 Proyecto de Investigación I+D+i "El cine y la televisión en la España de la post-transición" (CSO2012-31895), Ministerio de Economía y Competitividad, Gobierno de España; "Las coproducciones cinematográficas españolas: aspectos sociales y de documentación". Comunidad de Madrid-UC3M. Ayuda a la consolidación de grupos de investigación". Ref. 2011/00098/001.

Fundamentals, Databases and Television

Co-productions, Global Markets and New Media Ecologies

Doris Baltruschat

International co-productions enable filmmakers and television producers to pool finances, government subsidies, labour and talent for new project developments. Co-productions differ in their degree of government involvement (i.e. treaty co-productions), financial participation of non-treaty partners, and flexibility to structure co-venture type deals for cultural products to be distributed on the global market. The production technology dates back to the 1940s, but the turbulent economic, social and technological changes in the cultural industries during the 1990s gave co-productions an unprecedented boost. In particular, the dismantling of broadcasting monopolies in Europe, the ensuing re-regulation of the same along commercial mandates, digital convergences and the creation of multi-channel television services created ideal conditions for extending film and television production into international domains. At the same time, protective measures in the form of content regulations and cultural import restrictions aimed at the development of new markets to compete against the proliferation of U.S. media. One measure was the *Television without Frontiers* directive from 1992, which stipulated a 50% quota on foreign content to encourage the development of works by independent European producers. This initiative served economic as well as cultural purposes as governments sought to create economic opportunities for local industries, while collaborations were meant to foster a cultural identity – or in the case of Europe, a pan-European identity. Film and TV co-productions therefore played a vital role in the economic and cultural integration of Europe (Council of Europe, 1992). They were also important for establishing inter-regional trade between European nations and countries such as Canada and Australia.

The 1990s are synonymous with neo-liberal economics and trade liberalization, exemplified by the North American Free Trade Agreement (NAFTA) between the U.S., Mexico and Canada in 1993 and the overriding General Agreement on Tariffs and Trade (GATT), which became the World Trade Organization (WTO) in 1995. While France and Canada argued for the prerogative to establish national content regulations during the Uruguay Round, the U.S. pressed for a laissez faire approach to the international trade of cultural products. In the same vein, the U.S. called on European governments to lower cultural import quotas, which the Motion Picture Association of America termed as a "maimed, disabled theory…alien to the very objective of GATT, which is to reduce trade tension and break down trade barriers" (Jack Valenti, 1991, as cited in Given, 1995, p. 13). During this decade, the global market became a strategic priority for the U.K., France, Canada and Australia, and co-production was seen as a tool to finance high-quality productions for international distribution. Between 1995 and 2002, treaty co-productions between the U.K.

and Canada increased dramatically, but were then succeeded, in the mid 2000s, by co-financing deals between the U.K. and the U.S. and increasing intra-European co-productions. The following discussion traces the development of international co-production from a predominantly government and cultural policy directed approach to film and television to an increasingly flexible and profit-driven global production technology. In particular, the analysis reveals how media and cultural agents as part of global media production ecologies[1] are increasingly subjected to an international climate of trade liberalizations that stands in sharp contrast to cultural policies based on the advancement of cultural diversity[2].

A Global Production Technology for International Markets

Co-productions are governed by official treaties or consist of co-venture type arrangements between producers for the duration of film and TV production and distribution. In the scholarly literature, co-ventures are often referred to as co-productions as well to define different constellations of collaborative project development. For example, Jäckel (2003) cites examples of co-financing deals, such as presales to TV channels or foreign territories, and creative and financial collaborations between produces and broadcasters (p. 58). Morawetz, Hardy, Haslam & Randle (2007), on the other hand, equate 'co-producing' with 'co-financing' as collaborations on feature films are increasingly capital driven. In comparison, Miller, Govil, McMurria & Maxwell (2001) use the term to describe different types of collaborative work in film and television with an emphasis on the international division of cultural labour, which now defines global media production. This highlights that the terms 'treaty co-production' and 'non-treaty co-production' tend to be used interchangeably, even though distinct differences exist between these two production technologies, especially in regards to triggering public funding mechanisms. Non-treaty co-productions – better referred to as 'co-ventures' or co-financing deals – include collaborative business ventures between countries that do not have a treaty – such the U.K. and the U.S., and Canada and the U.S. – and co-productions that fall outside specifications outlined in a treaty. In turn, co-ventures allow for greater flexibility in production but may not be eligible for government funding.

1 The concept of 'media production ecologies' draws attention to activities, processes, lived realities and interdependencies that characterize the collaborative as well as competitive relationships between cultural producers. Production ecologies therefore encapsulate relational dynamics that exist between producers due to power differentials, access to resources, and the globalization of creative labour. In addition, they point towards the importance of technologies and tools – such as digital media and copyright – that now form an integral part of global production chains (also see Baltruschat, 2010).

2 The United Nations Educational, Scientific and Cultural Organization (UNESCO) adopted the 'Universal Declaration on Cultural Diversity' in 2002 to preserve the "common heritage of humanity" and cultural diversity, including biodiversity and cultural rights. Most importantly, the Declaration recognizes that cultural goods and services "which, as vectors of identity, values and meaning, must not be treated as mere commodities or consumer goods" (UNESCO, 2001, p. 11). Furthermore, the Convention on the Protection and Promotion of the Diversity of Cultural Expressions (UNESCO, 2005) promotes international cooperation, and encourages "the conclusion of co-production and co-distribution agreements" (p. 8) within the paradigm of fostering diverse cultural forms of expression.

The advantages of co-producing lie predominantly in the pooling of financial resources. Average production costs in Europe range between EUR 6–7 million (European Audiovisual Observatory [EAO], 2009). Co-productions, on the other hand, allow for productions with higher budgets. Co-productions also tend to be released in twice as many markets and, as a result, earn more admissions than national films (EAO, 2008). Access to international broadcasters and distributors is therefore key, especially since co-productions are embedded in production ecologies that are based on established relationships between media and cultural agents. Disadvantages of international co-productions relate to higher coordination costs such as long distance travel and dealing with additional government bureaucracies.

Another drawback to co-production is the potential loss over the creative process and cultural specificity. Co-production entails compromises in the treatment and style of content since different cultural backgrounds and methods of production inevitably influence overall project development. Specifically, creative compromises generate a context that links narrative development and genres to the conditions of the production technology itself. Since co-productions are meant to have a 'cross-border appeal' some storylines are more suitable, notably those that emphasize drama, human emotions and the dynamics of close relationships (Strover, 1995). Similarly, genres like science fiction, adventure and fairy tales are favoured for co-production as they transcend spatial and temporal boundaries; but typically, they tend to eschew any political or socially relevant content (Baltruschat, 2003).

Many co-productions feature globally recognized stars, which add to a co-production's appeal for broadcasters, distributors and audiences. However, the matching and mixing of actors and locations in some European co-productions have earned them the designation of 'Euro-puddings' because of their contrived narrative development. This results from allocating personnel and production facilities according to the level of participation from each country in order to achieve a balance in creative, technical and financial elements. The practice dates back to early co-productions in the 1950s and 1960s. Jäckel (2003a) describes how European co-producers typically used lead actors from each country to satisfy treaty stipulations. Also, co-productions, originally meant to create a distinct European cinema, later adopted Hollywood film practices, from launching stars to applying new technologies (i.e. colour film) and the reworking of previously released material. Similarly, in a study about more recent Australia France co-productions, Hammet-Jamart (2004) highlights the growing commercialization of international feature film co-productions in spite of an Australian cultural policy aimed at enhancing a domestic cultural industry. Her research reveals the "superficiality" of the Australian point system – meant to increase the country's "creative equity" in projects – by showcasing how the system is flexed to achieve economic targets rather than cultural objectives. Today, a focus on global distribution also leads producers to structure co-production deals that circumvent restrictions around financial and creative involvement from the U.S. For example, in the US $30 million production of the television series *Pillars of the Earth* (Bauer, 2010), producers used the more flexible German-Canadian co-production treaty. This allowed them access to government subsidies, but also enabled them to hire a writer and director from the U.S. As a result, the television series followed a distinctive U.S. style of editing, pacing and narrative progression, which in turn increased its appeal to U.S. broadcasters (MIPCOM, 2010).

The development of film and television programs is an elaborate and risky undertaking. Feature films, in particular, have high start-up costs, especially large-scale, first-time productions. Co-production therefore spreads the risks across partnerships between international producers, financiers and government agents; thus, stemming the impact of potential project failure. Within the broader context of the film and television industries, co-production is also linked to changing production practices, which are the result of new technologies, changing market demands and evolving production ecologies. First of all, film and television media are not renewable sources, but represent cultural products that are depleted once they have been consumed. Yet, since *re*-production costs are generally low, revenues can be recouped through DVD sales, video-on-demand and downloadable files for pay. Also, producers manage risk through creating product repertoires, serialization, sequels and prequels and their spin-offs. Other strategies involve the development of new technologies for 3D production. Innovation in this instance serves to differentiate feature film exhibition from the traditional viewing experience in order to draw audiences into the theatre space for a premium experience, which in turn increases profitability for theatre chains and distributors. In the same vein, the visual and special effects industries provide an important platform for the U.K. Since the early 2000s, post-production on global franchises such as the *Harry Potter* (Yates, 2007) series and the *Chronicles of Narnia* (Adamson, 2008), which are co-produced with large U.S. conglomerates like Warner Brothers and Walt Disney, has generated important revenues for its domestic film sector. Another significant development is the 'integrated approach' to film production, which links media project developments to broader objectives such as building industries across sectors, including the cultural industries, IT and knowledge based job creation and training opportunities as well as cross-promotion in the form of tourism (i.e. theme parks and movie tours) and image branding. Movie tours, in particular, represent a new industry that builds tourist attractions around franchises such as *Harry Potter* (i.e. walking tours in London, U.K.), the *Lord of the Rings* trilogy (in New Zealand), and the *Twilight* saga (in Portland, U.S., Vancouver, Canada, and Montepulciano, Italy, all shooting locations for the franchise). The integrated approach defines

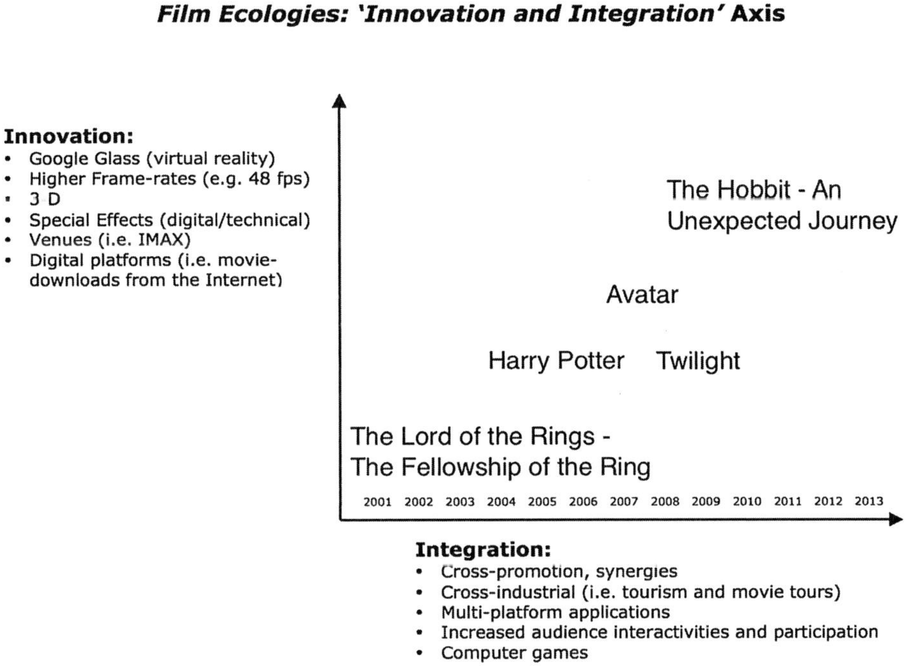

Figure 1: 'Innovation and Integration' Axis

film production, from the outset, as a business venture to benefit several industries at once in order to offset potential failure on the one hand, and to reap maximum returns, on the other. Film and television producers therefore increasingly structure their projects along an 'Innovation and Integration Axis', which facilitates the extension of production into new formats, technologies and industries (see Figure 1). As a result, international co-production now involves non-traditional partners in tourism, marketing and image branding as well as computer games development and multi-platform applications: thus, extending partnerships and alliances into new media production ecologies for short- or long-term project development, marketing and distribution.

The Rise and Decline of Treaty Co-productions

Canada's co-production treaty negotiations date back to 1963, when the country signed its first bilateral agreement with France for the production of feature films. Reasons for co-production included the notion that it would develop Canada's film industry through creating employment and exposure to more experienced partners, and that increased production would offset U.S. domination of Canada's film industry. Co-production was thus framed within an official policy for cultural protectionism. Between 1970 and 1985, Canadian producers averaged about four co-productions annually. Then, between 1986 and 2002, co-productions increased steadily until they peaked at over 100 per year. Co-production budgets also climbed to CDN $4.2-5.6 million (EUR 3.1-4.5 million). However, in stark contrast, co-productions declined rapidly in the mid 2000s due to changing international mandates and a growth in inter-European co-production activities. By 2005, Canadian co-productions had dropped by nearly 50% in comparison to numbers from the previous five years (Davidson, 2005) (see Figure 2).

This dramatic decline of Canada-European co-productions is the result of a combination of factors. Firstly, changes to expenditure requirements in the U.K. in 2003 impacted on international project developments. A temporary increase from 20% to 40% of minimum production spending requirements in the U.K. made collaborative projects very expensive for foreign producers. Secondly, a popular funding mechanism, the U.K. sale-lease-back,[3] was suspended in addition to the cancellation of U.K. equity funds by Inland Revenue in 2004.[4] Thirdly, European producers began to focus on inter-European co-productions since a common currency, a vast array of funding mechanisms (such as Eurimage and MEDIA)[5] and the close proximity of countries are conducive for collaborations on film and television productions. Also, European producers sought out co-producers in Eastern Europe because they offer established cinema traditions and a low-cost structure for production and locations. And finally, European co-productions fall under the European Convention on Cinematographic Co-production from 1992, which allows for participation from of non-signatory countries, such as the U.S., as long as the overall project promotes a European identity (Council of Europe, 1992).[6] As a result between 1998 and 2003, inter-European co-productions nearly doubled from 164 to 285, with U.K. projects growing from 37 to 99 and French projects from 78 to 114 (European Audiovisual Observatory [EAO], 2004).

3 Based on a tax deferral scheme, this mechanism enabled investors to reclaim previously paid taxes, which were then repaid over the duration of the lease.

4 Inland Revenue changed its tax deducting scheme to end alleged abuses of its existing co-production rules.

5 As of 2005, 182 different support mechanisms for feature film development exist in different European countries, amounting to EUR 1.3 billion (with the exclusion of tax incentives) (Morawetz et al.).

6 Co-producers from the U.S. are able to partake in a project as long as their financial investments do not exceed 30% of the total budget (Davenport Lyons, 2007).

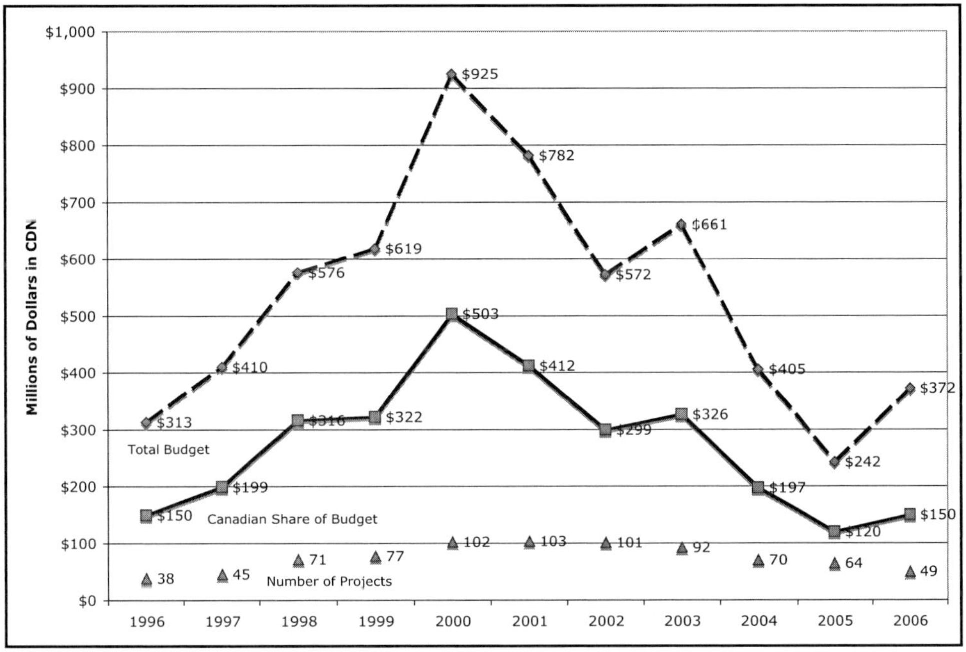

Figure 2: Co-production between European Partners and Canada, 1996–2006
Note. Based on data by Telefilm Canada, 1999; Baltruschat, 2003; Nordicity Group, 2006

According to Morawetz et al. (2007) key reasons for a steady increase in European co-production are a) the introduction of tax incentives to encourage private investments, and b) U.S. producers accessing European co-production mechanisms for big budget productions due to a shortfall of domestic funding opportunities. In the early 1990s, U.S. film financing became increasingly international through preselling distribution rights to international media companies (i.e. BMG or the German Kirsch Group) and insurance-backed securitization. However, due to high-risk ventures institutional investments from insurance companies failed in many instances with the result of a financing gap in the U.S. industry. Co-productions with European countries therefore provided a welcomed new revenue stream. At the same time, the introduction of tax incentives by European governments led to an inflow of capital into the film and television industries. This created a 'tax competition' between countries, which tried to match and overbid competitors' offers to attract investors. U.S. producers seized this opportunity to combine monies from multiple countries, leading to ever increasing budgets for movie production, and co-production for mainly economic reasons. For example, co-production budgets involving the U.K. increased from US $41.3 million in 2002 to US $77.6 million in 2003 (UK Film Council, 2004, p. 77). Also, U.K. feature film production generated US $1.91 billion in 2003, primarily due to U.S.–U.K. collaborations, which comprised 90% of foreign investment and 99 co-productions/co-ventures between the countries. In 2007, inward investments to the U.K. from U.S. studios amounted to US $1.04 billion with the result that foreign investments now account for 73% of U.K. production expenditures (Dawtrey, 2007).

According to a spokes person from the former U.K. Film Council[7] all co-production treaties are "cultural documents designed to be exploited for economic reasons" (interview with the author, July 27, 2005). Consequently, and in spite of their 'cultural' claim, they are increasingly used to develop film and television as global products rather than public goods. This emphasis on economic imperatives has to be placed within the neo-liberal context, which, since the 1990s, frames cultural production as a predominantly industrial exercise, even when cultural attributes are highlighted as the focal point. In other words, cultural arguments increasingly conceal economic directives aimed at expanding industries and increasing global market share. As a result, revenue streams, profits, prestige and audience attendance (or TV ratings) have become assessment tools by which the 'success' of cultural production is measured. These include, but are not limited to, the proverbial 'box office hits', often associated with Hollywood movies, the international recognition of genres based on the star system, and the establishment of film and television hubs connected to certain production centres (notably Los Angeles and Hollywood, but also Toronto due to its internationally recognized film festival, and Mumbai, India, a centre for Bollywood).

The Film Council's notion of co-production clearly highlights a new direction in co-production for the U.K., namely increased collaboration with U.S. film and television producers and investors. Under the European Convention, international co-productions can be structured along multi-lateral lines to allow for foreign investment in the form of U.S. funding and the use of 'international' stars, which are easily identifiable as Hollywood actors popularized through global promotional campaigns. According to a spokes person from the Council (interview with the author, July 27, 2005): "We recognized that if you're going to put together an independent film, it is almost impossible to raise the finance without a star who has an international reputation".[8] Consequently, feature films like *Troy* (Rathbun, Wilson & Petersen, 2004) and *Alexander* (Borman, Kilik, Schühly, Smith & Stone, 2004) are now, with a stretch of the imagination, considered 'European' because they are based on Greek myths and history. Similarly, *Cold Mountain* (Berger, Horberg, Pollack, Yerxa & Minghella, 2003), which starred Renée Zellwegger and Nicole Kidman, profited from the European convention on co-production as well as a low-cost location shoot in Romania. According to the Council (as cited in Terberl, 2005):

> [We are] encouraging investment into the UK that primarily comes from the major US studios. Films like *Harry Potter, Troy*, these very big US studio backed films. We encourage them to come into the UK to shoot, either through a, what is called *Schedule*

7 The U.K. Film Council will be closed by 2012 as a result of DCMS cost-cutting measures (Bennett, 2010).

8 The use of the star system in U.S.-U.K. co-ventures is evident in the numerous matching of British and American actors, especially in romantic comedies—notably the actor Hugh Grant (U.K.) with U.S. actors Andy MacDowell (Four Weddings and a Funeral, 1994), Julia Roberts (Notting Hill, 1999), Renée Zellweger (Bridget Jones, 2001 and 2004), Sandra Bullock (Two Weeks Notice, 2002), Drew Barrymore (Music and Lyrics, 2007) and Sarah Jessica Parker (Did You Hear About the Morgans?, 2009). A similar case can be made for Jude Law and Kate Winslet and to a lesser degree Colin Firth, Emma Thompson and Ewan McGregor (all actors from the U.K.).

> *1-structure*, which is where they do the majority of the work in the UK and spend it on UK or EU Commonwealth personnel. Or we encourage them to think about structuring it through co-production. (p. 80; emphasis in the original)

The prolific U.S. involvement in co-production arrangements with the U.K. and other European countries has a direct impact on treaty co-production partners. For example, the increasing use of 'stars' necessitates a new 'flexibility' in international co-productions with countries like Canada, which had to adjust its official guidelines to allow for increased U.S. involvement in the production of its publicly funded media – a clear departure from original mandates that emphasized cultural protectionism. This also shows how the so-called balance between economic and cultural imperatives actually represents a gradual shift towards predominantly industrial benefits. In this equation, cultural attributes are turned into international marketing tools to attract foreign production to domestic locations, which are the 'hub' and "centre of excellence for global film activity" (DCMS, 2005) and designated to enhance the international prestige of local industries, production facilities and talent. This is clearly exemplified by the 'Cultural Test', which was introduced in 2005 after consultation with U.K. industry representatives.

The Cultural Test highlights the complex balancing act to determine guidelines for British film certification in a global media market. The Test, which is based on a point system (31 points in total, 16 points are needed to pass), measures the degree of British 'cultural attributes' in a film to determine if it qualifies for tax subsidies. Originally the test emphasized the utilization of U.K. production services, but then had to refocus its target on British cultural attributes as a result of pressures from the European Commission (2006), whose permission was needed to align the new U.K. feature film tax incentives with EC State Aid Rules. Consequently, the DCMS increased the amount of points for the content of a film and decreased the point values for where the film was made. Yet, even though the test was revised because it placed "too much emphasis on the economic elements of film-making i.e. where the film was made and the persons employed to make it, and therefore had the capability of affecting intra-Community trade" (DCMS, 2006), the predominant focus remains on budgetary spending in the U.K. This is exemplified by the sequel to the *Chronicles of Narnia* titled *Prince Caspian*, which produced by Disney (U.S.) and Walden Media (U.K.), now qualifies as a British production because it is based on a British book, features lead actors from the U.K. and is generally "infused with a British sensibility" (Dawtrey, 2006). According to a statement by Disney (as cited in Dawtry, 2006):

> We are pleased to confirm that 'Prince Caspian' is expected to qualify as a British film under the government's new cultural points test. ... While the majority of filming will take place outside the U.K., the majority of the post-production and visual effects, which constitute a significant part of the overall production budget, will take place in the U.K. (p. 6)

The DCMS cultural test thus exemplifies the extent to which European countries like the U.K. have become integrated into the global market. As a result, treaty co-production partners have to adjust official guidelines in order to successfully navigate this new and challenging terrain of international co-production.

Summary and Conclusion

International co-productions became an important focal point for film and television industries in the 1990s. Yet, as the global market became a strategic priority, domestic film and television production sectors went through a period of downsizing in the form of cutbacks to public service broadcasting and cultural agencies.[9] Initially, treaty co-production proliferated. But then, in 2003, international treaty co-productions declined rapidly and were succeeded by inter-European co-productions and co-financing deals with U.S. partners. The dramatic decline of treaty co-productions highlights the volatility of this production technology, which interlinks cultural policies from international jurisdictions, and subjects producers to changing fiscal and cultural priorities in the global market place. It also highlights a shift in focus from collaborative cultural production to capital driven projects for international distribution. This change in priorities towards economic imperatives is the direct result of market deregulation and its devastating effects on public subsidies, which has led to the commercialization of the 'public good' and 'public space'. Closely linked to these developments is the process of 'normalizing' commercial sponsorship and branding, now synonymous with most forms of cultural production and events. Within the neo-liberal paradigm 'culture' is equivalent to 'industry' and, consequently, becomes an entity based entirely on profit motives and capitalist values. In other words, culture as a common, accessible form of practice for the celebration, documentation and reflection on the human condition – connected to particular moments in time and associated with experiences tied to specific locales – is undermined by a preemptive ideological framework.

The neo-liberal turn in cultural production is also reflected in cultural policy, which historically made a distinction between arts and commerce. In the 1990s, the traditional patronage of the arts, protection of the freedom of the press and public service broadcasting gave way to deregulating the public sector and prioritizing economies of scale, vertical and horizontal integration of corporations, and the maximization of audiences (Garnham, 2005). As noted, the cultural industries are defined by their high costs and risks in production, on the one hand, and low costs of reproduction and distribution, on the other. Within this paradigm, novelty is priced highly, as is the creation of needs to be satisfied by consumer and 'lifestyle' products. This in turn, favours large corporations with the ability to fund research and development for new product and service lines. It also provides the basis for their 'deep' involvement in cultural production and "the actual constitution of the cultural object itself in pursuit of corporate goals" (McGuigan, 2005, p. 235). Indeed, the increasing commercialization of cultural production is clearly evidenced in the exponential growth in branded entertainment in film and television. Since the late

9 Examples range from the BBC, which had to face increasing 'institutional flexibility', particularly through outsourcing and subcontracting of labour and the establishment of its commercial arm, BBC World, to the closure of the U.K. Film Council. In the case of Canadian cultural institution, the Canadian Broadcasting Corporation (CBC) faced a 30% budget reduction (over $414 million) by 2000 and the loss of 3000 jobs (Gurd, 1998, p. 47). Similarly, Telefilm Canada's annual parliamentary appropriation was reduced from $145 million in 1991–1992 to $78.5 million in 1999–2000.

1990s, product placements in television programs have grown by over 20 percent annually, with feature films not lagging far behind (Baltruschat, 2011).

Official co-productions create interdependencies between media and cultural agents, which can result in amplifying the risks associated with film and television production rather than mitigating it. The sudden collapse of treaty co-productions in the mid 2000s emphasizes that this production technology does not guarantee the development of stable, long-term film and television industries. On the contrary, the shift towards economic priorities led to changes in official co-production guidelines that undermined original mandates meant to reinforce media diversity. In addition, these developments blurred the boundaries between treaty co-production and co-ventures and consequently shifted the focus from collaborative cultural production to capital driven projects for global markets. International co-productions in the form of co-ventures and co-financing deals will continue to expand with the growth of multi-platform media and interactive program content in film and television. Driven by new creative partnerships across the cultural industries, co-production will thus move beyond official treaties and traditional alliances to open the doors to a wide variety of producers of video games, digital content and 3D entertainment. Consequently, these new production ecologies are going to define the media landscape of the future.

BIBLIOGRAPHY

Acheson, K. / Maule, C. "Convention on cultural diversity". *Journal on Cultural Diversity* 28 (2004), p. 243-256.

Acland, C.R. "Cinemagoing and the rise of the megaplex". *Television & New Media* 1.4 (2000), p. 375-402.

Baltruschat, D. "International film and TV co-productions: A Canadian case study". In: S. Cottle (ed.). *Media organization and production*. London: Sage Publications, 2003, p. 181-207

Baltruschat, D. *Global Media Ecologies: Networked Production in Film and Television*. New York: Routledge, 2010.

Baltruschat, D. "'Branded Entertainment'". In: G. Sussman (ed.). *The Propaganda Society: Neoliberalism and the Regime of Public Persuasion*. New York: Peter Lang, 2011.

Bennett, R. "Axing the Film Council: a move that impoverishes us all". *The Guardian* (26.7.2010), URL: http://www.guardian.co.uk/film/2010/jul/26/uk-film-council-abolished-reaction (05.08.2010).

Canadian Filmmaker. *To co-produce or not to co-produce?*, URL: http://www.canadianfilmmaker.com/content/view/81/33/ (05.01.2007).

Council of Europe. *European convention on cinematographic co-production (ETS No. 147)* 1992, URL: http://conventions.coe.int/Treaty/en/Reports/Html/147.htm (05.02.2006).

Davenport Lions. *The UK's co-production treaties and UK government and European Union subsidies*, URL: www.davenportlyons.com/html/legal_services/articles/film_tv/uk_co_production_treaties.doc (09.09.2007).

Davidson, S. "International copros drop by 50%". *Playback Magazine* (28.3.2005), URL: http://www.playbackmag.com/ (09.07.2005).

Dawtrey, A. "'Caspian' to qualify as U.K. movie. London companies to be given much of the effects work". *Variety* (13.12.2006), URL: http://www.variety.com/ (26.02.2007).
Dawtrey, A. "Majors fund British films. U.K. Film Council releases new statistics". *Variety* (12.11.2007), URL: http://www.variety.com/ (10.12.2007).
Department for Culture, Media and Sport (DCMS). *Estelle Morris announces tightening up of co-production treaties* (April 2004), URL: http://www.culture.gov.uk/global/press_notices/archive_2004/dems044_04.htm (02.062005).
DCMS. *The UK and international film co-production agreements*. London: DCMS, 2005.
DCMS. *British film fest gets green light* (2006). URL: http://www.culture.gov.uk/ (02.03.2007).
European Audiovisual Observatory (EAO). *Yearbook 2004, volume 3: Film and home video*, URL: http://www.obs.coe.int/oea_publ/ (12.06.2005).
EAO. *The circulation of European Co-productions and entirely national films in Europe, 2001 to 2007* (2008), URL: www.coe.int/t/dg4/cultureheritage/culture/film/paperEAO_en.pdf (10.11.2010).
EAO. Focus 2009. *World film market trends*. (2009), URL: www.obs.coe.int/oea_publ/market/focus.html.en?print (10.11.2010).
European Commission. *State aid: Commission approves revised U.K. film tax incentive scheme* (22.09.2006), URL: http://europa.eu (09.05.2007).
Garnham, N. "From cultural to creative industries. An analysis of the implications of the 'creative industries' approach to arts and media policy making in the United Kingdom". *International Journal of Cultural Policy* 11.1 (2005), p. 15-29.
Given, D.M. "'Plus ça change, plus c'est la meme chose': European coproduction remains viable, for now". *The Entertainment and Sports Lawyer* (1995), URL: http://www.phillaw.com/html/co-productions.html (12.01.2006).
Gurd, G. "Canada". In: Albarran, A. B. / Chan-Olmsted, S. M. (eds.). *Global media economics. Commercialization, concentration and integration of world media markets*. Ames, IA: Iowa State University Press, 1998, p. 33-50.
Hammett-Jamart, J. "Regulating diversity: Cultural diversity, national film policy and the international co-production of films". *Media International Australia Incorporating Culture and Policy* 111 (2004), p. 46-62.
Jäckel, A. *European film industries*. London: British Film Institute, 2003.
Jäckel, A. "Dual nationality film productions in Europe after 1945". *Historical Journal of Film, Radio and Television*, 23.3 (2003), p. 231-243.
McGuigan, J. "Neo-liberalism, culture and policy". *International Journal of Cultural Policy* 11.3 (2005), p. 229-241.
Miller, T. / Govil, N. / McMurria, J. / Maxwell, R. *Global Hollywood*. London: BFI, 2001.
MIPCOM. "The Pillars of the Earth" Co-production Masterclass, URL: www.mipcom.com (10.11.2010).
Morawetz, N. / Hardy, J. / Haslam, C. / Randle, K. "Finance, policy and industrial dynamics – The rise of co-productions in the film industry". *Industry and Innovation* 14.4 (2007), p. 421-443.
Nordicity Group Ltd. "Green paper: The future of television in Canada". Prepared for the The Banff World Television Festival 2006 (08.06.2006), URL: http://www.nglglobal.com/reports/The_Future_of_Television_in_Canada.pdf (10.07.2006).
Strover, S. "Recent trends in co-productions: The demise of the national". In: Corcoran, F. / Preston, P. (eds.). *Democracy and communication in the new Europe*. Cresskill, NJ: Hampton Press, 1995, p. 97-123.
Terberl, D. *Perspektiven europäischer Koproduktionen, auf Basis der bilateralen Koproduktionsabkommen unter der 'European convention of cinematographic co-production' am Beispiel von Deutschland und Großbritannien*. Unpublished master's thesis, Hochschule für Film und Fernsehen Konrad Wolf, Potsdam-Babelsberg, Brandenburg, 2005.

Telefilm Canada. "Co-productions: 20 years of co-productions on the international scene". *International Affairs* (1999), URL: http://www.telefilm.gc.ca/enaffint/coprod/20_ans.htm (10.10.1999).

UK Film Council. *Statistical yearbook 2003/04* (2004), URL: http://www.ukfilmcouncil.org.uk (12.06.2005).

UNESCO. *Convention on the protection and promotion of the diversity of cultural expressions* (20.10.2005), URL: http://unesdoc.unesco.org/images/0014/001429/142919e.pdf (12.03.2007).

FILMOGRAPHY

Alexander (2004). Dir. Oliver Stone. United States: Warner Brothers Pictures.

Cold mountain (2003). Dir. Anthony Minghella. United States: Miramax Films, MirageEnterprises.

Harry Potter and the order of the phoenix (2007). Dir. David Yates. United States: Warner Brothers Pictures.

The Chronicles of Narnia: Prince Caspian (2008). Dir. Andrew Adamson. United States: The Walt Disney Company.

The Pillars of the Earth [Television series] (2010). Prod. Rola Bauer. Germany: Tandem Communications.

Troy (2004). Dir. Wolfgang Petersen. United States: Warner Brothers Pictures.

CO-PRODUCTIONS ARCHIVE: ARCHIVING AND CATALOGING OF FILM CO-PRODUCTIONS

Sagrario Beceiro and Carmen Ciller

Nowadays, collaboration among production companies from different countries in a film production results in greater complexity when it comes to establishing the film's nationality, thereby posing different issues for researchers regarding what is considered a national or foreign film. In any case, co-production is an increasingly common mode of collaboration with important economic and cultural repercussions, regardless of its conception as a process of transnationalization or, on the contrary (and sometimes simultaneously), as a process of "glocalization" – and not globalization – an attachment to what is local, identitary, and multicultural (Pohl/Türschmann, 2007, p. 15-19).

The complexity and gradual increase of the international co-production phenomenon makes its research from different points of views important, and also increases the need to have trustworthy and verifiable data that are sometimes hardly accessible to researchers. The present chapter, thus, focuses on this latter issue.

The aim of this chapter contemplates two main aspects: an analysis of the current situation of the cataloging system of film co-production and an inquiry into the appropriateness of the creation of a specific database, a unique archiving and cataloging system, for the Spanish film co-productions with different Latin American and European countries from 1978, the beginning of democracy in Spain. The main objective of this data base consists in providing interested academics and researchers with reliable references about the evolution of the Spanish co-productions. It would also be appropriate to complement the creation of this database with an archive on legislation and bibliography, at least in the European and Latin American settings.

In addition, the study of these issues will allow for an approximation, albeit an introductory one, in order to understand the circumstances of production and international circulation of Spanish film co-productions, reflect on the legal framework in which these operate, compile relevant information about its repercussion, and single out its importance within the context of current globalization processes.

1. Co-production Agreements

It is quite customary for the definition of film co-production to be very much linked to the interests of each researcher or the specific elements to be analyzed (e.g. Borau, 1998; Moreno, 2008; Fuentes, 2011): economic and market purpose, co-operation and international relations tool, competitive strategy against American film, creative inquiry, component of diversity and multiculturalism, etc.

However, from the point of view of the present work, we are interested in a definition that highlights the obligations constituting the normative framework in which co-productions operate. To this end, we will use the definition by the *Instituto de la Cinematografía y de las Artes Audiovisuales* (ICAA) (Institute of Film and the Audiovisual Arts) of Spain, which understands international co-production[1] as a film work carried out in collaboration with foreign companies, in compliance with the conditions demanded by the specific laws in every country and the existing international agreements (multilateral and bilateral agreements).

This formula of legal co-operation to which ICAA makes reference allows the co-produced film to attain a nationality certificate from all the co-producing countries, access all types of grants for the film production, distribution, and exhibition under the same conditions as the rest of the native films, and it counts toward fulfilling the requirement of minimum share of screens exhibiting native films in those countries that have such protection mechanisms.

Additionally, the Film Co-production Agreements are ratified by two or more countries with the aim to achieve several objectives, among which are, obviously, to stimulate the development of the film industry of the participating countries, reconcile different legal frameworks and policies with regards to film, and contribute to the growth of economic and cultural exchanges.

Table 01. SPAIN: MULTILATERAL FILM CO-PRODUCTION AGREEMENTS
Ibero-American Film Integration Agreement Caracas, November 11, 1989.
Latin American Film Co-production Agreement Caracas, November 11, 1989.
European Film Co-production Agreement Strasbourg, October 2, 1992.

Spain has sanctioned two fundamental, multilateral agreements: the *European Film Co-production Agreement*, ratified by Spain in 1996, and the *Ibero-American Film Integration Agreement* (linked to the *Latin American Film Co-production Agreement*), ratified in 1992.

Both agreements are applied to the multilateral co-productions, but also to bilateral projects whenever there is no specific agreement among the countries participating in the co-production. Moreover, these multilateral agreements are applied in a subsidiary manner to those aspects that are not included in the agreements signed by two countries, so that the content of the latter may not contradict, in any case, their main clauses.

1 See: http://www.mcu.es/cine/CE/Industria/CoproduccionesInternacionales.html [Search: 05/10/2012]

Table 02. SPAIN: BILATERAL FILM CO-PRODUCTION AGREEMENTS

Germany Film Relationships Agreement between the Government of the Kingdom of Spain and the Federal Republic of Germany. Berlin: 02-11-00.	**Morocco** Co-production Agreement and film exchanges between the Kingdom of Spain and the Kingdom of Morocco: 04-27-98.
Argentina Hispanic-Argentine film relationships agreement: 08-28-69.	**Mexico** Film Co-production Agreement between the Kingdom of Spain and the United Mexican States: 01-30-04.
Brazil Exchange of Letters concerning Film Co-production, from 12-02-63.	**New Zealand** Film Co-production Agreement between the Kingdom of Spain and New Zealand. Madrid: 01-16-08.
Canada Film Relationships Agreement between the Government of Spain and the Government of Canada: 01-14-85. Exchange of Letters from 09-17-90 and 04-12-91 and annex, under which the Agreement is modified (07-11-91).	**Portugal** Film Relationships Agreement between the Kingdom of Spain and the Portuguese Republic. Madrid: 11-08-89.
Chile Memorandum of Collaboration concerning the co-production, promotion, dissemination, and conservation of the Film Heritage between the Ministry of Education, Culture, and Sports of the Kingdom of Spain and the National Council of Culture and Arts of the Republic of Chile.	**Puerto Rico** Memorandum of Collaboration between the Institute of Film and the Visual Arts of the Kingdom of Spain and the Corporation of the Development of the Arts, Sciences, and Film Industry of the Commonwealth of Puerto Rico: 05-27-03.
Cuba Film Collaboration Agreement between the Kingdom of Spain and the Republic of Cuba: 03-03-88. Effective as of: 01-31-90.	**Russia** Film Relationships Agreement between the Kingdom of Spain and Russia. Madrid: 10-26-90.
France Film Relationships Agreement between the Kingdom of Spain and the French Republic: 03-25-88. Exchange of Letters from 11-28-96 and 01-21-96, under which the Agreement is modified.	**Tunisia** Film Agreement between the Kingdom of Spain and the Government of Tunisia: 11-02-71.
Ireland Co-operation Protocol between the Institute of Film and the Audiovisual Arts of the Ministry of Culture of Spain and the Irish Film Council of the Republic of Ireland for the creation of film co-productions: 12-26-08.	**Venezuela** Film Co-production Agreement between the Kingdom of Spain and the Bolivarian Republic of Venezuela. Madrid: 06-20-96.
Italy Hispanic-Italian Agreement signed in Bologna on 09-10-97.	

Source: Personal compilation based on ICAA data

To this date, Spain has hardly signed any agreements with African (only Morocco) or Oceanian (only New Zealand) countries, and it has not subscribed to any agreements with the Asian continent. Even though it is possible for new bilateral agreements with Asia, Africa, or Oceania to be added, the most plausible reasons for this evident shortage may be, at least as a first approach, the clear absence of cultural connections, the difference in economic and industrial models, and the heightened discrepancies in the film producing routines between continents.

Nonetheless, it is also evident that it is not only an issue of tradition or culture, but of industrial and commercial importance, as well. Thus, European countries with a film market that is larger than the Spanish one in size and economic weight, such as the French market, have already signed bilateral agreements beyond the historical relationships that bind them to certain Asian, African, or Oceanian countries. Other cases, such as that of the United Kingdom, are similar to or even more limited than the Spanish one (See Table 03).

Table 03. BILATERAL FILM CO-PRODUCTION AGREEMENTS (Year 2011)

		FRANCE		
ALGERIA ARGENTINA AUSTRALIA AUSTRIA BELGIUM BRAZIL BULGARIA BURKINA FASO CAMEROON CANADA	CHILE CZECH REPUBLIC COLOMBIA DENMARK EGYPT FINLAND GEORGIA GERMANY GREECE GUINEA	HUNGARY ICELAND INDIA ISRAEL ITALY IVORY COAST LIBANON LUXEMBOURG MEXICO MOROCCO	NEW ZEALAND NETHERLANDS POLAND PORTUGAL ROMANIA RUSSIA SENEGAL SOUTH KOREA SPAIN SWEDEN	SLOVAKIA SWITZERLAND TUNISIA TURKEY UK VENEZUELA FORMER YUGOSLAVIA
		ITALY		
ALBANIA ALGERIA ARGENTINA AUSTRALIA AUSTRIA BELGIUM BELGIUM (FRENCH COMM.)	BRASIL BULGARIA CANADA CHILE CHINA CUBA CZECH REPUBLIC	FRANCE GERMANY FORMER YUGO- SLAVIA HUNGARY INDIA ISRAEL MACEDONIA	MEXICO MOROCCO NEW ZEALAND PORTUGAL ROMANIA RUSSIA SLOVAKIA	SOUTH AFRICA SPAIN SWEDEN SWITZERLAND TUNISIA URUGUAY VENEZUELA
		GERMANY		
AUSTRALIA AUSTRIA BELGIUM BRASIL	CANADA FORMER YUGO- SLAVIA FRANCE HUNGARY	INDIA ISRAEL ITALY LUXEMBOURG	NEW ZEALAND PORTUGAL SOUTH AFRICA SPAIN	SWEDEN SWITZERLAND
		UNITED KINGDOM		
FRANCE CANADA	AUSTRALIA NEW ZEALAND	SOUTH AFRICA	INDIA	JAMAICA

Source: Personal compilation based on cineuropa.org[2] data

2 See: http://cineuropa.org/2011/dd.aspx?t=dossier&l=es&tid=1364&did=144475 [Search: 10/05/2012]

These data show that film co-production is a complex activity in which "globalization" is many times fulfilled in the form of an association/contribution by reasons alluding to geographic and historical affinities or a singular access to economic and/or technological resources, and in a creative process where conflicts and readjustments abound, continuously conditioning the same (Moreno, 2008, p. 96).

Following this line of analysis, and though it is not the explicit aim of this work, it is necessary to point out that the creative possibilities mentioned above, the diversity, and the cultural hybrids are key issues to take into account whenever an audiovisual production that has been created according to these prescriptions is analyzed. Other key issues are the different forms of co-production (minority/majority, financial, etc.), in addition to the corresponding legislation and grant, promotion, and protection programs in each geo-political environment. There is a European data base, KORDA (http://korda.obs.coe.int), which belongs to the European Audiovisual Observatory and catalogs the public organisms of 36 European countries according to their support programs and grants for film and audiovisual works. This database is applicable to co-productions and also includes specific grants for co-productions between member countries and with third parties.

2. Cataloging System and Databases

Data compilation, the research of resources, or the access to updated and trustworthy information, is vital today for researchers who are analyzing the importance attached to co-productions in the audiovisual sector in general, and in the film industry in particular. There are currently numerous references and databases, albeit partial and incomplete, of a very diverse nature. As we will see next, this diversity clearly hinders the analysis and contrast between sources.

If we analyze the information we have and what shortcomings we have observed in the reference databases that have been consulted, we ought to consider a national and regional dimension. At a national dimension, we registered the main Spanish database, carried out by the ICAA, having established itself as one of the most reliable sources for an initial compilation of information. The obtained results and tables have been directly contrasted with other transnational databases and sources. This comparison has shown the differences among sources according to the origin and purpose for which the compiled data were created. Once this initial step was completed, where the difficulty of merging the data in a specific database on co-productions was confirmed, we decided to contrast this reality with available references and databases from other European and Latin American countries. This last phase is still in progress because of the significant limitations that have been detected among them, the difficult access to the contents and sources in some cases, and the different problems about their joint or unified conceptualization, among other reasons.

A) ICAA Database

The database of films rated for their opening at Spanish movie theaters belonging to the Spanish ICAA is what provides us with the most complete information. It collects data on Spanish co-productions, but it is not conceived as a specific database, and therefore, presents some shortcomings which we will comment on below.

Table 04. SPAIN-LATIN AMERICA CO-PRODUCTIONS, 1978-2009 (Sample of countries participating in the Ibermedia Program)	
Argentina	144
Bolivia	2
Brazil	9
Colombia	18
Costa Rica	0
Cuba	52
Chile	21
Ecuador	2
Guatemala	0
Mexico	110
Panama	2
Peru	12
Puerto Rico	7
Dominican Republic	1
Uruguay	11
Venezuela	27

Source: ICAA Database, films that premiered in Spanish movie theaters

Table 05. SPAIN-EUROPE CO-PRODUCTIONS, 1978-2009 (Sample of countries: EU15)	
Germany	75
Austria	6
Belgium	30
Denmark	3
Finland	1
France	285
Greece	6
Ireland	8
Italy	205
Luxembourg	7
Netherlands / Holland	2/ 15
Portugal	64
United Kingdom	103
Sweden	2

Source: ICAA Database, films that premiered in Spanish movie theaters

The following are some issues to take into account regarded the data collected in the official ICAA database that justify the need to create a specific database on co-productions:

1. While being the most reliable and complete database that is currently available, it does not constitute a specialized source in co-productions, and therefore, these are not differentiated from the rest of the films. Co-produced films should be isolated in a joint search of countries according to the specifications established by the tool, e.g., Spain-Brazil.

2. The ICAA database makes reference to films that have premiered, and not to the co-productions that may have been carried out without reaching the Spanish movie theaters. A feature film co-produced by Spain that has not been premiered in Spain for one reason or another does not appear in this database.

3. Some of the co-productions are multi-party, and the data being provided lead us, in some cases, to certain confusion that may only be resolved by observing each case individually, e.g., a Spain-Argentina-Brazil co-production often appears counted twice: as a co-production with Argentina and as a co-production with Brazil.

B) International / Transnational Databases

For a comprehensive overview of co-productions (whether or not they have premiered in Spanish movie theaters), it is necessary to cross the ICAA database data with other sources and databases.

In the case of Latin America, there is the possibility of crossing the data with the IBERMEDIA database and with those of the *Fundación del Nuevo Cine Latinoamericano* (New Latin American Film Foundation), which keeps a database on the distribution of films in the Latin American setting. In the case of Europe, this is possible with the European Union's LUMIÈRE database and the data on the financing of co-productions of the Council of Europe's Eurimages Fund.

The IBERMEDIA Database (www.programaibermedia.com) collects the data of those co-productions financed by this organism since 1998. Its webpage is currently under construction and only allows access to data from up to 2007. Regarding the database of the *Fundación del Nuevo Cine Latinoamericano* (www.cinelatinoamericano.org), it does not allow searches of co-productions, and only collects data of films from a dozen countries as long as the film distributor and the countries where the film has opened are entered into the search engine. Because of this difficulty, it has been decided to reject this source.

The European Audiovisual Observatory's LUMIÈRE database (http://lumiere.obs.coe.int), in collaboration with the MEDIA program, offers the available data on European films that have premiered in European movie theaters since 1996. Its operation is similar to the ICAA database, but the included items are very diverse in relation to the different countries due to the need of crossing different national/state traditions for counting the data. In addition, this database is still a work-in-progress, and although it is still significant and detailed, the inclusion of a considerable amount of information is still pending.

Eurimages (www.coe.int/t/dg4/eurimages) is the Council of Europe's fund assigned to the co-production, distribution, and exhibition of European films. Its page contains very synthetic data of the European co-productions that have been co-financed by Eurimages since 1989.

The main problem of combining data through the databases of ICAA, IBERMEDIA, LUMIÈRE, and Eurimages consists in the fact that its nature and justification are very different. Consequently, they are scattered and show little coherence for researches specific to co-productions. Difficulties are made evident, among others:

- In the time period: the ICAA database covers the entire period being analyzed in the present project, but Ibermedia only contains data since 1998, and Eurimages offers, at least momentarily, the data of co-financed co-productions since 1989.
- In the typology of entered data: some sources list the co-productions according to the production year, and some others, according to the year of exhibition. Another example is that, during the last years, the data collected by the Ibermedia listings only reflect the nationality of the main production company and the title of the feature film.

Another secondary problem is the mistakes of the data obtained from these sources and databases, which means that, in some isolated cases, there could be discrepancies about the nationality/ies of a particular feature film depending on the source being consulted. It may also be observed in Table 05 that the search in the ICAA database provides two different results according to our search specifications, such as Holland or the Netherlands.

C) National Databases

In order to conclude the search of co-productions databases, we have also analyzed the data and national or state databases, reaching the following conclusions:

- The existence and/or availability of data on film co-productions is quite varied according to the statistic and research tradition of each country, market and film industry size, and even political-geographical situation.
- There is a clear distinction between the European and Latin American settings. The former includes a myriad of accessible databases about film through the web (although not specific about co-productions), whereas the latter provides more limited accessible data that are circumscribed to a few countries (initially, those of larger geographical dimensions).

During the first stage of the work, and in order to avoid the overburden and overlap of the information, only those data with countries that are the main co-producers with Spain have been crossed. In Europe: France, Germany, Italy, United Kingdom, and Portugal. In Latin America: Argentina and Mexico.

In France, the data from the CNC (www.cnc-aff.fr) and Unifrance (http://es.unifrance.org) are being crossed. The same is occurring with the German Films Service (www.german-films.de) in Germany; the ANICA (www.anica.it) in Italy; the BritFilms (www.britfilms.com) in the United Kingdom; the ICA (www.ica-ip.pt) in Portugal; the INCAA (www.incaa.go.ar) in Argentina, and the IMC (www.imcine.gob.mx) in Mexico.

The main problem stemming from the crossing of data of different countries is associated with the incongruence in the data of some feature films provided by the sources: films appearing as co-production in one source and not in another, different participation rates in the production, etc. For example, on Table 06 we can observe the data incongruence between the French CNC and the Spanish ICAA.

Table 06. FEATURE FILMS: CO-PRODUCTIONS, YEAR 2009 Sample: SPAIN-FRANCE (and 3rd countries)			
El niño pez (The fish child)	L. Puenzo	ARG/ FR	Acc. to ICAA, Spain also co-produces
Agua fría de mar (Cold water of the sea)	P. Fabrega	FR/ SP	Does not appear in ICAA
La Yuma	F. Jaugey	NIC/ MEX/ SP/ FR	Does not appear in ICAA
El último verano de la Boyita (The last summer of la Boyita)	J. Solomonoff	SP/ ARG/ FR	Appears in ICAA as ESP/ ARG co-production
¡Mejor que nunca!	D. Payás	SP/ IT / FR	
La sal de este mar (Salt of this sea)	A. Jacir	FR/ SW/ SP/NETH/ UK/ EEUU/ PA-LEST/ BELG	Acc. to ICAA: FRA/ CHE/ ESP/ BEL/ NLD
La posibilidad de una isla (Possibility of an island)	M. Houellebecq	FR/ SP/ GER	
Vengo con la lluvia (I come with the rain)	T. Anh Hung	FR/ UK/ SP/ CHI-NA/ IRL	
Petit indi (Little indi)	M. Recha Batalle	SP/ FR	
La bestia en el corazón (Don´t tell)	C. Comencini	IT/ UK/ SP/ FR	Yr. acc. to CNC: 2005 / Yr. acc. to ICAA: 2009
Napoleón y yo (Napoleon and me)	P. Virzì	IT/ FR/ SP	Yr. acc. to CNC: 2006 / Yr. acc. to ICAA: 2009
Celda 211 (Cell 211)	D. Monzón	SP/ FR	
La mujer sin piano (Woman with-out piano)	J. Rebollo	SP (90.00%) / FR (10.00%)	Yr. acc. to CNC: 2009 / Yr. acc. to ICAA: 2010
Triage	D. Tanovic	IRL/ FR/ SP	
Buscando a Eric (Looking for Erik)	K. Loach	UK /FR/ BELG/ IT	Acc. to ICAA, Spain also co-produces
Singularidades de una chica rubia (Eccentricities of a blond-haired girl)	M. de Oliveira	PORT/ SP/ FR	

Source: CNC/Unifrance and ICAA

Some of these incongruences have a simple solution, but others highlight the work that still remains to be done in terms of data verification and the need to incorporate an analysis of the legislation on co-productions that is applicable in each of the countries taken into account, for this may be the key for certain divergences (requirements for a country to recognize a film as co-production, the inclusion of co-productions with minority participation, etc.).

3. Design of a Co-Productions Database

The proposed design of a co-productions database is still a work-in-progress. So far, largely generic data about the co-produced feature films have been compiled, according to the data by the ICAA: year, title, director, genre, participation (with percentages, whenever available), production companies, distributor and box-office receipts in Spanish movie theaters.

From those co-productions compiled in the LUMIÉRE database, we have only used the data referring to those co-productions with Spain's participation and that have been premiered on screens in the EC. The collected data in this case are: year of production, title, director/s, and spectators. In the case of the IBERMEDIA and EUROIMAGES programs, only the year of grant concession, title, and production companies have been available for compilation.

Table 07. DESIGN OF CO-PRODUCTIONS DATABASE

BASIC DATA (Source: ICAA)	Other Data (Source: LUMIÈRE)
→ *YEAR* → *TITLE* → *DIRECTOR* → *GENRE* → *PARTICIPATION (% if available)* → *PRODUCTION COMPANIES* → *DISTRIBUTOR* → *SPECTATORS (Spain)* → *BOX-OFFICE RECEIPTS (Spain)*	→ *SPECTATORS (Europe)* **Other Data (Sources: IBERMEDIA/ EUROIMAGES)** → *YEAR OF GRANT CONCESSION* → *PROJECT TITLE (non-definitive)* → *PRODUCTION COMPANY (subsidized)*

In view of the available data, tables compiling the basic data of every co-production in a unified manner are being elaborated: author, title, etc. The fundamental idea consists in that once the database project is in an advanced stage, more information may be included for each film, such as the countries where it premiered, the spectators in each co-producing country, or the grants that its co-production received.

This design poses different additional difficulties. For example, it is necessary to further reflect on the data that ought to be incorporated to be useful for research; how those projects that received grants for the co-production, but that did not premiere in commercial theaters or were not even completed, are shown; how we can resolve the incongruences among sources, etc. A considerable amount of work is still pending before reaching a definitive and useful design for researchers who may be interested in its use in the future.

4. Possible Contributions of a Co-productions Database

A project such as the present one should be set out in the direction of two priorities: the final design of a specific database about co-productions and the creation of a new archive about legislation and bibliography in the European and Latin American settings.

A specific database about co-productions being designed with this purpose would be aimed at allowing access to a set of data that are basic for the research on the current importance of co-productions, their historical evolution, results, etc.

Among the main contributions, the following should be noted:

- To create a database specialized in co-productions (it is already something unique).
- To facilitate the search of the data of any co-production carried out in the last decades for researchers.
- To relate two geo-political settings: Latin America and Europe.
- To know the circulation of feature films co-produced in the European and Latin American settings (capacity to premiere in the co-producing countries and/or third countries).
- To discern the received amounts/effective results from the different programs aimed at fostering co-production (Ibermedia, Eurimages, and other programs and/or state subsidies).

Meanwhile, the creation of a compilation archive that is specific about legislation, on-line sources, and academic bibliography about co-productions in the European and Latin American settings would be aimed at facilitating the research of legislation, data, and sources about co-productions for researchers.

Thanks to the creation of these tools: a compilation archive on legislation and bibliography, and a specific database on co-productions, we could help the exploration of this emerging model of collaboration between different countries and industrial, social, and cultural traditions, as well as singling out the multiple data about the results and the evolution of the Spanish co-productions. As has been commented on, researchers could extract detailed information on, for example, about how many of these feature films are premiered in third, non-co-producing countries; whether the grant programs such as Ibermedia or Euroimages have the initially expected impact, considerably contributing to a greater penetration of the co-produced films in the international market; or whether the increasing evolution in the number of Spanish co-productions is uniform or, on the contrary, if it occurs in a different manner according to the country and the continent. All this information is necessary in order to get a sense of and investigate into the future evolution of film co-production in Spain.[3]

3 This work has been made possible by the help of the Research Projects "Media co-productions in the European context: Identities and cultural transnationalization processes" (AT2009-0020, Ministry of Science and Innovation, Government of Spain, Integration Actions Program), "Spanish film coproductions: social and information aspects" (2011/00098/001, Grants for the Consolidation of Research Groups, Community of Madrid/Carlos III University of Madrid) and "Cinema and Television in Post-Transition Spain (1979-1992)", Ministry of Economy and Competitiveness, Government of Spain (CSO2011-15708-E).

BIBLIOGRAPHY

Barriales-Bouche, S. / Salvodon M. A. (eds.). *Zoom In, Zoom Out: Crossing Borders in Recent European Cinema*. Newcastle: Ed. Cambridge Scholar, 2007.

Borau, J.L. *Diccionario del cine español*. Madrid: Ed. Alianza, 1998.

Caballero, R. "Producción, Coproducción e Intercambio de Cine entre España, América Latina y el Caribe". *Informe Avances en Investigación*. Madrid: Ed. Fundación Carolina CeALCI, 2006, URL: http://www.fundacioncarolina.es/es-ES/publicaciones/avancesinvestigacion/Documents/produccioncoproduccioneintercambio.pdf (20.06.2012).

Enrich, E. *Legal Aspects of International Film Co-productions. Observatorio Europeo Audiovisual (OEA)*, Bruselas, mayo 2005, URL: http://www.obs.coe.int/online_publication/expert/coproduccion_aspectos-juridicos.pdf.en (20/06/2012).

Fuertes, M. "Marco teórico para el análisis de una política pública cinematográfica en los nuevos espacio del siglo XXI". *Chasqui. Revista Latinoamericana de comunicación* 113 (2011), p. 16-21.

Fuertes, M. / Mastrini, G. (eds). *Industria cinematográfica latinoamericana. políticas públicas y su impacto en un mercado digital*. Buenos Aires: La Crujía Ediciones y AECID, 2011.

Moreno, J. M. "Diversidad audiovisual e integración cultural: analizando el programa IBERMEDIA". *Comunicación y Sociedad* 9 (2008).

Pohl, B. / Türschmann, J. (eds.). *Miradas glocales: cine español en el cambio de milenio*. Madrid: Ed. Iberoamericana, 2007.

THE HARD ROUTE TO EUROPEANNESS. THE CASE OF THE SERIES *PEPE CARVALHO*

Manuel Palacio

Let us imagine that we are keen to know the nationality of particular films, or of the filmmakers that put them together; perhaps because with this data we could find out how they connect to their roots, which grow deeply into the sediment both of culture and history. So then; what nationality is *Un Chien Andalou,* the short film signed by Luis Buñuel and Salvador Dalí? Let us think about it for a moment: the funds for the production were Spanish, the original script was written in Spanish, it was shot in French studios with French actors and the original title and title cards are in André Breton's language. So, I think that without creating any tension one can say that the famous Surrealist film is a European production, even though at that point in time little was said about Europeanness. Although the truth is that once finalised, the first decade of the 21st century, with Europe in an economic and social situation unlike any it has known since the European institutions began, it seems fitting to consider those processes that, on the surface or from the cultural depths, give meaning to the collective transmission of European values, to a particular common identity, to Europeanness. It is quite possible that it is precisely in the analysis of those processes that one can reveal some of the burdens that the process of European construction suffers, and indirectly, the differences that control politicians' daily actions. In this sense, one cannot forget what some recent surveys show, how visible the seams of the suit of Europeanness have become and how turbulently the waters of Europeanness flow.[1] In short: it seems evident that the economic and financial crisis is veering towards nationalism in each of the countries and less towards Europe. This is because in spite of the fact that Europe seems to withstand as a basic idea amongst its citizens, the perception these citizens have about what is happening shows strong divergence between different groups and especially between southern Europeans and those from other places.

In the following pages we wish to talk about Europeanness or its shortcomings, from what can be seen in audiovisual products. It has not been long since Michel Bruter, in his already classic *Citizens of Europe? The emergence of a Mass European Identity* (2005), whilst establishing different variables to measure Europe's cultural identity processes, talks about concepts such as the circulation of news, of symbols of integration (flag, passport, euro...) and the spreading of languages. Nevertheless, the British essayist makes little mention of what is happening in the audiovisual media or the role that media plays in social processes. From our point of view, this absence limits the reliability of his analysis, because without doubt, cinema and television (and, of course, the internet) form an integral part of the eve-

1 See for example "European Unity on the Rocks" by the Pew Research Center, 2012.

ryday life of Europeans; or that the media, finally, constitute one of the central cultural elements in the elaboration of a public space that is shared by all European citizens. Our objective, in short, is to observe the manner in which the audiovisual media are interwoven into the collection of actions that are working towards the idea of Europe as a community. But once the guiding theme has been stated, it appears to be rather broad; this can be confirmed by a simple consultation of the ample international bibliography. Consequently, I consider it necessary to deal with one aspect that is superficially narrower, such as the way in which critics and analysts collaborate, as spurs or brakes, in the processes of transmitting the idea of European identity, of Europeanness.

The Audio-Visual Media

The privileged place occupied by television and cinema in modern European history cannot be doubted. The images and narrations broadcast by both these media unquestionably form part of the continent's public space. Nowadays this experience may be less visible but for generations of Europeans, their first everyday example of their Europeanness was being a viewer of Eurovision. Also forgotten, but possibly just as useful to recall, is that the bilateral or trilateral agreements for filmic co-productions or the creation of Eurovision in 1950 are parallel and complementary milestones of the various processes that took place at the end of the Second World War which, needless to say, started developing the idea of a common Europe. I would dare to say this another way: when the founding fathers began to create the idea of Europe in the ruins of cities devastated by war, film and television formed part of the seminal project that gave some meaning to the common road ahead. Cinema, because it is capable of creating images and stories shared by Europeans; and television, because it works with the idea of a network that unites, as later tourism and football would do.

How can we forget that before we had a flag, a passport, or the euro, television and films gave us some of our first shared symbols? Many Europeans cannot forget such eurovisual memories like the European TV channels broadcast signals such as, of course, that of the Eurovision Song Contest. Similarly, the Eurovision programmes and broadcasts have merged into a sort of European public space, shared by all of those who combine television viewing and an interest in transnational events or anniversaries; amongst many others one can mention the New Year's Concert by the Vienna Philharmonic Orchestra, the Four Hills Tournament ski jumps or the Games without Frontiers. The cinema experience is different from that of television but it has, nevertheless, some aspects in common with the other. Undoubtedly, European film companies have created such recognizable styles (so different between each other) that one need not be a great expert to detect some characteristic traits in the stories created for the big screen by Italian, French or British cinema: this is, in short, what is known collectively as European cinema, as opposed to that of Hollywood (refer to, at this point, the Sorlin 1991 classic).

When, during a second stage of the European Institutions in the1980s, Europe is conceived as a place from which values of freedom and coexistence can radiate to the world, European cinema and television will take their part: no one can doubt that diverse promotion policies were very present since then. To know the way Europe is communicated through the audio-visual media requires an answer to questions about contemporary transnationality. However, there are different ways of observing transnationality as a characteristic phenomenon of Europeanness in the second stage. One of the most common alterations that give meaning to the changes and new communicative European processes is related to the policies of representation. Audiovisual analysts have mainly done research with a greater emphasis on the quantitative aspects of the processes of communicating Europe: the number of appearances by Eastern Europeans, and the stereotypes of Westerners shown, amongst others.

Also, work has been done, though less of it, regarding extraterritoriality on the continent and the new transnational processes. In this sense, although the studies carried out in the past regarding the international reception of the American series *Dallas* are famous, little is known about what happens when what we consider a model example, the international (European) television format *Big Brother* circulates throughout European countries; in other words, communicatively speaking, what happens with the combination of absolute uniformity in the idea of an international format with the national differences presented by aspects which are not at all unimportant, such as: the scenario of the home in which the television programme unravels, significantly different in each country; the diverse psychological characteristics of the contestants; or the time of day that the programme is shown.

It is easy to note that European co-productions have been installed as the privileged position through which to think about Europeanness. For several decades film co-productions have become a common practice in the European film industry: first in the fifties and sixties based on bilateral agreements and later as part of the European Convention on Cinematographic Co-Production and Eurimages's Co-productions Support Fund. With other public policies to foment the European television industry, Europe has generated similar economic collaboration between countries. The initial rule on which co-production is based is simple: the co-financing agreements, promoted by the European programmes, must be established among at least three partners from at least three different countries. The objective is that the combination of efforts by the partners allows them to take on projects that are more economically ambitious; and that it may even act as a defence measure in their own market against the habitual aggressiveness of the American audiovisual industry. The case of television is not in principle very different from what occurred in film. As from the seventies, fiction television co-productions began to proliferate; with them came a concept that reduces the legitimacy of the work not only of television co-productions but also of film: *europudding*. Those productions combine scenarios, actors and actresses from several countries in order to achieve a supposed flavour beyond what the national public is used to, in an attempt to find the lowest common denominator shared by a very diverse public.

It is not a question of reconstructing in this text the genealogy of the word *europudding* but it seems unquestionable that its very appearance and circulation for several decades shows a somewhat elitist attitude when it comes to thinking about the audiovisual media. It is true that co-productions, understood in the strictest sense as collaboration in terms of capital, technical and professional means to create an audiovisual product, may offer little in the way of creating a European identity or as a mechanism for building a European public space; in fact, in many cases they are nothing more than a commercial project with financial and economic advantages so that the co-produced work can gain easier access to the markets and various subsidies established by legislative regulations. This is something almost contradictory in its very essence if we also consider that traditionally, the identity of cinema and television, of a culture as a whole, was based on the stable borders of the nation-states, that one value of all audio-visual creators consists of being well-rooted in his/her native culture and of not being attached to something much more generic, such as the European identity.

Yet co-productions are a basic element in the process of communicating Europe and creating an identity and European public space, above all if we accept the cultural component which always exists in a co-production. Needless to say, so-called multicultural co-productions require a re-examination of the concept of national television or cinema. The symbolic space in which multicultural co-productions must move is one in which the identities that erase national borders cross over, thus occupying a space that is not foreseen by the official narratives of the Nation State; it is a new, ambivalent space between our own image of ourselves and another that reflects the ambivalence inherent to the construction of a collective identity and that breaks the canons of "official" interpretations. There are two examples that illustrate the limits of this and they both come from the beginning of the first decade of the 21st century, when one could not perceive any circumstances that could modify the collective and positive perception that Europeans had of communitarian institutions. One of them is the film *L'auberge espagnole* (Cedrick Klapisch, 2002) and the other is the TV series *Napoleon* (Yves Simoneau, 2002). It is true that both works are very different in terms of target audience, budget or mode of production. However, we do find some substantial coincidences. The most obvious is that they are both co-productions, the first one is Spanish-French and the second one is a French-British-German-Canadian-Italian-American conglomerate. However, we cannot overlook that the narrative components of both productions emanate from the transnationality of the experiences of Europeans: in the film the binding cement is made up of the troubles experienced by a group of Erasmus students who travel to Barcelona from different parts of Europe; and in the television series it is the political realignment of the whole of Europe in the context of the Napoleonic Wars at the beginning of the 19th century.

Even if, in the critical reception, it is easier to negotiate multiculturality immanent to European transnationality in a film that has a hint of auteur than in a television serial production addressed to a massive television audience, this was not an obstacle for the forbidden word to appear in some commentaries. This occurs in the progressive British newspaper *The Guardian*, which publishes an article on the film by Cédrick Klapisch entitled "Eurostar and the Europudding" (Xan Brooks, 2003). On television it is unusual to find products that fulfil a multicultural or transnational function. This is probably because contemporary (national) television takes place in a public space determined by established social signals and with established canons of interpretation; and as if that is not problematic enough, on the small screen, dubbing into another language is habitual and reduces the credibility of the multicultural aspects of the programme. Therefore in *Napoleon*, which seeks to be historically correct, as on the list of collaborators, one can find the French historian Max Gallo, only French and English are used, languages spoken by the Prussians, Spaniards, Austrians, Russians and Poles that appear on the footage.

A curious aspect needs mentioning: in contemporary television, the predominance of the market has reduced conventional co-productions but the exchanges of formats have increased. Thus, in order to solve the problems related to "national" peculiarities in television viewing, the industry has found solutions which already existed in the field of cinema but which were not as common on the small screen. It is no longer necessary for finished programmes to travel across Europe: ideas can travel instead. Nowadays, exchanges of programmes among European countries frequently occur when a format that is successful in one country is bought and then adapted to fit a different national context, taking into account the unique characteristics of that context: the duration of the programs in evening timetables, acting traditions, social situations, linguistic turns of phrase, etc. The internationally well-known case is that of the Colombian telenovela *Yo soy Betty, la fea* (1999-2002), which has been adapted in more than two dozen countries.

However, the conversion of a series to another (European) context requires that important decisions be made. Regarding one of the first Spanish examples of this type of conversion, the adaptation of *Médico de Familia* (*The Family Doctor*) to the Italian television market, where it was shown with great success on RAI with the title *Un medico in famiglia* (1998-), the well-known Italian producer Carlo Principini declared in the press:

> (The) new format is 50% Spanish influence and 50% Italian mentality. That explains why the Andalusian maid from the Spanish series has relinquished her position to a Neapolitan maid. This way we can also understand why one of the most important characters is developed through the indescribable charisma of the grandfather (Lino Banfi). (Amon, 1998b)

Obviously, the passage of a series or entertainment format from one cultural and social context to a completely different one establishes a dialect between, on the one hand, the international processes of transnationalization, and on the other, the local characteristics of reception. Also, it should not be overlooked that the meanings constructed in the place of the adaptation are not necessarily the same as those constructed in the place of origin. An interesting case is the series *Cuentame como pasó* (2001-; *Tell me how it happened*), which is undoubtedly the television series with greatest repercussion in the whole history of television in Spain. However, the Portuguese (*Conta-me como foi*) or Italian (*Raccontami*) are testimonies of how each country found a different solution to the initial opening presentation: the arrival of the first television set in the family home. In Spain, the principal family buys their first television set in 1968 (casually coinciding with the only time that Spain won the Eurovision Song Contest); in Italy in 1960 during the Olympic Games in Rome; finally in Portugal some time at the end of the sixties. We could also mention here the case of *Los Serrano* (2003-2008), an enormously successful family comedy that has been exported to countries such as France and Slovenia and that has had adaptations made for the Czech Republic, Portugal, Greece and Italy. What is interesting is that while *Los Serrano* was still on, the official webpage of the Spanish version of the series published references to the similarities and differences between the original and the Italian translation (*I Cesaroni*, 2006-), even showing online some key moments in the development of the story, such as the misunderstandings created by the physical attraction between two 'siblings', which make the viewer think about these relationships from a 21st century European morality viewpoint (the young adults are born from different parents who have entered into a second marriage after ending their previous ones; consequently, the young people are not blood relations but step siblings.) The contrasting European sexual habits and their televisual representation have recently provided another example: in 2012, the Spanish series *Física y Química* was removed from Italian television due to the high degree of erotism in the television fiction of Spanish origin.[2]

How can we combine the way we see the audiovisual images that come from the national public space and the canons of interpretation left by history to establish a, let us say, European or multicultural reading? There is no easy answer. Nevertheless, it seems clear that there must be shared responsibility among the various agents of the communicative processes, from the schools all the way to the moment in which the viewers receive the final product, so that the pro-European commitment does not become the responsibility of the producers or creative teams alone. In this new cultural territory of European public space it is essential to make the changes in mentality and sensitivities that European multiculturalism demands. In order to learn lessons and draw conclusions, we can observe the case of a European television co-production: *Pepe Carvalho* (1999), a Spanish-Italian-French series with six episodes lasting about ninety minutes each, based on the adventures of the private detective of the same name, created by Manuel Vázquez Montalbán (the series is available in Spanish on DVD). Years later, a second season with four episodes was made in which neither the Italian nor the Spanish partners as such did not collaborate, although a Spanish regional television station did, consequently turning it into a simple French-Spanish region co-production, thereby losing part of its European vocation. Significantly, it has not been broadcast to the Spanish territory as a whole.

Pepe Carvalho

The writer from Barcelona Manuel Vázquez Montalbán is probably one of the contemporary writers whose work has been most widely translated into other languages. In fact, over decades, he has become one of the most important Spanish references of the Iberian detective novel. This privileged place is not surprising due to the writer's view of the world: leftist, antifrancoist, nihilist, smart gourmet, makes him a life model for many readers, especially in countries like Spain and Italy, countries where the author enjoyed great prestige until his unexpected death in 2003. In this sense, during the first years of the 1990s, specifically at a time when the television co-production we are referring to was made, there was an accumulation of recognition in the shape of prizes: in Spain he won the "Premio Nacional de

2 See http://www.liberoquotidiano.it/news/957212/Porno-Rai-in-fascia-protetta-droga-sesso-ammuchiate.html.

Narrativa (1991)" (National Prize for Narrative (1991)); in an international context he achieved the European Union Prize for Literature (1992); and in Italy he was awarded the international Flaiano Prize (1994). When he received the European prize, Manuel Vázquez Montalbán made some statements on European lines which help one understand the cultural ties that bound him to a certain relationship between European regions. "I accept the prize as a symbol of a future European culture, which must be profoundly mixed, euroasian, euroafrican, euroamerican" (Muñoz Diego, 1992).

The bestknown literary character by the writer from Barcelona is the private detective Pepe Carvalho, identified by many as the true alter ego of his creator. In the eighties and nineties several adaptations were made for film and television, based on the detective's works. However, the writer was not satisfied with the results and there were notable disputes with some of the adapters. During the second half of the nineties the conditions seemed to have changed. The detective's antifrancoist feeling is starting to wane; on the other hand, on the European continent a new television model is settling in, one which is far from the conventional forms of public television service and which oblige the very same public broadcasters to seek new social positioning. It is not surprising, then, to use the notoriety of Manuel Vázquez Montalbán and pick up the adventures of the detective in order to produce a European series and attempt to achieve the success of the series based on the French Navarro or the Italian Montalbano (an indirect homage, by the way, to Vázquez Montalbán himself).

Spanish, French and Italian producers initiated a television co-production about the adventures of the detective Carvalho. The production process for *Pepe Carvalho* was the usual: the production company Cartel (one of the larger ones in the Spanish audiovisual industry) in collaboration with the Institut de Cinema Catalá (Catalan Film Institute – a public institution) reached an agreement with Tele 5, the Spanish television station with a majority interest in the Italian company Mediaset/Fininvest, to develop an adaptation of some of the detective stories written by Manuel Vázquez Montalbán. Several partners were added to the initial Spanish nucleus which, according to official information, contributed 40% of the production costs. One partner was Italian (Solaris Cinematografica), and another, French (Tanaïs Productions), with each contributing 30% of the budget. The directors had the freedom to develop each episode as they though fit. Consequently, there were no unifying criteria. The episodes, depending on where they were set, were filmed by directors with somewhat established careers in the film industry in their respective countries, such as the Spaniards Enrique Urbizu and Rafael Monleón, the Italian, whose father was Slovenian, Franco Giraldi (who directed two episodes), the Algerian Merzak Allovache and the Frenchwoman Emmanuele Cuau. The initial meetings were held in Madrid, in Cartel's offices. There was no pre-set language; the attendees spoke Spanish or Italian, but translation was available. Filming of the first episode began in Barcelona, where the interior sets were located (for example the detective's office or his house), continued with scenes shot in France and in Italy and ended in Barcelona with the final episode. It goes without saying that during the shoot, the actors performed in their mother tongues and were later dubbed by local actors, who in some cases emphasized the accent and in others used a more neutral version of the language employed.

To increase its Europeanness, from the beginning, the creators thought of reducing the national aspects of the original text, fomenting multicultural elements instead. The most obvious operation was eliminating the scent of Spain (Barcelona) from the original stories to convert it with touches of Europeanness; thus, the plots of the various episodes begin in Pepe Carvalho's offices in the Catalan capital but later, the adventures involved in solving the cases take the detective, his girlfriend, and, occasionally, his assistant to different areas of France or Italy. Despite the fact that in the different episodes there were no examples of multilingualism, which would have been a natural situation since the action took place in various countries, there were, in fact, healthy cultural confrontations. Clearly, a central element was the choice of actors who played the characters from Vázquez Montalbán's stories. Needless to say, the main roles were played by actors and actresses who were well-known in their respective countries: the Spanish/Catalonian actor Juanjo Puigcorbé (as a Pepe Carvalho with attitudes and behaviours that were more cosmopolitan than Catalonian), the Italian actress Valeria Marini (as Charo, the detective's girlfriend, who in the series, apparently due to the actress's demands, did not work as a prostitute but ran an independent nightclub, and who, imitating *Pretty Woman,* enjoyed making sophisticated purchases) and the French/Algerian actor Jean Benguigi (as Biscuter, Carvalho's assistant and faithful defender of the idiosyncrasies of the F.C. Barcelona football and Catalan gastronomy). Omero Antonutti, Maurice Benichou, Manuela Arcuri and Walter Vidarte also appeared in some of the episodes.

Rubén Amón, the correspondent in Italy for the daily newspaper *El Mundo*, published an article on the filming of the "Italian" episodes of the series. In the article, he includes some declarations made by the director, Franco Giraldi:

> Pepe Carvalho is a Mediterranean detective who represents the challenge that a greater Europe presents to American agents forged in the James Bond style. He is a man who loves life, who eats, smokes, and lives by his own philosophy. He is an ex-CIA agent, ex-political prisoner, ex-communist, basically a post-modern character trying to conquer globalization. (Amón, 1998a)

Regardless of the fact that everybody knows that James Bond is European and that the Mediterranean has several different shores, Giraldi does point out some characteristics of the European public space which is one of the points that we have been discussing in these pages. In the French newspaper *Le Figaro*, the actor Jean Benguigui reflected on the mutual pleasure of working with other Europeans: "I was born in Algeria and working with Italians and Spaniards attracts me considerably" (Nataf Isabelle, 1999).

The series was shown throughout 1999/2000 on the broadcasting station Tele 5 in Spain, on Raidue in Italy and on ARTE in France. The production companies intended to guide the viewers' and critics' readings of the show by positioning it as a European series, indirectly working toward the creation of a European public space, and this was reflected in the press releases that were prepared for the launch of the series in Spain, as we can see in the following headline that appeared in the daily newspaper *La Vanguardia* (a historic masthead of the Spanish press, published in

Barcelona) that said: “Tele 5 opens the European series *Pepe Carvalho* on Sunday” (no by-line, *La vanguardia*, 2000).

In general the critics were not positive. Nevertheless, in the context of these pages, what is notable is not *Pepe Carvalho’s* negative reception but how the notes regarding the critics’ reception do not take into account the European vocation of the co-production; instead they give greater weight to the, let us say, national interpretations. We shall take a look:

In Spain, the Catalonian J.M. (Josep Maria) Baget Herms, who was, for decades and until his death, probably the most well-known television critic in Spain, wrote a commentary on the episode entitled “El delantero centro será asesinado al amanecer/ Il Centravanti è stato assassinato verso sera/ L’avant centre sera assassiné à la tombée du jour” (Franco Giraldi). In this chapter, the scriptwriters substituted Barcelona just before the Olympic Games of 1992 for Perugia “before the celebration of the 2000 Jubilee”. The detective storyline is centred on football and real estate speculation, themes very familiar to television viewers in almost all European countries, but other aspects are also present: drugs, father-son relationships, the philosophy of the “loser”, or the pride that comes with being part of a small town. None of these possible hooks were mentioned in Baget Herms’ critique, which was very focused on developing the stereotypes of the Italophobia present in Spain, and he wrote without further comments:

> Outside of his context (from Barcelona-Spanish), Carvalho becomes a less than believable character, and in the “El delantero centro será asesinado al atardecer (The centre forward will be murdered at dawn)” we again find him in Italy, the supposed adviser to an athlete who’s received a death threat, no less, which affects a subject close to his heart, the world of football. However, the storyline lacked credibility and fell into the most conventional stereotypes regarding real estate speculation linked to stadiums and the famous *appalti* (in Italian in the original); that is those tenders for public building projects that, in Italy, are always won by firms with close ties to the Mafia. Basically, *Pepe Carvalho* seems to be more a series with Berlusconian roots, although with this transplant the character and his legions of followers have lost out. (Baget, 2000)

In Italy there is talk of another Mediterranean detective, heir to Montalbán. Most of the critics focus on the differing ways (Spanish and Italian) of understanding life and the difficulty of mixing the Spanish character with the Italian stories. In *Storia della Televisione italiana*, of which several editions have been published in Italy, Professor Aldo Grasso focuses his comments on the first episode, “El hermano pequeño/ Il Fratellino/ Le petit frère” (Enrique Urbizu), which is set in the city of Barcelona and deals with the links between the illegal financing of political parties and certain cases of economic corruption. Grasso’s entire reflection is based on a comparison between the values of Vázquez Montalbán’s text and the various deficiencies of the adaptation. In his words:

> Abandoned to the affected performance of Juanjo Puicorbé (his assistante being better than him) and the always unbelievable Valeria Marini, the adventures of a socialist Spanish politician, scapegoat of a corrupt intrigue, reveal the sordid side of reality, one of the most interesting stories of the Spanish writer, become disheartening artificiality. One of the most interesting sides of the story is the complete and ironic reflection on the media (…) what remains is the background of Barcelona, and its Catalan magic. (Grasso, 1999, p.673)

Critical reception in France (Nataf, 1999; Waintrop, 1999; Borde, 1999; Baudou, 1999) does not even contemplate themes related to the nationality or the Europeanness of the project. In some media like *Le Figaro* the series is presented exclusively as a Spanish-Italian co-production (Isabelle Nataf, 1999). They speak totally in code about images that in France one may have of Spain: Don Quijote y Sancho Panza (Carvalho and his aide Biscuter). In France, on the French-German channel ARTE's webpage, we can find commentaries on all of the episodes of the series, which result in a very useful source of information.[3] In general they are very descriptive and lacking in references to Europeanness, mostly contered on the Spanish personality of Carvalho's universe. Let us choose the commentaries about an episode set in Paris: "La soledad del manager/La solitudine del manager/La solitude du manager" (Merzack Allovache), with a storyline about illegal arms trafficking (missiles sold to Saddam's embargoed Iraq!) by multinational companies with offices in France, indirectly controlled by a neo-Nazi organization in the heart of Europe. The interpretation, which is made on the ARTE institutional site is altogether a French one. Although police racism is not avoided here, no mention is made about the significance of Valeria Marini on the streets of Paris; nor is there any venture beyond the description of the exotic behaviour of the Spaniards, represented by Carvalho's assistant Biscuter, played, as was previously mentioned, by the French-Algerian actor Jean Benguigi:

> Pepe Carvalho is confronted with two unfathomable entities: a multinational company and new technologies. Pepe Carvalho swims counter current and paradoxically it is Biscuter who is the intercessor in this modern world. The Parisien spree is an opportunity for a veritable Biscuter festival, he fears homesickness and embarks with, amongst other victuals, a "jamon Serrano" (the best Spanish ham), finding choucroute inedible and dons a Pulp Fiction cap. Another wink, the French racist cop played by Maurice Benichou, who addresses Pepe talks to him about "the Mediterranean arrogance. (Pepe Carvalho, *Cinema & Fiction*)

In short, we are looking at a co-production in which, from the start, the producers included all of the characteristic mechanisms required to satisfy the supposedly average tastes of European audiences: locations in very well-known places, actors or actresses who are popular in their home countries, among other particular features, attempting to create a European work that plays with multiculturalism. But it seems clear that these ideas do not reach the critics and audio-visual analysts very easily, as they establish their opinions and criteria on the fixed, stable identity of the nation-state, no matter how much the old concept of a national cultural space may be very eroded by globalization and transnationalisation nowadays.

This situation is worrying due to the role that social mediators must fulfil in the processes of communicating Europe and converting them into cultural ties that give meaning to the common identities based on the everyday life of Europeans. If one of the effects of contemporary transnationalisation is the modification of limits and forms in which social and cultural signs circulate, critics and analysts have a role to fulfil in the task of transcending the readings where only national public spaces predominate. This is one way to erase national borders and occupy a previously un-

3 *Pepe Carvalho*, http://www.arte.tv/fr/Les-films/558778.html.

precedented and ambivalent space in the construction of a collective European identity.[4]

BIBLIOGRAPHY

Amón, R. "Pepe Carvalho a la italiana". *El Mundo* (5.11.1998) (a), URL: http://www.elmundo.es/1998/10/05/television/05N0088.html (20.6.2009).

Amón, R. "La hora del doctor Martini". *El Mundo* (6.12.1998) (b), URL: http://www.elmundo.es/1998/12/06/television/index.html (20.6.2009).

Baget, H. "La nueva estética de Pepe Carvalho". *La Vanguardia* (28.3.2000), URL: http://hemeroteca.lavanguardia.com/preview/2000/03/28/pagina-10/34068353/pdf.html (10.6.2009).

Baudou, J. "Pepe Carvalho met les pieds dans le plat". *Le Monde* (19.9.1999), URL: http://lemondefr./cgi-bin/ACHATS/ARCHIVES (24.6.2012).

Borde, D. "Le polar fait l'Espagne". *Le Figaro* (11.9.1999), URL : http://recherche.lefigaro.fr/recherche/access/lefigaro_print-afficher (24.6.2012).

Brooks, X. "Eurostar and the Europudding". *Guardian* (8.5.2003), URL: http://www.guardian.co.uk/film/2003/may/08/features (24.6.2012).

Bruter, M. *Citizens of Europe? The emergence of a Mass European Identity*. Basingstoke: Palgrave Macmillan, 2005.

"European Unity on the Rocks", Pew Research Center, Washington (29.5.2012), URL: http://www.pewglobal.org/2012/05/29/european-unity-on-the-rocks/ (20.6.2009).

Grasso, A. *Storia della televisione italiana*. Milan: Garzanti, 1999.

Muñoz, D. "Vazquez Montalbán gana el Premio Europeo de Literatura con la novela *Galíndez*". *El País* (27.11.1992), URL: http://elpais.com/diario/1992/11/27/cultura/722818810_850215.html (7.7.2012).

Nataf, I. "Un privé très public". *Le Figaro* (10.9.1999), URL: http://recherche.lefigaro.fr (7.7.2012).

Palacio, M. "Elogio posmoderno de las coproducciones". *Cuadernos de la Academia* 5 (1999), p. 221-235.

Pepe Carvalho. Cinema & Fiction. URL: http://archives.arte.tv/fr/archive_34058.html (18.6.2012).

"Porno Rai in fascia protetta: droga, sesso, ammucchiate". *Libero* (14.3.2012), URL: http://www.liberoquotidiano.it/news/957212/Porno-Rai-in-fascia-protetta-droga-sesso-ammuchiate.html (11.6.2012).

Sorlin, P. *European cinemas, European societies: 1939-1990*. New York: Routledge, 1991.

"Tele 5 abre el domingo la serie europea *Pepe Carvalho*". *La Vanguardia* (17.2.2000), p.11.

Waintrop, E. "Sur Arte, le héros de Montalban perd sa saveur. Les six épisodes oublient l'atmosphère trouble des romans". *Liberation* (10.9.1999), URL: http://liberation.fr/medias/0101291769-sur-arte-le-heros-de-montalban-perd-sa (21.6.2012).

4 This work has been made possible by the help of the Research Projects: "Media co-productions in the European context: Identities and cultural transnationalization processes" (AT2009-0020, Ministry of Science and Innovation, Government of Spain, Integration Actions Program) and "Cinema and Television in Post-Transition Spain (1979-1992)", Ministry of Economy and Competitiveness, Government of Spain (CSO2011-15708-E).

EUROPEAN TRANSNATIONAL TV FICTION: REMAKING *LIFE ON MARS* IN SPAIN

Concepción Cascajosa Virino

The emergence of transnational television has been one of the most significant developments in the media industry over the past three decades. With the international (often global) circulation of programmes and fiction series, the adaptation of formats and the generalization of co-production, television (a national-based medium in the origin) has reflected the new reality of a world interconnected in economic, social and cultural aspects. In Europe this must necessarily be understood as part of the European integration process, to the extent that transnationalization was a target set in policy rules as the Television Without Frontiers directive and the Euroimage Co-production Program. For Fickers and Johnson (2010, p. 4), the history of transnational television in Europe is a valuable way to observe this complex process:

> Television can catalyse or inhibit processes of political or cultural change; it can function as the social cement of a nation and foster collective individuation and participant isolation. When looking at the flows of television - for example, at television formats or programmes - television can at the same time stimulate cultural diversity and standardize narrative or aesthetic conventions; it can both - by the way of subtitling or dubbing - promote the other and make it feel familiar.

These transnational flows have developed in Europe along with a television industry which left behind public monopolies and gained strength through new channels and production companies. In Spain, the result of this new framework has been clear: the country has successfully managed to export many TV programmes and some fiction and nonfiction formats have been adapted in other European countries, while at the same time establishing business deals to adapt foreign formats. The purpose of this chapter is to analyze one such example of adaptation, the fiction series *La chica de ayer* (*The Girl From Yesterday*, Antena 3, 2009), based on the successful British cop drama *Life on Mars* (BBC1: 2006-2007). Our intended goal is to show how transnational TV works in practice and the way any adaptation bring into play a complex web of commercial, industrial and cultural elements.

Transnational TV in Europe: Now and Then

In an in-deep study of the symbols used to project the idea of a European identity (such as a common currency, a flag, an anthem and even an "Europe Day"), Johan Fornäs (2012, p. 2) has already noted how the rise of modern media not only can't be ignored, but it is critical to how the European identity is built in a fragmented context:

> Europe is no self-evident cultural or social unit. (...) A shared European public sphere is only in its infancy. But community may possibly not need to build on every member participating in exactly the same forum. Since the differentiation of television and other media forms into many divergent platforms and channels, this is not even true for any nation. Instead, Europe, like today's nation states, is crystallised by loosely combined 'sphere of publics' -networks of communication where no single medium or arena gathers all citizens but where their mutual exchanges produce a dynamic and heterogeneous totality, which is also not quite closed to the outside, but has permeable boundaries.

It seems clear, then, the role that the television was destined to play in the process of European integration. Despite the occasional false steps (such as the lack of agreement on a single color transmission system and the adoption of PAL and SECAM in different countries), there was a strong push to create a common ground for the development of television after the Second World War. So a group of twenty-three public broadcasters formed in 1950 the European Broadcasting Union (EBU) in order to establish a framework for exchange of programming and technical support. Although from the cultural point of view the most publicized offering of the EBU has been the much discussed Eurovision Song Contest, a more long-lasting legacy was the shared ident of the EBU with its twelve stars and an the music from Marc-Antoine Charpentier's "Prelude to *Te Deum*", a real symbol of the belonging to something that, step by step, was taking shape as an economic and political entity, Europe. For a country traditionally isolated like Spain, joining the EBU preceded in many years the integration in the (then) European Economic Community. But in a period where Francisco Franco's dictatorship took its first steps towards a gradual openness, it is difficult to question that the regular broadcasts of international football matches, musical contests and royal weddings were symptomatic of a new relationship with the rest of the continent. Spain had not yet completed its national network, but was already linked to Europe.

As already introduced, the idea of Europe as a marketplace was the basis of 1989 "TV Without Frontiers" Directive, which was adopted in the face of the early Eighties technological revolution and the growing deficit with the US in media trade[1]. The economical, the political and the cultural are intertwined factors here. In hindsight, the European circulation of media content has proven to be a difficult task. Faced with the popularity of the national-produced content and good production values of the American products, programmes from other European countries appears to be in no man's land. Again, the case of Spain may be illustrative, as in prime-time the only fiction series airing on the main channels are still scarce. Except from some international miniseries, after a review of the TV schedules of 2011 and 2012, we only could find in prime-time the British heritage dramas *Downton Abbey* (BBC, 2010-) and *Upstairs, Downstairs* (BBC: 2010-2012), while some action dramas from Germany, led by the long-running *Alarm für Cobra 11* (*Cobra*

1 "Whereas it is therefore necessary to promote markets of sufficient size for television productions in the Member States to recover necessary investments not only by establishing common rules opening up national markets but also by envisaging for European productions where practicable and by appropriate means a majority proportion in television programmes of all Member States". Television without Frontiers (TVWF) Directive, Council Directive 89/552/EEC of 3 October 1989, p. 3.

Alert, RTL: 1996-), have found a niche in the morning hours. European fiction is more common in pay-TV and thematic channels, where more British, German, Italian and French series are often seen, but sometimes, as in the case of the Danish crime drama *Forbrydelsen* (*The Killing*, DR1: 2007-), as a secondary effect of the production of an American remake. As Philip Schlesinger (1993, p. 12) stated taking account of the cultural policies and collective identities in Europe:

> What these observations suggest, then, is that there is something inherently improbable about asking people to consume television as if they already had a European imagination. We could term this the fallacy of distribution, according to which it is supposed that distributing the same cultural product leads to an identity of interpretation on the part of those who consume it.

In a situation in which public policies have failed to get European television to be watched regularly outside their countries of origin, co-productions have been called to play a prominent role. Co-productions are an investment in national culture for governments and a transnational marketplace opportunity for producers, but sometimes these factors can be reversed: "Some governments may have a primary goal of strengthening a national film industry for economic reasons, while some producers may use international co-production money to make their artistic visions possible" (Selznick, 2008, p. 17). But it is true that co-productions, understood in the strictest sense as collaboration in terms of capital, technical and professional means to create a media product, offer little in the way of creating a European identity or as a mechanism for building a European public sphere. In fact, in many cases they are nothing more than a commercial project with financial and economic advantages so that the co-produced work can gain easier access to the markets and various subsidies established by national regulations.

The problem is, often the combination of factors in the design of the co-production has resulted in a cultural cocktail of bitter taste, and expressions such as "Europudding" or "Euro-Trash" began to be used to define productions where each producer tried too hard to give his national flavor to the final result. As an example, see this ironic definition of the so-called "Europudding":

> Take a story that crosses the borders of two or more Member States in the European Community. . . . Preferably historical subjects are recommended. (Take care not to favour any single national perspective or choose a subject that could offend the national sensibility of any of the other EC Member States). . . . Add a writer and director from these same Member States then gently solicit investment from their domestic television networks. . . . Fold in the appropriate number of actors and technicians from each country. . . . Yield: Two hours plus of a deal driven fictional 'screen entertainment' devoid of distinctive contour or flavour (William Fisher in *Sight & Sound*, quoted in Selznick, 2010, p. 32).

Perhaps this is the reason why recent co-productions have tended to eliminate these too obvious strategies in the hope of achieving a more successful result in creative and economic terms, contradicting the intended cultural effects of the public policies that patronized co-productions in the first place.

While the co-productions have tried to adapt to a changing media landscape and its own internal contradictions as cultural artifacts, television marketplace have gradually been more and more dominated by the selling, buying and adaptation of formats. That is, the remakes of programmes from other countries, sometimes news formats, but generally entertainment programmes and fiction series. For Albert Moran (2004, p. 258),

> a format can be used as the basis of a new programme, the programme manifesting itself as a series of episodes, the episodes being sufficiently similar to seem like instalments of the same programme and sufficiently distinct to seem like different episodes. Similarly, behind industrial/legal moves to protect formats, lies a complementary notion that formats are generative or organizational. Thus, from one point of view, a television format is that set of invariable elements in a programme out of which the variable elements of an individual episode are produced.

Perhaps one of the most characteristic features of television formats is that every country has the ability of create and export formats and their success or popularity is not linked directly to the strength of the television industry when they were born. A study on the international circulation of formats between 2006 and 2008 revealed that the country which exported more formats in this period was the United Kingdom (146, well above the United States with 87), while several European countries achieved excellent results exporting formats, such as the Netherlands (35), Sweden (22), Germany (21) and Spain (17). For a country whose television industry is virtually unknown in the rest of the continent, it is striking to learn that Norway exported seven formats[2]. The dynamics established in the process of locating different cultural and social narratives structures to specific national contexts have been a topic popular between researchers in the field of Television Studies, especially when dealing with planetary success as the Dutch reality TV competition programme *Big Brother* or the Colombian telenovela *Yo soy Betty, la fea* (*I am Ugly Betty*, RCN: 1999-2001). But other examples, as the one analyzed in our case study, have not gone unnoticed.

Spain and Transnational TV: Going the Distance

The Spanish television system was born as a public monopoly that ended in the 1980s when the door was opened for three new private channels: Antena 3, Telecinco and Canal +. Although Canal + decided to be a premium channel and based its programming on sports and recent movies (with a very limited investment in original content), Antena 3 and Telecinco early found in the production of original fiction series a main attraction for the audience. These fiction series were carried out by independent production companies of new creation, like the successful Globomedia, which replicated the American TV working system, employed young professionals with little previous experience, and seek a wider audience appealing to the whole family. These fiction series (mainly comedies) not only successfully connected with the Spanish audience, but soon they began to be exported to other countries, as was the case of the first ratings hits of private TV in Spain, *Farmacia de guardia* (*Duty Chemist*, Antena 3: 1991-1995) or *Médico de Familia* (*Family Doctor*, Telecinco: 1995-1999). Until that time, with the exception of a very few

2 The study is available at: http://www.international-television.org/tv_market_data/international-tv-format-ranking-and-trading_2006-2008.html (15-06-2012).

series broadcast in Latin America, Spanish productions were virtually unknown in the international TV marketplace.

The next logical step was to think that Spanish TV was producing formats able to be exported to other European countries, many years after the popular quiz and game show *Un, dos, tres...* (*One, Two, Three...*, TVE1: 1972-2004), created by Narciso Ibáñez Serrador, was sold for local versions in four European countries: Great Britain (ITV: 1978-1988), the Netherlands (KRO: 1983-1986), Germany (ARD: 1984-1987) and Portugal (RTP: 1985-1990). But the conversion of a Spanish series to another European context requires that important decisions be made. Regarding one of the first Spanish examples of this type of conversion, the Italian adaptation of *Médico de Familia, Un medico in famiglia* (RAI, 1998-), Milly Buonanno (2009, p. 266) noted:

> Despite a degree of cultural affinity between Spain and Italy, the adaptation of the format entailed considerable work of 'cultural localization'. Greater emphasis was deliberately placed on the family group, a shift that can be perceived immediately from the title. This was changed from the original professional qualification of the protagonist – un médico de familia, equivalent to family doctor or GP – to 'a doctor in the family', thus anchoring his role in the family community.

More recently, Spanish viewers were able to watch special episodes about the adventures of the families of the Italian (RAI, *Raccontami*, 2006-2008) and Portuguese (RTP1, *Conta-me como foi*, 2007-2011) versions of the historical series *Cuentame como pasó* (*Tell Me How It Happened*, TVE1: 2001-) and how they resolved the initial presentation that began the story: the arrival of the first television in the family home. We could also mention here the case of *Los Serrano* (*The Serranos*, Telecinco: 2003-2008), an enormously successful family comedy that has been exported to countries such as France and Slovenia, and that has been remade in Portugal (TVI, *Os Serranos*, 2005-2006), the Czech Republic (*Horákovi*, Ceská Televize, 2006-2007), Italy (Canale 5, *I Cesaroni*, 2006-) and Greece (*Eutixismenoi Mazi*, Mega, 2007-2009). More recently, the action cop drama *Cuenta atrás* (*Countdown*, Cuatro: 2007-2008) was remade in Germany as *Countdown: Die Jagd beginnt* (RTL: 2009-2011).

But the good health of the fiction produced in Spain has not been an obstacle for buying fiction formats from other countries. In this dual model, producers have tried to keep a balance between developing original ideas and adapting formats of proven success. Some of these formats have originated in Latin America, for example the soap-operas *Soy Bea* (*I am Bea*, Telecinco, 2006-2009) and *Lalola* (*Lalola*, Antena 3: 2008), the melodrama *Sin tetas no hay paraíso* (*Without Breasts, There's no Paradise*, Telecinco: 2008-2009), and the detective comedy *Hermanos y detectives* (*Brothers and Detectives*, Telecinco: 2007-2009), coming from Colombia and Argentina. At the same time, there have been remakes from U.S. series, with recent examples such as *Matrimonio con hijos* (*Married with Children*, Cuatro: 2006), *Mesa para cinco* (*Party of Five*, La Sexta: 2006), *Las chicas de oro* (*The Golden Girls*, TVE1: 2010) and *Cheers* (*Cheers*, Telecinco: 2011). In the past few years, it has been also the turn of the thriving European fiction, with varying results. While the French high-concept comedy *Camera Café* (*Coffee Camera*, M6: 2001-) was remade with great success as *Camera Café* (Telecinco, 2005-2009), the Italian police procedural *R.I.S, Delitti imperfetti* (*R.I.S, Imperfect Crime*, Canale 5: 2005-) was the basis for the failed *R.I.S .Científica* (Telecinco: 2007). The following pages will be devoted to analyzing one of these versions of European fiction, *Life on Mars* and its Spanish remake *La chica de ayer* in 2009. In the same year, private channel Antena 3 found in British television a mine for new projects, remaking in a short period *Life on Mars* and *Doc Martin* (ITV: 2004-), which was the inspiration for *Doctor Mateo* (Antena 3: 2009-). Our analysis of this case study will show the advantages and risks involved in a typical process of adaptation.

From Sam to Samuel: *Life on Mars* Becomes *La Chica de Ayer*.

Life on Mars arrived in the British TV screens in January 2006 as an original twist on the cop drama formula. It was the new offering for the BBC of the burgeoning production company Kudos Film and Television, who had already surprise audience and critics with *Spooks* (BBC1: 2002-) and *Hustle* (BBC1: 2004-), stylish and clever reinventions of the spy drama and the grifters stories. The creator and two of the writers of *Hustle* (Tony Jordan, Ashley Pharoah and Matthew Graham) developed the basic concept for a new series: a present-day repressed but brilliant Manchester Detective Chief Inspector, Sam Tyler (John Simm) is hit by a car, but when he wakes up, discovers that he has been transported to 1973. While trying to discover the reason of this weird occurrence and the way back to 2006, Tyler keeps solving cases applying modern police techniques developing a surprising friendship with his reactionary boss, a force of nature named Gene Hunt (Philip Glenister). *Life on Mars* quickly became a ratings success in Great Britain and a favorite of the TV critics. It also won the International Emmy for Best Drama Series and the audience award at the BAFTA TV Awards. However, even before the premiere of the second season, BBC announced that the series would not be extended beyond the eight new episodes produced (it is a common practice in Britain that even most successful series only last a couple of seasons).

But the impact of *Life on Mars* in contemporary television has gone beyond this short existence, to the point of becoming a small cultural landmark. The narrative gimmick on which the programme is based works at the service of a reinvention of the police drama, a mainstay on British TV. The choice of the 1970s as the setting for the series is a clear reference to the decade in which the genre lived a particular Golden Age with the popular *Z-Cars* (BBC1: 1962-1978), *The Sweeney* (ITV: 1975-1978) and *Law & Order* (BBC2: 1978). Some of these programmes, particularly *The Sweeney*, receive direct or indirect allusions in *Life on Mars*, as many reviewers noted. It is undeniable that much of its appeal lies in its effective use of nostalgia in the representation of the decade, from the David Bowie's song that inspired the title (that was used in the key scene of the episode, where it plays in Sam's car before the accident in 2006 and after that in 1973) to the trademark leather jackets and sideburns wore by the characters. *Life on Mars* embodies television's efforts to explore the memory of the past, mainly from his own past through the resurrection of old programmes, the success of formats that used archive footage, the constant rerun of old seasons, the popularity of DVD editions, and the proliferation of old TV clips on YouTube and other video services, proving Amy

Holdsworth's claim (2008: 139) that the TV medium is "lost in memory". Accusations that the portrayal in *Life on Mars* of the 1970s police behavior as unrealistic, hyperbolic and ironic can be answered from this point of view (Chapman, 2009).

Although the final episode of *Life on Mars* was broadcast in April 2007, that did not mark the definitive end of the series. As if they were regretting the premature ending of the series, the producers decided to create a sequel that would follow the misadventures of the charismatic Gene Hunt. *Ashes to Ashes* (BBC1: 2008-2010) took the action to London in the 1980s with an narrative concept very similar to the previous series, but this time was the agent Alex Drake (Keeley Hawes) who awoke in 1981 after being shot in 2008. In addition, *Life on Mars*, like many other British television programmes, was subject of two remakes: an U.S. version, also titled *Life on Mars* (ABC: 2008), and the Spanish series *La chica de ayer*.

The Spanish adaptation was carried out by independent production company Ida y Vuelta (the former production company Boomerang), which has also developed the dramas *Motivos personales* (*Personal Reasons*, Telecinco: 2005), *Génesis, en la mente del asesino* (*Genesis, in the Mind of the Murderer*, Cuatro: 2006-2007), *Círculo Rojo* (*Red Circle*, Antena 3: 2007) and *Acusados* (*Defendants*, Telecinco: 2009-2010), all which came to represent the renovation that Spanish television fiction was experiencing in terms of narrative structures, themes and stylistic features. Kudos trusted Ida y Vuelta with its most valuable property, but as with the American remake, the company was also interested in taking part in the production and, this way, to extend its international operations. Dario Madrona, creator of *Génesis* and *Acusados*, developed the new series and wrote the first episode, while Ignacio Mercero, a veteran producer, took showrunning duties and direct the first episode. A key point of the adaptation process was to find a lead actor who would give some distinction to the new Sam Tyler, now named Samuel Santos. After they couldn't reach an agreement with the movie heart-throb Eduardo Noriega, the producers settled on another popular film actor, Ernesto Alterio, who except for the expensive miniseries *Vientos de agua* (*Winds of Water*, Telecinco: 2006), had not worked in TV in more than ten years. To play his love interest, Ana Valverde, the producers hired Manuela Velasco, who had just won a Goya (the Spanish Oscar) for Best New Actress for her work in the hit horror film *REC* (2007, Jaume Balagueró and Paco Plaza).

After buying the rights to remake the programme (and maybe because it was part of the deal), Antena 3 broadcast *Life on Mars* in its sister digital channel Neox with modest results. As discussed earlier, adaptations of European series were becoming a trend on Spanish TV, but it was truth that few of these adaptations could provide the pedigree of *Life on Mars*. But we must add another key element to explain the interest in *Life on Mars*. It was a historical programme, a genre that was then fashionable in Spanish fiction thanks to the success of *Cuéntame cómo pasó* and *La señora* (*The Lady*, TVE1: 2008-2010). And the 1970s, where *Life on Mars* took place, was a key period in the recent history of Spain. After forty years of ruling the country with a iron hand with the help of the Spanish Army and the Catholic Church, dictator Francisco Franco died in 1975 and the country took the path to democracy led by King Juan Carlos I and prime minister Adolfo Suárez. But in the 2000s, the Spanish Transition became the subject of frequent discussions and political debates. Many left-wing politicians, commentators and scholars started to argue that it was a process less idyllic than previously thought and that the compromise to achieve democracy left many issues unresolved, including the crimes committed during and after the Civil War. The passing of The Law for the Recovery of the Historical Memory, a signature legislative action by socialist Prime Minister Rodríguez Zapatero in 2007, was the controversial climax of these public debates.

La chica de ayer showed very quickly highlighted the challenges and obstacles posed by the process of cultural adaptation. One of the central features of *Life on Mars* was its treatment of nostalgia through the use of cultural artifacts, but these could completely lose their meaning in Spanish culture. That was the case of the David Bowie song that gave the series its title. The chosen replacement, "La chica de ayer" ("The Girl From Yesterday"), by the beloved band *Nacha Pop*, was paradigmatic of musical renewal in the Madrid pop scene in the 1980s, the "Movida". Besides the nostalgia for the period, the title of the song allowed to emphasize the love story between Samuel Santos and Ana Valderde as a key element in the series. The problem was that the song "La chica de ayer" was not released until 1980, making impossible that Samuel Santos would be listening to the song when he wakes up in 1977. The answer to this situation was to use the Queen song "Bohemian Rhapsody", originally released in 1975 and far more popular among the Spanish audiences than the David Bowie track. The result of this musical mess is obvious: *La chica de ayer* did not find the link between past and present through a song that could express the deep alienation of its main character.

That any cultural adaptation is almost never innocent must also be noted. The first indication of a much deep cultural transformation was the choice of 1977 as the year in which Samuel Santos wakes up. In an interview included on the DVD release of *La chica de ayer*, executive producer Ignacio Mercero offers the following reason:

> We had to adapt it a bit to the Spanish society. The original series took place 73. We thought that the year 73 was still a very dark year in Spain. Franco was still alive and we wanted to be more positive. And we thought that the year 1977 was a year in which people in Spain were very excited. It was the Transition, democracy arrived. We were about to vote the Constitution.

The year 1977 also appears as a time of optimism in a prologue scene included in the first episode aimed to explain the premise of the series, just in case the Spanish viewers are too dumb to understand it (an example of the low consideration that Spanish executives and producers have of TV audiences). Breaking the fourth wall, Samuel Santos speaks directly to viewers:

> They say that 1977 was a great year. Well, it is true that there were no mobile phones or MP3 players. Of course, there was no Internet. And finally, divorce, gambling and many more things were still forbidden. But that year the first democratic elections were held. On the streets there was an air of optimism. Betis [a modest football team] won the first King's Cup, formerly known as the Generalissimo's Cup. That year *Star Wars* was released and all radio stations played "Gavilán o paloma" ("Hawk or Dove").

Producer Ignacio Mercero talks about illusion, while Samuel Santos refers to an optimism sparked by epic sport victories, special effects movies and catchy tunes. It is very possible that the Spaniards could have felt hope or optimism following the passing of the Political Reform Act in December 1976 and the prospect of the first democratic elections in June that year. But they were also feeling fear. Historian Álvaro de Soto (2005, p. 33-34) has noted that the political violence was so present throughout the Transition process that it became a key feature of it. Mariano Sanchez-Soler even titled his book about the period *La transición sangrienta / The Bloody Transition*, where he established in almost six hundreds the fatal casualties by the violence exercise by the police forces and extreme left and right-wing organizations (2010, p. 17-20). Almost nothing of that is present in the eight produced episodes of the series, which prefer to ignore the bloody events happening in the streets of Madrid in this period. Not only the series as a whole forgets the past, its main character does it as well. While the original series Sam Tyler was a reformer of the police force, somebody who even in a difficult circumstance behaves like a modern cop, already in the first episode of *La chica de ayer* Samuel Santos acts as a vigilante and tries to kill a detainee who he thinks will kidnap his girlfriend in the future. Later he acts without remorse where the same detainee is killed in self-defense by a fellow cop, who asks for the cleaning lady to sort out the mess. But in the context of the Spanish Transition and 1977, the scene is hard to swallow when remembering the dark episodes of detainees tortured and killed in police precincts and jails during and after the dictatorship. It is not an isolated fact. *La chica de ayer* turns a just released left-wing political prisoner and the son of the leader of a workers' union into cold-blooded murderers in subsequent episodes. The use of the "buddy-cop" movie formula in *La chica de ayer* masks a convenient and conservative representation of the past. The progressive beat of *Life of Mars* is lost in translation.

Conclusion: An After-Life

As noted above, *Life on Mars* ceased production after only two seasons, longer than its two remakes, both of which were canceled after one season. *La chica de ayer* premiered on Antena 3 on April 26 2009, in the privileged slot of Sunday prime-time. While the representation of the recent Spanish past is clearly problematic, the series excelled in formal elements (camera work, editing, use of music and dialogue) and offered a riveting performance of Antonio Garrido as Gallardo, the Spanish Gene Hunt. The rating initial results were good (a 19.7% share and nearly four million of viewers), but the series lost a third of viewers in the second episode, a decline that continued in the following weeks[3]. In a context of increased competition on Spanish TV, *La chica de ayer* was more a disappointment than an outright failure. Neither the historical setting nor the presence of famous film actors ensured a commercial success as big as to justify the high budget of the series. Ironically, it was the ambition of *La chica de ayer* what caused its early end. In an interesting closing to its existence, *La chica de ayer* now enjoys a kind of after-life together with *Life on Mars*. In December 2009, both a "Complete Series" edition of *Life on*

3 The rating information is taken from: http://www.formulatv.com/series/la-chica-de-ayer/ (14-05-2012).

Mars and *La chica de ayer* were released on DVD the same day by Universal Pictures. The distributor also released a combo pack containing the first season of *Life on Mars* and the only produced season of *La chica de ayer*. With this unique experiment, the remake, which used the first season of the former series as basis for most of the scripts, was cast as a complementary alternative to the original. A viewer could enjoy a meticulous recreation of the 1970s England before enjoying a nostalgic trip to the Spain of the Transition, with its more recognizable references (or the other way around). It shows that when transnational TV crosses borders the process of adaption tends to reveal cultural differences, yet at the same time open doors to understand what we have in common and think of ourselves. [4]

BIBLIOGRAPHY

Buonanno, M. "A Place in the Sun: Global Seriality and the Revival of Domestic Drama in Italy". In: Moran, Albert (ed.). *TV Formats Worldwide: Localizing Global Programs*. Bristol: Intellect, 2009, p. 255-270.

Chapman, J. "Not 'another bloody cop show': *Life on Mars* and British television drama". *Film International* 7.2 (2009), p. 6-19.

Fickers, A. / Johnson, C. "Transnational Television History: A Comparative Approach. Introduction". *Media History* 16.1 (2010), p. 1-11.

Fornäs, J. *Signifying Europe*. Bristol: Intellect, 2012.

Moran, A. "The Pie and the Crust. Television Program Formats". In: Allen, R. C. / Hill, A. (eds.). *The Television Studies Reader*. London: Routledge, 2004, p. 258-266.

Sánchez Soler, M. *La transición sangrienta. Una historia violenta del proceso democrático en España (1975-1983)*. Barcelona: Ediciones Península, 2010.

Schlesinger, P. "Wishful Thinking: Cultural Politics, Media, and Collective Identities in Europe". *Journal of Communication* 43.2 (1993), p. 6-17.

Selznick, B. *Global Television: Co-Producing Culture*. Philadelphia: Temple University Press, 2008.

Soto, Á. *Transición y cambio en España, 1975-1996*. Madrid: Alianza Editorial, 2005.

Television without Frontiers (TVWF) Directive, Council Directive 89/552/EEC of 3 October 1989.

---

4 This work has been made possible by the help of the Research Projects "Media co-productions in the European context: Identities and cultural transnationalization processes" (AT2009-0020, Ministry of Science and Innovation, Government of Spain, Integration Actions Program), "Spanish film coproductions: social and information aspects" (2011/00098/001, Grants for the Consolidation of Research Groups, Community of Madrid/Carlos III University of Madrid) and "Cinema and Television in Post-Transition Spain (1979-1992)", Ministry of Economy and Competitiveness, Government of Spain (CSO2011-15708-E).

The Transnational In Europe

Coproductions between France and Italy during the post-war period: the building up of a transnational audience?

Camille Gendrault

"Our two markets could become one. If our experiment is successful, producers in France and Italy would have access to a market of ten thousand screens which could lead to greater and more regular earnings on their films."[1] This is how Salvo D'Angelo, a well-respected Italian producer working at the time with the Roman company Universalia on the production of *Fabiola* – a film directed by the Italian Alessandro Blasetti but with French actors (Michèle Morgan, Michel Simon, Henri Vidal) in the leading roles – presented the project involving "very close coordination amongst the French and Italian film industries"[2] to a special correspondent from the trade journal *Le Film français* in March 1948.

Salvo D'Angelo was certainly not the only one from his profession, in Italy as well as in France, working towards setting up a genuine joint policy of filmmaking between these two countries. There had of course always been very active ties between the two film industries, as can be seen from the many exchanges, collaborations and trips back-and-forth by film professionals on both sides of the Alps, although they had weakened somewhat by the final years of the Second World War. As a flood of Hollywood films hit the European markets in the first years after the war, it was a question however of going much further: agreements were reached, the initial version of which was signed between France and Italy as early as October 1946, allowing a film at that time to benefit from the status of coproduction if any foreign financial backing was used in making it. This provided a considerable advantage since what it meant in concrete terms was that the film in question could benefit from the same conditions which applied to Italian films in Italy and French ones in France. This was of course also true with regard to the terms of access to each of the national markets, which were thus opened up to the film without any of the usual restrictions relating to import quotas and screenings of foreign films.

As we know, the principle of coproductions has since spread and become a common practice in many other film industries beyond Italy and France. West Germany and Spain also ended up signing coproduction agreements with France and Italy beginning in the early 1950s. Nonetheless, throughout that decade, France

1 "Nos deux marchés peuvent n'en faire qu'un. Si notre expérience réussit, les producteurs de France et d'Italie se trouveront devant un marché de dix mille salles qui permettront une rentabilité beaucoup plus grande et beaucoup plus régulière de leurs films."

2 M.B. [Maurice Bessy]. "Pour une politique franco-italienne de production". *Le Film français*. Paris, No. 171, 19 March 1948, p. 9 : "une coordination très étroite des cinématographies française et italienne".

and Italy clearly stood out as the two European countries jointly undertaking the most coproductions. In October 1960, the French *Bulletin d'information du Centre National de la Cinématographie* (CNC) counted no less than 408 coproductions covering the period from 1949 to 1959, which amounted to nearly one-third of all films being then produced in France; 79% of these coproductions were carried out with Italy.[3]

While this golden age of coproductions between France and Italy lasted well beyond this period, since it was not until the early 60s that the phenomenon underwent a veritable explosion before declining drastically in the mid-70s, it is essentially these early years when the idea was introduced and took off, progressively at first before becoming more patently obvious, that we would like to concentrate on here. However, we will not be retracing the different stages involved in building up this coproduction policy, as this has already been done.[4] Nor will we be presenting a table showing all of the films produced under this framework. The purpose of this article is quite different. Rather, it aims in fact to determine to what extent the growing importance of coproductions during this period actually reshaped the outlines of the Italian and French markets, producing a transnational market like the one envisaged in 1948 by producers such as Salvo D'Angelo.

With this in mind, as well as the fact that a market "can be defined first and foremost as a place for exchanges" where "the wants of consumers (…) meet those of the producers"[5] (Creton, 1997, p. 22), readers will be invited to shift their attention from the actual filmmaking to the audience. The focus will be on whether a transnational audience between France and Italy was indeed built up during the post-war period in light of how the French public received these coproductions. However, our subject will necessarily be limited in scope, if only because it would be untenable to discuss all three hundred and fifty odd films coproduced during the period being examined in this paper. We have therefore chosen to focus our attention on the biggest box office successes and, among these, certain comedies in particular which stir up specific lines of questioning which tie in with the development of a taste in films which cuts across borders.

The Rapid Rise of Coproductions with Italy at the French Box Office

The rapid rise of coproductions between France and Italy in the early 1950s is very obvious. First off, in terms of sheer numerical volume. If we look at the figures provided by Aldo Bernardini (Bernardini, not dated), which are now considered the reference in this field, we can see that the number of coproduced films over the next few years only rarely numbered more than ten (and even in these cases, making it to eleven with difficulty), but then it clearly began to increase starting in 1952 (17 ti-

3 Not signed. "La coproduction en France (Résultats d'exploitation)". *Bulletin d'information du C.N.C.* Paris, No. 65, October 1960, p. 162-164. By way of comparison, during this period, there were 326 coproductions with Italy, while the coproduction figures given for other film industries are the following: Spain: 23; Germany: 20; other countries: 39.

4 See in particular Burucoa, 1995.

5 "[Un marché] se définit d'abord comme lieu de l'échange" où "les désirs des consommateurs (…) croisent ceux des producteurs".

tles) and especially in 1953 (33 titles), even going so far as to break the fifty mark the following year. After the hesitant initial steps of the immediate post-war period and the first legal texts signed in 1946, we can therefore consider that the system set up and consolidated in 1949, at which time new, more detailed agreements were concluded, started gaining real momentum around 1952-1953. This new momentum was especially substantiated by the films' success in terms of numbers of moviegoers. If we look at the films which ranked in the top 20 at the French box office,[6] the phenomenon is quite noticeable: until 1952, French-Italian coproductions very rarely made it onto this list, with only one or two films at best; and yet, in 1952, as many as six films coproduced by the two countries appeared on the list with similar results over the next three years. For the rest of the decade, their place among the biggest box office successes in France was constant, never going below six and, in 1959, coming very close to an even ten; that is to say, half of the films listed among the biggest box office successes.

It is these films which are of primary interest to us in this paper insofar as they can assist us in determining the growing importance of coproductions in terms of what was considered the most popular type of cinema during this time in France.[7] A closer examination must also be made of what kind of films they are and what they tell us of the French public's taste regarding coproductions; but first, we must consider in what way these coproduced films were identified as such – and therefore in what way they were identified by the cinemagoers at the time – and how this new practice was then perceived.

Approaching the question of coproductions from this angle – that of audience response – shifts the attention paid up to now by studies devoted to this issue which, for the most part, considered it from the point of view of filmmaking. We were therefore compelled to consult other sources. Thus, if Barbara Corsi's research on coproduction policy (Corsi, 1996 et 1999) essentially used contemporary (Italian) corporate magazines as sources since what was of primary interest to her was looking at the phenomenon from the point of view of the film industry (Italian side), it is understandable that we chose to use the flip side in our approach by studying almost exclusively the popular (French) film magazines of the period. Of these, we decided

6 The records used here are the ones published by Simon Simsi (Simsi, 2000). Besides the fact that coproductions were not always identified as such– an omission which we have corrected in our own analyses– these lists nonetheless present the inconvenience of grouping together figures that were accumulated up until the year of publication which could sometimes, in the case of films which became surrounded somewhat by hype afterwards, skew perspectives to some extent.

7 Our use of "popular cinema" here perhaps requires further explanation. All those who have worked on this topic have felt the need to underline the vague nature of this concept which is not easily defined. See notably Pierre Sorlin (1995, in particular p. 357) as well as Richard Dyer and Ginette Vincendeau (1992, p. 2-3). Here, we use the term "popular" according to its Anglo-Saxon meaning (Translator's note: as opposed to its French usage), namely: appealing to a large number of people. In the words of Yannick Dehée (2012, p. 553), it therefore signifies "neither a production of the working classes, nor one necessarily intended for the working classes" but rather "a mass production which reaches its target" ("ni une production des couches populaires, ni forcément destinée aux couches populaires" mais plutôt "une production de masse qui atteint son but").

to favor in particular the weekly publication *Cinémonde*, one of the most widely read at the time.[8]

Identification and Promotion of Coproductions between France and Italy

Even though the publication *Cinémonde*, richly illustrated with photos, was largely devoted to news of movie stars, it at least still reported on some of the discussions sparked by the introduction of coproductions in the early years and contributed to nurturing the debates. From this viewpoint, it must first be remarked how the principle of coproduction itself was questioned in the beginning. This is why, in 1947, the magazine's special correspondent in Rome wondered with a certain perplexity about what role and responsibilities were to be taken on by each of the two countries when shooting a particular film:

> I left Jean Marais in Milan in order to go to Rome to meet with Christian-Jaque and Viviane Romance, who are working in different studios shooting films with a "French percentage" that is in fact fairly uneven. On *La Chartreuse de Parme*, we know that the entire crew is French. The French presence is much smaller on the crew of *Le Carrefour des Passions*[9], especially since Henri Calef, who started the film, had to pack up and go following several incidents which we will be reporting on next week...[10]

Above all, coproductions, which then had to deal with certain specific problems, were not at all considered to be a gage of quality of a film, as pointed out by this critic of *Rocambole* (Jacques de Baroncelli, 1948):

> What is likely the most to blame in *Rocambole* results from the conditions in which this film was made. As it was shot in Italy, with Italians making up half of the cast, a large number of scenes had to be redubbed. It's noticeable. It's even annoying. Perhaps it is because the dubbing is not very good.[11]

And although the problems linked to shooting films in several languages seem to have later been resolved insofar as they are no longer cited, an article published in

---

8 The work carried out by Delphine Chedaleux was of great help in the drafting of this article and consisted of indexing the magazine *Cinémonde* as part of the National Research Agency's (Agence Nationale de la Recherche) French program (2012-2014) "Cinepop 50" on mainstream cinema and film buffs in post-war France, directed by Geneviève Sellier, Professor at the Michel de Montaigne University - Bordeaux 3. http://cinepop50.u-bordeaux3.fr/. On the magazine *Cinémonde* as a source for a study on response, see Burch; Sellier, 2009.

9 This film came out in Italy in 1948 under the title *Gli uomini sono nemici*. The director Henri Calef, not listed in the credits, was in fact replaced in the middle of shooting by the Italian Ettore Giannini.

10 Leprohon, Pierre. "Avec les Français de Rome". *Cinémonde*. Paris, No. 683, 2 September 1947, p. 13: "J'ai laissé Jean Marais à Milan pour aller retrouver à Rome Christian-Jaque et Viviane Romance qui s'emploient sur des studios différents, à tourner des films dont le "pourcentage français" est, en fait, assez inégal. Pour La Chartreuse de Parme, on sait que l'équipe technique tout entière est française. Elle est beaucoup plus réduite dans Le Carrefour des Passions, surtout depuis qu'Henri Calef, qui l'avait commencé, a dû prendre le chemin du retour à la suite d'incidents dont nous vous entretiendrons la semaine prochaine... ".

11 Spade, Henri, "Rocambole", *Cinémonde*. Paris, No. 716, 20 April 1948, p. 8: "Ce qui est sans doute le plus à blâmer dans Rocambole ressort aux conditions dans lesquelles ce film a été réalisé. Tourné en Italie, avec une interprétation à moitié italienne, il a donc dû être doublé pour une grande partie des scènes. On le sent. On en est gêné. Sans doute parce que le doublage n'est pas très réussi."

1952 in reference to *Fanfan la Tulipe* (Christian-Jaque) still mentions, without really getting into specifics, "the difficulties which crop up in all 'Franco-foreign coproductions'".[12]

Another point worth noting is that the articles – even when they express certain reservations, as in the latter cited – progressively reveal how the principle of coproduction is slowly becoming part of the discourse on film. With each successive issue, we can thus observe, if not the dawning of the term itself of coproduction, at least its rising popularity. In 1947, it was used from time to time but still only appeared exceptionally and in reference to the "collaboration" and the "exchanges of artists" involved. Instead, mention was usually made, in a fairly vague manner, of "Franco-Italian cinema" or even "Franco-Italian filmmaking".[13] Likewise, on advertising materials, for example the posters for *La Chartreuse de Parme*[14] and *Rocambole*[15], the term used is that of "associated production". As late as 1952, the term coproduction, even though it had been assimilated, did not seem to be the one most commonly used if a double-page spread listing the film titles of the year, from which the magazine's readers were asked to select their favorite, is any indication: among the categories used ("French films", "dubbed films" and among the latter: American, Argentinean, British, Mexican, etc.), the one of interest to us is listed as "French speaking films made abroad (Franco-Italian coproductions)".[16]

The Promotion of Latinity

Nonetheless, as early as 1947, even if the term – and especially the usage that it designated – was not yet widespread, some staff members of *Cinémonde* took up the cause of coproductions and were already picturing the promising future of a practice destined to spread to other countries. Thus, Lo Duca, in an article which sets up a short Voltaire-inspired tale by narrating a discussion between two characters named "The Innocent" and "The Distinguished but Devastated Producer" ("Le Producteur Distingué mais Catastrophé"), had the first proclaim loudly and strongly: "Work together, French and Italian, and you'll see that others will join you in no time."[17] In this context, there were those who first looked towards Spain, such as

12 Not signed. "Voici notre opinion sur les films nouveaux". *Cinémonde*. Paris, No. 922, 4 April 1952, p. 16: "les difficultés qui naissent de toutes les 'co-productions franco-étrangères'".

13 For example in: Leprohon, Pierre. "Cinémonde en Italie 3: l'Italie carrefour du cinéma international". *Cinémonde*. Paris, No. 666, 6 May 1947, p. 9; Lo Duca. "Ce qui crève les yeux ou Cinéma franco-italien". *Cinémonde*. Paris, Special Cannes issue (not dated), 1947, p. 31; Bessy, Maurice. "Pour que Fabiola soit chrétienne il en coûtera un demi-milliard… et Michèle Morgan est devenue une patricienne du IIIe siècle". *Cinémonde*. Paris, No. 711, 16 March 1948, p. 5-6.

14 Poster signed by Eric, 1947, 160 x 240 cm, printer: Paris: Courbet.

15 Poster for Rocambole, 1ère époque signed by Jean Jacquelin, 1947, 120 x 160 cm, printer: Paris: C.F. – Imprimerie de la Cinématographie Française.

16 Not signed. "Les victoires du cinéma français, grand prix de Cinémonde". *Cinémonde*. Paris, No. 912, 25 January 1952, p. 14-15.

17 Lo Duca. "Ce qui crève les yeux ou Cinéma franco-italien". *Cinémonde*. Paris, Special Cannes issue (not dated), 1947, p. 31: "Travaillez ensemble, Français et Italiens, et vous verrez les autres se grouper à vous à brève échéance." It may be noted that Joseph-Marie Lo Duca revisits the topic of coproductions in 1954, defending the principle behind them, in comments

the critic Pierre Leprohon, who took up the reflections made on this issue by a particularly influential leading figure of French culture at that time, namely Marcel Pagnol:

> We know that a major Franco-Italian production was recently shot at the Farnesine studios in Rome: *La Danse de mort*, directed by Marcel Cravenne, with Eric von Stroheim, Maria Denis, Denise Vernac, Massimo Serato and Roberto Villa. It will then be the turn of the Italian actors to shoot abroad: Pagliero and Anna Magnani in France and Fosco Giachetti and Maria Denis in Spain. This exchange of artists is a very welcome development as it will help increase knowledge and familiarity of the actors in the different countries of the "Latin Bloc", which was dreamt of this winter by Marcel Pagnol in Monte Carlo and is already being implemented in reality by Mr Scalera[18], the coproducer of *La Vie de bohème*, *Carmen*, *Rocambole* and *La Chartreuse de Parme*.[19]

These remarks were therefore a continuation of the thinking expressed at the "International Latin Film Congress", which had in fact convened in Monte Carlo in September 1947 at the initiative of Pagnol,[20] and can be seen as rather representative of the increasingly weighty rhetoric of Latinity from this period which greatly helped in promoting Franco-Italian coproduction policies in its early years. The pages of *Cinémonde* echoed this line of thinking on several occasions. As a result, when the producer of *Fabiola* cited at the beginning of this paper was invited to share his views on the question of coproductions, this time for the popular magazine, the article ends with this rallying cry: " – Let us work for Latin civilization, stated Salvo D'Angelo."[21] Again in 1952, when the director Henri Decoin was interviewed for an article on the shooting of *Amants de Tolède* (1953), he adopted the same approach:

> The age of national films has passed. […] I shot two films in Spain because that's what popped up. We must persevere down this path of international agreements and conquer all the markets. […] Let me come back to Spain. Has serious thought been given to the 'Latin Bloc' that we form with Spain and Italy? How much consideration

printed in *Cahiers du cinéma*, a magazine which he helped set up (Lo Duca. "'Pool'" du cinéma européen, coproduction et manœuvres...". *Cahiers du cinéma*. Paris, No. 36, June 1954, p. 28-32).

18 On the image of the "international" production house built by La Scalera in the last years of the 1930s, notably through its French subsidiary, see Alberto Farassino et al., 1986.

19 Leprohon, Pierre. "Cinémonde en Italy 3: l'Italy carrefour du cinéma international". *Cinémonde*. Paris, No. 666, 6 May 1947, p. 9: "On sait qu'une grande production franco-italienne a été tournée récemment au studio de la Farnesine, à Rome : La Danse de mort, réalisée par Marcel Cravenne, avec Eric von Stroheim, Maria Denis, Denise Vernac, Massimo Serato et Roberto Villa. Les acteurs italiens, à leur tour, vont aller tourner à l'étranger. Pagliero et Anna Magnani en France, Fosco Giachetti et Maria Denis, en Espagne. On ne peut que se réjouir de ces échanges d'artistes, car ils contribueront à faire connaître les uns et les autres dans les divers pays de ce "bloc latin" dont Marcel Pagnol rêvait cet hiver, à Monte-Carlo, et que M. Scalera, le coproducteur de La Vie de bohème, Carmen, Rocambole et La Chartreuse de Parme, envisage déjà sur le plan des réalités".

20 On this issue, reference can be made in particular to Barbara Corsi, 2001, p. 92-94.

21 Bessy, Maurice. "Pour que Fabiola soit chrétienne il en coûtera un demi-milliard… et Michèle Morgan est devenue une patricienne du IIIe siècle". *Cinémonde*. Paris: No. 711, 16 March 1948, p. 5-6: "– Travaillons pour la civilisation latine, dit Salvo D'Angelo".

> has been given to the distribution our films could have if we were to cooperate more closely with the film industries in these two countries?[22]

The common denominator of Latinity was thus strongly underscored in the remarks made by those working in the industry during these years. Bearing this concept in mind,[23] even if it therefore seemed natural that the Italian and French film industries should work together, it was not done in fact solely for economic reasons; in other words it was not necessarily because they formed the two film industries in Europe which carried the most weight in the post-war period and which shared many similarities in terms of their markets. Another reason also given, and even primarily, was the great cultural proximity linking the two countries.

A Similar Taste in Comedy?

Success in economic terms of the transalpine coproduction policy as it was carried out during the post-war period, which validated its becoming as developed as much as it did afterwards, also seemed to confirm that such cultural proximity did in fact exist. In this regard, *Le Petit Monde de Don Camillo* (Julien Duvivier, 1952), which was the first in the series of films featuring Don Camillo (Fernandel), forever at odds with the communist mayor Peppone (Gino Cervi), and which earned extraordinarily good ticket sales as soon as it was released, stands out as one of the best examples of success resulting from this formula. Such success can be quite surprising as comedy is often seen as having a strongly national, or even regional, component, which makes genre films hard to export.[24] Insofar as it fell under this type of comedy, the fact that this coproduced film was such a success, with similar results for the sequel *Le Retour de Don Camillo* released the following year (and also directed by Julien Duvivier), quite pointedly raises the question of whether or not a transnational audience was being built up.

> I am certain that the success of the series (*Don Camillo* was the box office champion of its film season and the other films in the series placed high on the same list) provides a good indication for understanding how Italians – or at least a large number of

22 Decoin, Henri. "Decoin, l'Espagnol". *Cinémonde*, Paris, No. 936, 11 July 1952, p. 11: "Le temps du film national est révolu. […] J'ai tourné deux films en Espagne, parce que cela s'est trouvé comme ça. Il faut persévérer dans cette voie des accords internationaux et conquérir tous les marchés. […] J'en reviens à l'Espagne. A-t-on songé au 'bloc latin' que nous formons avec elle et l'Italie ? A-t-on songé à la diffusion que connaîtraient nos films si nous coopérions plus étroitement avec les productions de ces deux pays ?" The tripartite coproductions with Spain began to really take off in 1962, as noted by Thomas H. Guback (1969, p. 190).

23 This was a concept which was not new and which was to last long after the period being studied. Already, in the 1930s, the notion of a "Latin film" as advocated by Luigi Freddi, appointed head of the Directorate General for Italian Cinematography in 1934, struck a chord in France (see Peyrusse, 1986, p. 174-178). In the early 1980s, the "Latin Axis" line of reasoning was widely used again, particularly by its main promulgator, Daniel Toscan du Plantier, in order to justify the choice of Italy by Gaumont as part of its international expansion strategy, as emphasized by Vicky Postler (2005, p. 100-102 and p. 265-267).

24 See for example Thomas Elsaesser's remark (1992, p. 78) made in an aside concerning the beginning of Lubitsch's career: "Lubitsch soon abandoned comedian's comedy and concentrated on directing, perhaps precisely because the 'Meier' type he had helped bring to the screen proved geographically and ethnically too limiting, cutting out potentially important audiences and becoming – as much popular European comedy seems to have been – inexportable."

> them – consider the fundamental problems of politics or religion. [...] To the extent where it talks about politics, even in a comedic way, in one of the most politicized countries; insofar as it brings together the major protagonists of Italian society – the communist and catholic masses – this series tells us many things about ideologies and especially attitudes in Italy in the 1950s.[25] (Gori, 1987, p. 122)

Indeed. But when Gianfranco Gori, who worked extensively on ties between cinema and history, made this analysis more than thirty years after the release of *Le Petit Monde de Don Camillo*, he seemed to forget that the film's amazing success had been replicated in France where it very clearly stood out at the #1 spot at the box office. This is undoubtedly even more interesting! So what should be concluded from this? Does the film also tell us "many things about ideologies and especially attitudes" in France "in the 1950s"? We think it is more relevant, in keeping with the focus of this study, to consider to what extent certain aspects of the film may have contributed to it being such a huge success on both sides of the Alps at the same time.

In particular, we are thinking of the way in which the fictional setting is represented, namely a village in the plains of Po. As a matter of fact, the film refrains from showing any picturesque scenery that would emphasize the Italian nature of the surroundings. As Gianfranco Gori would himself remark, the landscape of "unending well-tended countryside" ("campagne sans relief et bien cultivée") which is lingered over in the opening scenes of *Le petit Monde de Don Camillo*, and which we can assume is characteristic of this film as well as the others in the series, does not appear to be specifically Italian or "typically Italian": "It is a countryside that could be anywhere" in "a film from out of the blue"[26] (Gori, 1987, p. 123). More generally speaking, as also pointed out by Gori, the film in no way presented a national or local identity but instead was centered on a generic opposition between town and country. This, we might add, is what helped to make the universe portrayed in the film one which would be as familiar to a French moviegoer as an Italian one. The fact that a French audience could watch one of its favorite actors, Fernandel, in the title role of parish priest of course helped to bring it even closer to home and made it easier to embrace this world. In this regard as well, the transnational balance was thus skillfully managed since the comic duo leading the film's cast and constantly quarreling throughout the film was in fact Franco-Italian.

A Comedy with a Double Approach

The same principle is at work in another coproduction which came out several years later, *La loi, c'est la loi* (Christian Jaque, 1958), in which Fernandel was

25 "Je suis certain que le succès de la série (Don Camillo a été le champion des recettes de sa saison cinématographique, et les autres films du cycle se sont placés en bonne position) en fait un bon indice pour comprendre comment les Italiens – ou une bonne partie d'entre eux – considèrent les problèmes fondamentaux de la politique ou de la religion. [...] Dans la mesure où elle parle de politique, même si c'est sous forme de comédie, dans l'un des pays les plus politisés ; dans la mesure où elle fait se rencontrer les grands protagonistes de la société italienne – les masses communistes et catholiques – cette série nous dit beaucoup de choses sur les idéologies, et surtout sur les mentalités dans l'Italie des années cinquante."

26 "Il s'agit là d'une campagne indéterminée", d'un "film de nulle part".

paired this time around with a comic actor equally famous in his own country, which had not been the case of Gino Cervi when *Le Petit Monde de Don Camillo* was first released: the Neapolitan Totò. This film is probably even more pertinent to the crux of our thesis since the village in the story is a town straddling France and Italy and the whole plot plays around the idea of borders to emphasize the absurdity of it and finally to render it meaningless. Once again, the main characters complement one another and are both equally essential in order for the comic plot gag to work since one of them (Totò) plays a smuggler and the other (Fernandel) a customs officer chasing him, one being Italian and the other French. Like the films portraying the struggles between Don Camillo and Peppone, *La loi, c'est la loi* also sets up a confrontation between the two protagonists, representing two distinct groups, defined in this case by their respective nationalities, before putting the village community first in the end. That being said, we might wonder whether, in this case, this film shouldn't be seen as being more bi-national than transnational.

When watching the French version, one is first surprised by the use of both French and Italian which peppers exchanges throughout the film. Of course, the majority of the dialogue is still in French and this is the language spoken most often by the character played by Totò. However, this is not done at all systematically and Italian regularly creeps into the dialogue. It happens a great deal and thus, the words pronounced in one language by one of the speakers may be repeated in another by the person with whom he is speaking. This can of course be somewhat startling but what is more surprising is discovering, upon watching the Italian version afterwards, that *La loi, c'est la loi* is set up as a film – and a comedy – with a double approach.

All you have to do is compare the first few minutes of the film in each of its two versions to grasp the concept. The film opens with a shot of a mountainous landscape panning off to the right while a narrator, in voice-off, begins to introduce what we are looking at before introducing himself. In the French version, it is the voice of Fernandel who tells us:

> Those are the Mediterranean Alps. But careful, eh, to the left they're French; to the right they're Italian. You don't notice any difference? And what about the border? You don't see it? […] And that bit of border… that's me, Ferdinand Pastorelli, customs officer, with twenty years of loyal service, who has the honor of ensuring it is respected by closely monitoring the sector of Assola.[27]

After the long opening shot which lasts more than a minute, the camera pans down to a village below: "Speaking of which, look, here it is, the small pretty bit of country where I was born and where I've lived for forty-five years."[28] The voice-off does not stop there: it also takes the time to introduce the film's first confrontation between the two protagonists by presenting his adversary as well. Zooming in on

---

27 "[…] ça, c'est les Alpes méditerranéennes, Mais attention, hein, à gauche elles sont françaises, à droite elles sont italiennes. Vous ne faites pas la différence ? Et la frontière, alors ? Vous ne la voyez pas ? […] Et celle-là de frontière, c'est moi, Ferdinand Pastorelli, brigadier des douanes, vingt ans de service, qui ai l'honneur de la faire respecter en surveillant étroitement le secteur d'Assola."

28 "Tiens, justement le voilà ce joli petit pays qui m'a vu naître et où j'habite depuis quarante-cinq ans."

the shot of a man walking through the mountains and from which Totò is recognizable, it continues: "That one (…) is the yellow jersey of fraudsters. Giuseppe La Paglia, who insidiously takes part in reprehensible smuggling activities."[29] And yet, even though the Italian version shows us the exact same sequence, it is Totò's voice, and therefore that of the aforementioned Giuseppe La Paglia, that we get to hear and which then proceeds to narrate the diametrically opposite point of view. For this character, who clearly lets the viewer know from the outset that "this is not [his] region, that [he] wasn't born here" but that "this small village here below" is the one "where [he's] lived for many years", "all would [of course] be much better if the customs officers weren't there. And especially, the French officer who's known [him] for quite some time and who [he] fondly considers to be his best enemy. But like the regional proverb says, 'there is always a worm in the pear and a customs officer at the border.'"[30]

Thus, with these opening remarks, the film's narrator is clearly shown, depending on the version being watched, as being either on the Italian side or the French side. And the dialogues which follow in each of these versions are in keeping with this, leaning more towards one or the other of these two languages. Each of the two actors accordingly finds himself with a national audience rooting for its favorite: Italian for Totò, French for Fernandel. We can speculate on how much of it was deliberately calculated to let the two different audiences respond to the film as a national product in order to guarantee the best ticket sales possible in both markets. Indeed, it would seem that building up a transnational audience was far from being a foregone conclusion.

Preference Given to National Productions

When looking at the films ranked in the top twenty at the French box office over the entire period, although coproductions between France and Italy increasingly make it to this list as the years pass, one aspect is striking: this almost systematically applies only to coproductions directed by French directors and whose leading actors were French. For example, in 1955, the list includes, to the exclusion of all other coproductions that year between France and Italy, the six following films: *Le Comte de Monte-Cristo* directed by Robert Vernay, *Napoléon* directed by Sacha Guitry, *Les Grandes Manœuvres* directed by René Clair, *French Cancan* directed by Jean Renoir, *Ça va barder* directed by John Berry and *Chiens perdus sans collier* directed by Jean Delannoy. One notable exception is however worth mentioning: the huge success in 1952 of *Anna*, a melodrama directed by Alberto Lattuada and starring Silvana Mangano in the title role, which came in at number thirteen in the year's list of box office hits. It seems nonetheless to be the exception that proves the

29 "Celui-là (…) c'est le maillot jaune des fraudeurs. Giuseppe La Paglia, qui se livre sournoisement à des activités répréhensibles et contrebandières."

30 "Questo non è il mio paese, non sono nato qui […] quel paesino laggiù dove vivo da parecchi anni. […] Certo andrebbe megio se non ci fossero i doganieri. E in particolar modo il brigadière francese Pastorelli Ferdinando che mi conosce da lunga pezza e che io considero affettuosamente il mio miglior nemico. Ma come dice un proverbio di queste parti 'c'è sempre un verme nella pera e un doganiere alla frontiera.'"

rule. Moreover, as Pierre Sorlin recalls, "the success of a few films is not necessarily significant as it is often the result of a savvy film distribution."[31] (Sorlin, 2000, p. 31). On the other hand, what the annual box office rankings do show which is very revealing is that, other than a strong showing by films from Hollywood, French audiences indicated a clear preference for national productions.[32]

Of course, the fact that films which were 100% made in Italy also managed to make their way at times onto these lists (for example, *Riz amer*, as early as 1949, also with Silvana Mangano) mitigates somewhat the finding of such a national preference. Likewise, more generally speaking, we can note the ever growing number of Italian films distributed in France over the years – increasing from a total of 151 films in 1950 to as many as 268 in 1959[33] – part of the credit for which must undoubtedly go to the support of coproduction policies: by familiarizing French audiences with actors and actresses of Italian cinema, for instance, it certainly helped films from this industry to penetrate the French market. It should also be specified that the Italian film industry was able to spark particular interest amongst certain specific audiences, as the historian Fabrice Montebello demonstrated by looking at the audience response to Italian films and the exceptional box office receipts they earned in areas where Italian immigrants were concentrated (Montebello, 1997).

That being said, as a whole, when looking at the larger scale of the number of spectators reached all across the national territory, market shares for Italian cinema remained limited (an average of 4.6% for the period in question[34]) and much lower than those for domestic films, which attracted many more moviegoers. The fact that coproductions ranking in the top twenty at the French box office were generally films with a majority of French involved and not a majority of Italian cast and/or crew only confirms this conclusion.[35] This is why we prefer to err on the side of caution and not be too hasty by concluding that the healthy economic functioning of the coproduction formula as a whole points to a "cross-fertilization process between Italian and French popular cultures" (Jäckel, 2003, p. 235). And it would be even more prudent to not conclude from all this, by following the well-trodden path of rhetoric on Latinity, that "the system worked well because the two countries shared cultural affinities – a common background of Romance cultures and languages as well as the Catholic religion and comparable schemes of incentives" (Jäckel, 2003, p. 240). In actual fact, the greater the impression on the part of French audiences that the coproduced film was indeed a national production, the greater the success

31 "[...] le succès de quelques films n'est pas nécessairement significatif, il résulte souvent d'une habile distribution."

32 On this point, see in particular Montebello, 2005, p. 32-42 and p. 145.

33 Here, we are using the figures given by Glas and Gyory, 1992, p. 106.

34 Average calculated using annual market shares broken down by nationality as indicated in Simsi, 2000.

35 It should be noted that, if Italian box office receipts for the same period are examined, the reverse does not necessarily hold true. Of course, further studies of the questions raised by such a distortion would be needed. Italian audiences seemed indeed to be more receptive to French cinema than French audiences to Italian cinema.

of the film.[36] The case of *Le Petit Monde de Don Camillo* appears to be a case in point.[37]

Appropriation

Whereas the *Catalogo Bolaffi,* published in Italy in 1967, explained that, although directed by a non-Italian director, "in all respects, it can be considered a film which is wholly Italian" – "it is typically Italian, not only because it was shot in Italy with a crew that was mostly Italian, but because its wit and character faithfully portray the Italian novel that it is based on"[38] (Levi et Rondolino, 1967, p. XIX and p. 58), the discussions surrounding *Le Petit Monde de Don Camillo* on its release in France were more primarily attuned to the French sensibility, and even more specifically a Provencal one, being portrayed. Thus, in the full-page article on the film published by *Cinémonde* in May 1952, not much mention was made of the fact that the film had been shot in Italy and used Italian actors (only Gino Cervi is very briefly mentioned). Most of the focus was on Fernandel's performance, and a novelist from the 19th century, famous for his typical southern characters, was brazenly invoked to lend it even greater weight: "Alphonse Daudet would have recognized in [Don Camillo as played by Fernandel] his priest of Cucugnan relocated to the other side of the Alps."[39] In an issue published two weeks later, no less a figure than Marcel Pagnol was referred to: "*Le Petit Monde de Don Camillo* is in keeping with the finest Mediterranean traditions of which Pagnol was the first poet and Rossellini the talented copyist."[40] And, a bit further in the text, the reference was made even plainer: "The spats between the Communist mayor Peppone and the priest Don Camillo have now entered the repertoire of classic squabbles, in the Pagnol-Raimu style of humor."[41] The phenomenon of cultural appropriation sparked by the film on the French side can thus be clearly seen, and it was tenaciously embraced as part of the well-established tradition of portrayals of the South of France. Indeed, the accent used in the French version not only by Fernandel but by most of the characters seemed to encourage this thinking, as pointed out by several critics at the time. Some of them did not entirely approve of such a choice, like Louis Chauvet who

36 In this regard, it seems significant, even if not specifically referred to, that in a list compiled by Anne Jäckel of coproduced films which won an award at the International Cannes Film Festival, all were directed by a French director without exception (2003, p. 235).

37 In Anne Jäckel's article, this film and the others which followed from the same series were used as an example. In our opinion, however, the series should instead be cited as an isolated case, most noteworthy for its usefulness as a counter-example.

38 "[…] a tutti gli effetti può considerarsi un film interamente italiano" – "è tipicamente italiano, non solo perché ambientato in Italia con una troupe soprattutto italiana, ma perché nello spirito e nella lettera riflette fedelmente il romanzo italiano da cui è tratto."

39 Not signed. "Dans *Le Petit Monde de Don Camillo* Fernandel est un don du ciel". *Cinémonde.* Paris, No. 930, 30 May 1952, p. 7: "Alphonse Daudet aurait reconnu en [Don Camillo interprété par Fernandel] son curé de Cucugnan passé de l'autre côté des Alpes."

40 Bessy, Maurice. "Notre opinion sur les films nouveaux". *Cinémonde.* Paris, No. 932, 13 June 1952, p. 15: "*Le Petit Monde de Don Camillo* se rattache à cette pure tradition méditerranéenne dont Pagnol fut le premier poète et Rossellini le doué copiste".

41 "Les démêlés du maire communiste Peppone et du curé don Camillo font désormais partie d'un répertoire de la brouille, style Pagnol-Raimu."

wrote in *Le Figaro:* "It can be somewhat odd to hear these inhabitants alongside the Po River, whose faces seem "authentic", speak with a Provencal accent."[42] Other critics however appreciated it precisely for the connection it created and which gave a French dimension to the film: "The dubbing is excellent and the idea of having Italian actors speak French with a whiff of aioli is amusing. The spirit of Daudet, and perhaps the ghost of Pagnol, is almost palpable."[43] The film – which was an Italian majority coproduction, financially speaking, with a cast made up of almost all Italian actors, with only four exceptions – thus accomplished the feat of being considered Italian by Italian audiences and French by French audiences. This is far from being the case of all the films coproduced during the period under examination.

The operating results of the coproduction policy actively carried out between France and Italy during the post-war period are absolutely conclusive: in October 1960, the CNC Newsletter indicated that the films coproduced under this framework represented 40.5% of total receipts earned in 1958 for the French market (compared to 19% in 1952) and 32.5 % of those added up for the same year for the Italian market (compared to 10% in 1952). Should it be considered though that a transnational audience had indeed been formed? That goes perhaps one step further than we are willing to take. A closer study of the annual box office rankings reveals to what extent the French public clearly favored any coproduced films which it identified as primarily French insofar as the directors and leading actors were associated in people's minds with a national film.

Of course, this was by no means an absolute rule: the huge success achieved at the French box office by *Anna* and *Le Petit Monde de Don Camillo*, even though they were productions with a majority of Italians, is proof of this. We could thus be tempted to see these examples as proof of popular Italian-French successes, or even to point to them as indicators of the strong cultural affinity between the two countries, a myth nurtured frequently by the rhetoric on Latinity. Yet, it so happens that these two films also met with success internationally, well beyond their specifically transalpine success, and were able to make inroads into many markets, including the American market, a long way from the Alps.

Of course, it is not a question of denying the wider intercultural dimension which characterized the French market during this period. This is all the more true since it was actually the foreign market most receptive to Italian cinema at the time.[44] Yet, the preference shown by French audiences for domestic productions - perceptible in the operating results even when they were coproductions, as we hope to have made sufficiently clear – is such that it would be difficult to conclude that a transnational audience had indeed been established. Furthermore, this assessment seems to concur with the conclusion reached by the major players in the film industries themselves, from both sides of the Alps, scarcely ten years after the very first agree-

42 Chauvet, Louis. "Les Films nouveaux". *Le Figaro*. Paris, 6 June 1952: "On trouve un peu bizarre d'entendre ces riverains du Pô, dont les visages semblent 'authentiques', parler avec l'accent provençal."

43 Guyo, Pierre-Jean. "*Le Petit Monde de Don Camillo*". *La Croix*. Paris, 14 June 1952: "Le doublage est excellent, et l'idée de faire parler aux acteurs italiens un français fleurant bon l'aïoli, est amusante. Il y avait du Daudet, peut-être du Pagnol dans l'air."

44 A point emphatically made by Christopher Wagstaff (1996, p. 163).

ments. In 1957, after a meeting with his Italian counterpart Eitel Monaco, the Director of the CNC Jacques Flaud in fact declared:

> We have reached a point where we have decided that what really matters is that France has helped Italy to make films befitting of its particular genius and artistic traditions, and vice versa. This system, which essentially amounts to a financial coproduction, seems to have produced happy results.[45]

Therefore, paradoxically, what the transnational coproduction policies carried out in the fifties distinctly reveal is first and foremost the clear delineation of very distinct national audiences: the markets do not overlap. Thus, in conclusion, it can be seen that a clear distinction needs to be made between transnational productions and transnational films and that any hasty impulses to consider these coproduced films as the expression of a popular European cinema need to be held in check. And this applies double to the idea of a popular European cinema which is specifically Latin in character.[46]

BIBLIOGRAPHY

Bernardini, A. *Filmografia delle comproduzioni italo-fancesi, 1947-1993*. Annecy: Rencontres du cinéma italien d'Annecy – Bonlieu Scène nationale, not dated.

Burch, N. / Sellier G. "Le courrier des lecteurs de *Cinémonde* dans les années 50 : la naissance d'une cinéphilie au feminine". In: Burch, Noël / Sellier, Geneviève. *Le cinéma au prisme des rapports de sexe*. Paris: Vrin, 2009, p. 67-90.

Burucoa, C. "Les conditions juridiques et historiques des coproductions (1946-1995)". In: Gili, J. A. / Tassone A. *Paris Rome, Cinquante ans de cinéma franco-italien*. Paris: La Martinière, 1995, p. 32-65.

Corsi, B. "Eutanasia di un'unione". In: Brunetta, G. P. (ed.). *Identità italiana e identità europea nel cinema italiano dal 1945 al miracolo économico*. Torino: Edizioni della Fondazione Giovanni Agnelli, 1996, p. 69-86.

Corsi, B. "L'utopia dell'unione cinematografica europea". In: Brunetta, G. P. (ed.). *Storia del cinema mondiale, Vol. 1, L'europa Miti, luoghi, divi*. Torino: Einaudi, 1999, p. 721-735.

Corsi, B. *Con qualche dollaro in meno. Storia economica del cinema italiano*. Roma: Editori Riuniti, 2001.

Creton, L. *Cinéma et marché*. Paris: Armand Colin, 1997.

Dehée, Y. "Populaire". In: Baecque, A. de / Chevallier, P. (eds.). *Dictionnaire de la pensée du cinéma*. Paris: PUF, 2012, p. 553-556.

Dyer, R. / Vincendeau, G. "Introduction". In: Dyer, R. / Vincendeau, G. (eds.). *Popular European Cinema*. Londres and New York: Routledge, 1992, p. 1-14.

---

45 Bazin, André and Doniol-Valcroze, Jacques. "Entretien avec Jacques Flaud". *Cahiers du cinéma*. Paris, No. 71, May 1957, p. 4-15, cit. p. 14: "On est arrivé à considérer que ce qui importait était que la France aide l'Italie à faire des films conformes à son génie et à sa tradition artistiques, et inversement. Ce système qui se réduit, dans le fond, à une coproduction financière, semble porter d'heureux fruits."

46 This contribution has been translated by Penelope Yim.

Elsaesser, T. "Author, Actor, Showman; Reinhold Schünzel and *Hallo Cesar*!". In: Dyer, R. / Vincendeau, G. (eds.). *Popular European Cinema*. London and New York: Routledge, 1992, p. 72-86.

Farassino, A. et al. "La Scalera Film". In: Magrelli, E. (ed.). *Sull'industria cinematografica italiana*. Venezia: Marsilio, 1986, p. 211-229.

Gori, G. "Giovanni Guareschi, un héros ambigu". *Les cahiers de la cinémathèque*. 46-47 (1987), "Europe 1945-1965", p. 121-130.

Glas, G. / Gyory, M. *Statistiques du cinéma en Europe*. Paris: CERICA, 1992.

Guback, T. H. *The International Film Industry. Western Europe and America since 1945*. Bloomington: Indiana University Press, 1969.

Jäckel, A. "Dual Nationality Film Productions in Europe after 1945". *Historical Journal of Film, Radio and Television* 23.3 (2003), p. 231-243.

Levi, O. / Rondolino, G. *Catalogo Bolaffi del cinema italiano: tutti i film italiani del dopoguerra*. Turin: Bolaffi, 1967.

Montebello, F. "Spectacle cinématographique et classe ouvrière: Longwy 1944-1960". Doctoral thesis in history, not published, Université Lyon 2, 1997.

Montebello, F. *Le cinéma en France*. Paris: Armand Colin, 2005.

Peyrusse, C. *Le cinéma méridional: le Midi dans le cinéma français (1929-1944)*. Toulouse: Eché, 1986.

Postler, V. *De Gaumont Italia à Arte; la politique culturelle française en Europe*. Paris: Connaissances et Savoirs, 2005.

Simsi, S. *Ciné-Passions. Septième art et industrie de 1945 à 2000*. Paris: Dixit, 2000.

Sorlin, P. "Popular Films or Industrial Byproduct? The Italian melodramas of the 1950s". *Historical Journal of Film, Radio and Television* 15.3 (1995), p. 349-359.

Sorlin, P. "Ce qu'était un film populaire dans l'Europe des années cinquante". In: Bertin-Maghit, J.-P. (ed.). *Les cinémas européens des années 50*. Paris: Editions AFRHC, 2000, p. 19-46.

Wagstaff, C. "Il cinema italiano nel mercato internazionale". In: Brunetta, G. P. (ed.). *Identità italiana e identità europea nel cinema italiano dal 1945 al miracolo économico*. Torino: Edizioni della Fondazione Giovanni Agnelli, 1996, p. 141-171.

TRANSNATIONALITY AND HISTORY: REPRESENTATIONS OF EAST AND WEST IN THEO ANGELOPOULOS' LAST TRILOGY

Irini Stathi

Introduction

The aspiration to be a "citizen of the world" reaches far back, at least to Socrates, if we can believe Plutarch before Martha Nussbaum's (1997) proclamation. At a time when there is so much talk about globalization, Linda Bosniak has written an important article that reviews writings on citizenship to explore what "denationalized" citizenship looks like in the present and might look like in the future. Bosniak argues:

> Recently [...]. Citizenship has begun to exceed the boundaries of the nation-state, they argue, and is increasingly taking nonnational forms. Whether described as "transnational," "postnational," or "global," the new forms of citizenship are understood to be denationalized in some way (Bosniak, 2000, p. 454).

To examine this affirmation in the context of today's cinema in Europe can be useful in understanding the way in which we treat the human condition through film creation and production. Theo Angelopoulos is clearly one of the directors who reflect continuously on the various changes that have occurred in Europe over the last decades. In his cinema, borders, boundaries and people's movement are essential in representing contemporary life; the line is blurred between the East and West as cultural territories promoting the fusion of the two poles. In so-called European culture (the formation of Western culture during the Renaissance) and nowadays in the form of the European Union (EU), efforts have been underway to construct a regionally framed supranational citizenship: a European citizenship. This development no doubt significantly challenges the conventional correspondence that we ordinarily assume exists between citizenship and national membership, and alerts us to possibilities for non-nation-centered arrangements.

Angelopoulos has always been clear in representing a "community of place" in his early cinema: he indicates a place-bound community formed within the particularity of a specific geographical space, which becomes a lived place articulated through the social relations of the people that inhabit it, as well as through their cultural values and meanings, the emotional, perceptual and symbolic investments produced therein. It gives rise to a discourse on place and identity (Morley and Robins, 1995; King, 1997; Massey, 1997 and 1998; Carter, Donald and Squires, 1993) which is connected to a discourse on history, place and identity as represented in films like *The Reconstruction* (*Anaparastasi*, 1970) and The *Traveling Players* (*O thiassos*, 1975). Later, both the "community" and the "place" are expanded in order to represent the complex status of the human condition as well as the multiple aspects of the places he refers to in his films. Cinema is probably the very means by which Angelopoulos represents the fusions between the different cultures and ideologies not only in Europe, but also all over the world. The nature of the means (unification of space and time) the freedom that it gives artists to move within these cultures, and the force of realistic representation gave an important advantage to the film in terms of depicting reality. Angelopoulos' characters in this sense become a kind of "citizens of history"; a history seen from the point of view of people who are moving because of the vagaries of history.

The Representation of History

The representation of historical reality in Angelopoulos is underscored because of the verification – and, at the same time, the denunciation – of the numerous ruptures, divisions and diversities which Greek people suffered during the 20th century; violent expatriations at the beginning of the century, the dictatorship of Metaxas in the 1930s, World War II (Italian invasion, German occupation, Civil War), political exile and finally the Dictatorship of the Colonels and the political exile that ensued (1967-1974). In the last few years, Angelopoulos seemed to have left history in the background (though without forgetting about it) and had extended his thinking by surveying, among other things, the degradation imposed by neo-barbarism across the wider region of the Balkans, where peoples experienced the trauma of both world wars and the conflicts in the area in earlier times, which influenced not only the Balkan peninsula, but the entire continent of Europe, and perhaps even the international community.

At the same time, through such choices, Angelopoulos reflects on the influence of history on the Greek people and his characters: Greeks who lived for centuries in the Mediterranean and the Balkans are then scattered all over the world through migration, exile and displacement. Angelopoulos considers the Mediterranean to be not only the birthplace of Hellenism, but also the birthplace of what we call Western culture (Angelopoulos, 1995; Stathi, 2008). In this way, his conception of Greekness is a notion which is "in between"; connecting the two worlds: East and West.

The various shifts from one place to another in Angelopoulos' films are caused by history and the great conflicts of the century, and are shifts from the inchoate East towards the amalgamated West. These could be considered a kind of allegoric journey through history and myth, where the parables mirror the times Angelopoulos himself lived inspired by history on the one hand and a kind of attempt towards multiculturalism (pluralism of identities) on the other. Angelopoulos' cinema proposes becoming conscious of the facts, both historical and individual; starting from a gradual stylistic catharsis, it finishes by showing the big revolutionary failures and the impossibility of a reconcilement between the two poles of the world, as well as the impossibility of a reconcilement between cinema and the visible world. Angelopoulos, as a true child of cinematic modernism, views history as a burden, by virtue of which changes are effected in substantial elements of his own identity, as well as that of nations and peoples.

But cinema is the present, and Angelopoulos' cinema especially is the present: "Cinema belongs to the specific epoch, which is determined by a specific conception of history as a category of a common fate," (Rancière, 1998, p. 45). In cinema, a meeting with history is, primarily, the conservation of a certain perception about cinema: a vehicle which keeps us connected to certain forms of the past into the present, through representation. It's what Angelopoulos did on the screen but also beyond the screen. From the time of *The Reconstruction* and up until his very last film, *The Dust of Time* (*I skoni tou chronou*, 2008), Angelopoulos positions himself, politically, clearly at the center of the problematic of the years in which he is working. His relationship with Greece's political history made him the filmmaker who seeks the real meaning of the uprising, which, in his early films, is transformed into a revolutionary desire. From *Voyage to Cythera* (*Taxidi sta Kythira*, 1984) onward, his characters move across the strict borders of the Greek nation and become creatures of a unified world with common problems and desires registered as disillusionment and painful discoveries of the century's disabilities, during which the much-desired change was never effected.

Thus, in Angelopoulos' later work, the notion of citizenship becomes increasingly "denationalized" and alludes to new forms of citizenship that go beyond the nation and are poised to replace the old. Phrases have been coined for these alternatives: "global citizenship", "transnational citizenship", "postnational citizenship".[1]

Citizenship, Nationality and Denationalization

To understand the nature of the various transformations in Angelopoulos' work, we seek to capture a substance through the terms mentioned above. The presence of multiple factors, groups and communities, partly strengthened by transformations in the Greek state in the 1990s, created a series of problems regarding the notion of citizenship, both as real situation and metaphor. The growth of immigrant waves from Albania, initially, and from Asia secondly enabled the formation of cross-border cultures and precarious identities in entire communities, so aptly described by Angelopoulos in *The Suspended Step of the Stork* (*To meteoro vima tou pelargou*, 1991). This involved various political projects, as well as human rights and environmental issues, which influenced cinematic expression and engendered or strengthened alternative notions of community and membership, and the consequent impact on the human condition.

One of the implications of these developments is the possibility of post-national forms of citizenship (Soysal, 1994; Jacobson, 1996 and Isin, 2000). Cinema is an area where these changes are presented as the formulation of a citizenship outside the confines of the national state. In the dominion of Angelopoulos' representation, this notion lies in artistic expression: in *The Suspended Step of the Stork*, the character's identity is abolished and he is reduced to a figure that does not belong to any nationality: with no name, no home, no language, and no clear identity, his situation describes the inherent and permanent bond of the subject to the sovereign. The phrase "No man may abjure his country" (Turner, 2000) traditionally was perceived

1 See Bosniak, 2000, p. 454.

as insoluble or at least exclusive. But while the bond of insoluble allegiance was defensible in times of limited individual mobility, it became difficult in the face of large-scale migration which was part of the new forms of industrial development.

In this reading of Angelopoulos, we are dealing with two distinct dynamics rather than only the emergence of locations for citizenship outside the frame of the national state. We distinguish from post-national what we would narrowly define as denationalized. The difference between them is a question of scope and institutional embeddedness. The understanding in the scholarship is that post-national citizenship is located partly outside the confines of the national (Sassen, 2000). In considering denationalization, the focus moves on to the transformation of the national, including the national in its condition as a fundamental element of citizenship. Thus it could be argued that post-nationalism and denationalization represent two different trajectories. Both are viable, and they do not exclude each other. The one is that Angelopoulos addresses the transformation of the national, specifically under the impact of globalization and several other dynamics, and tends to substantiate inside the national. The other has to do with new forms that we have not even considered. These might emerge out of altered conditions in the world located outside the national, rather than out of the earlier institutional framework of the national. Thus Soysal's focus on the European Union, for example, captures an innovation located outside the national. In Angelopoulos, the term denationalization helps capture something that remains connected to the national, as constructed historically, and is indeed profoundly imbricated with it, but in order to do this we will have to historically define new terms for their perception.

It seems that what changes the sense of citizenship today, in Angelopoulos' cinema as well, is the notion of a multi-border reality and the continuous endeavor to cross borders. The problematic of the borders, boundaries and limits arises early on in Angelopoulos' thinking on the modern condition of European multiculturalism, but also on exclusion and discrimination.

From where we stand on these issues, there is a third possibility, beyond these two. It is that citizenship, in Angelopoulos, even if situated in institutional settings that are "national", is something that may conceivably change if the meaning of the national itself has changed. In so far as conflicts, wars or globalization itself have changed certain features of the territorial and institutional organization of the state, or the identity of citizens, the institution of citizenship – its formal rights, its practices, its psychological dimension – has also been transformed even when it remains centered in the national state, i.e. the version of citizenship in *Weeping Meadow* (*To livadi pou dakryzi*, 2004) and *The Dust of Time* or the version of the brothers Manakia in *Ulysses' Gaze* (*To vlemma tou Odyssea*, 1995). For instance, here, the transformation concerns much more the particular conditions of the characters than the territorial or institutional transformation of state power and authority.

Bosniak suggests how history might illuminate the prospect of a denationalized conception of citizenship. She asks us to look critically at the fundamental assumption that "thinking of citizenship in national terms is part of our political common sense" (2000, p. 449). She urges us to unpack "various understandings we maintain of the concept of citizenship" (Bosniak, 2000, p. 452), including the diverse meanings and experiences it conveys in the present. In the same spirit, Angelopoulos asks us to look at immigrants or refugees (Greek or foreign) who are crudely transformed into global entities that entered the societies where they arrived in order to live there, but never represent an integral part of them.

Transnational Filmmaking: The East and the West

Probably the very first transnational filmmakers in Greece are the brothers Manakia[2], who lived between Thessaloniki, Ioannina and Bitola (Monastiri), filming the different nationalities and cultures within the Ottoman Empire. Their nationality is also discussed: born in Avdela (Greece), working in Bitola (Montenegro and Serbia), and then maintaining a studio in Ioannina and living the last years of their life in Thessaloniki (Greece), they are deeply aware of the fact that people during that period in this area are citizens of an extended geographic and cultural space. The fragile borders formed and abolished continuously in this area undermine a sense of territorial stability, which in turn serves to strengthen nationalist mentalities. Borders have become places where the rule of law can be suspended at any time and unsanctioned violence applied.

The complexion of the various populations living around these borders is the result of displacement and forced exodus, ethnic cleansing, discrimination and oppression. It is as if the nation-state sits on the shoulders of every citizen, observing and responding to his or her every move. Even though politics in the region have changed in recent years, a culture of mistrust, secrecy and dissimulation vis-à-vis the nation-state persists. Within the confines of nationalistic discourses in the Balkans, borders guard against difference and the threats this poses to the nation's ethnic purity. However, in this particular border area, these ethnic aspirations are compromised, and the population bears witness to the region's multi-ethnic complexity and non-homogeneity.

Angelopoulos tried to describe all these problems in his Trilogy of the Borders (*The Suspended Step of the Stork*, *Ulysses' Gaze* and *Eternity and a Day* [*Mia eoniotita ke mia mera*, 1998]). In these films, the border both as "limit and threshold" (Stathi, 2008, p. 292-293) forms an unusual identity for the people who live around it and the main query is "where is the homeland?" For instance, the question "We crossed the border and we're still here. How many borders must we cross before we get home?" (Angelopoulos, 1991), appears as a paradox when we think of real borders; if we think, however, of the limitations and the alienation of the people, then we realize that the borders are inner, existential and concern people's real identity.

The Balkans and the Mediterranean, besides being "home" to Angelopoulos, have long held an ambiguous place in the negotiation of boundaries between the East and West, the North and South (Tzanelli, 2009, p. 1). Historically speaking, the two regions, and especially the Mediterranean, have repeatedly figured as a "host" for migrant populations, transient groups such as traders and travelers and, in the aftermath of wars in the Middle East and the political re-organization of the

2 Angelopoulos makes a reference to their work in the opening scene of *Ulysses' Gaze*.

former Soviet sphere, as a "passage" for refugees. This openness to the flow and movement of both people and cultures has led policy- makers to treat the region as a distinctive and sometimes troubling domain, one that occupies the supposed "margins" of Europe. This way of thinking has long been reflected in academic scholarship, as well as in artistic expression which has discussed the Balkans and the Mediterranean variously as the "crossroads of civilizations", a cultural "melting pot", a "buffer zone" between East and West (Herzfeld, 2002), a space of East-West dialogue (Ribas, 2005, p. 7), an idea that can destabilize and challenge European unity, and a region that holds the key to the construction of a new "Eurasian" coalition and identity (Delanty and Rumford, 2005, p. 189-190).

In the contemporary context, that of accelerated global flow and movement, immigration into and emigration from the regions is again a central issue for its developing societies, giving these older debates a new urgency (Tzanelli, 2009, p. 1-2). This pattern of heightened international movements, far from creating societies that are open and accommodating, has rendered Balkan-Mediterranean societies focal points for tensions between established populations and "newcomers" who are often subjected to patterns of cultural, political and economic exclusion. Thus, we see a paradoxical situation emerging: on the one hand these societies have increasingly porous borders, and play host to an ever greater diversity of cultures and identities; on the other hand, the processes of human movement activate defensiveness and hostility, producing rigid distinctions between us and them. It is this tension between the ideal of inclusion and the reality of exclusion which Angelopoulos examines in his films. The wider territory, but also the spirit of the Balkans and the Mediterranean is vividly represented in the Greek director Theo Angelopoulos' work. The question of identity and belonging of his characters determines his whole oeuvre and recreates the various myths and legends (expressed through literature and poetry since antiquity) in order to explain and understand the modern-day condition of this transitional territory.

Transnationality and the Desire to Belong

Especially the Mediterranean is itself divided: there is an economic division between the relatively prosperous North and the relatively impoverished South. The region also partakes of a divide within Europe as a whole, which is commonly differentiated between its northern societies (supposedly industrialized, rational, organized and advanced) and its southern counterparts (often viewed as underdeveloped, agrarian and disorganized). This view of the southern Mediterranean as the "other", not yet fully a part of the Europe, has if anything been consolidated by recent developments. The movement of populations from disadvantaged regions of the world (Eurasia, Asia and Africa) to the "front line" of Europe confronts Mediterranean societies with profound economic and political challenges, further accentuating their supposed difference in the eyes of their northern counterparts.

Yet, contrary to the rhetoric of "anti-immigration", politicians and elements of the popular press, patterns of movement and mobility are not an "unfortunate accident" or the result of any weakness of will in guarding borders. Rather, they are an integral element of the workings of the global economy, and have been since at least the late 19th century, when the so-called "great transformation" (Polanyi, 1944) created a market society in which the needs of the capitalist economy began to direct the policies of states. Angelopoulos was working on all these problems in his last film, which was interrupted by his violent death. Readdressing the theme of refugees and immigrants in *The Suspended Step of the Stork*, he added a problematic on the current situation, introducing art and the theater as an element which delimits the multi-diversities or also the transnationality of Greek society today.

In a special issue of the journal *Ethnic and Racial Studies*, Steven Vertovec suggests that, while there have been a variety of uptakes on transnationalism, there has "not surprisingly [been] much conceptual muddling", which has led to an unproblematic articulation of transnationalism as referring "to multiple ties and interactions linking people or institutions across the borders of nation-states" (Vertovec, 1999, p. 447, 448). Such a proposition has been taken up in several different disciplines, including film studies, and we argue that it finds a direct manifestation in Angelopoulos' cinema. Hence, we hear the call to reconsider cinema beyond the borders of the nation-state, as a transnational cultural industry, as the forces of globalization have made it impossible to speak of cinema within such a categorical schema.

In setting up this proposition, we seek to problematize the categorization of Angelopoulos' last *Trilogy* (including the unfinished third part) as transnational cinema. Entering into this is the idea of an expanded identity of his characters, determined mainly by history and ideology. Very often, transnational cinema is defined and used in reference to cinema made by displaced filmmakers living in exile or as members of a diaspora, or used as a mode of expressing the interstitial and artisanal modes of production, distribution and consumption. This cinema is marked by the use of hybrid stylistic forms, patterns of identification and ideological concerns, and is "defined by [... the] affirmation of difference" (Roberts, 1998, p. 78) as a mode of resistance to the homogenizing forces of globalization.

Angelopoulos is not a filmmaker of the diaspora; he is profoundly aware of belonging to the Mediterranean, both territorially and culturally. However, his characters very often are characterized by the loss of identity. In *Ulysses' Gaze* (1995), the protagonist, a Greek-American filmmaker named A. (his name reduced to a single letter) who is searching for the first gaze ever registered in the Balkans, is a person who has lost his identity, roots and home because of the antenatal movements from East to the West.

In a sense, we can think of these clusters/themes as providing a framework for articulating the notion of transnationality in Angelopoulos' cinema to correspond to the traffic and forces of globalization. On the other hand, these clusters/themes also function to bracket transnational cinema within the jurisdiction of globalization, thus limiting it. Such a view, as suggested by Angelopoulos, is somewhat amnesiac. In his historicization of Greek cinema, Angelopoulos disrupts the categorization of such a cinema as a regional cinema and demonstrates that Greek cinema has always been transnational: here, the conception moves away from views affirming transnational cinema as "merely the mixing of local and foreign elements, characters, styles, and speech in particular films" toward one that sees it as involving "a deeper interrogation of the modes of cultural production [...] that involves [...] a rethinking of the hierarchy between center and periphery" as D'Lugo (2003, p. 104) underlines.

The proposed suggestion dismantles the notion of transnational cinema from its historical specificity (as a response to globalization) and opens up the category so that cinematic productions that were transnational in both form and content, prior to the emergence of contemporary globalization, can be conceptualized within this schema. At the same time, it calls for a reconsideration of transnational cinema as disrupting and contesting established center-periphery relations, again opening the category so that it is not simply couched in terms of the contest of center-periphery relations such as local-global and national-global.

It is these suggestions that we need to latch onto in order to propose the need to rethink the category of transitional cinema, the categorization of Angelopoulos' last cinema as a transnational cinema, the notion of a panhellenic national cinema and the normative construction of the nation in the post-war period. In other words, Angelopoulos' cinema functions to contest the legitimacy of a multiplicity of center-periphery relations: the regional-national cinema distinction and the unproblematic imagining of the Greek nation in specific terms.

Transnationality in the Trilogy

The *Trilogy* started with the *Weeping Meadow*, where the idea of Greekness is as expanded as the roots of the protagonists who come from Odessa but maintain an imaginary relationship with antiquity and the heritage of that antiquity as memories of "marbles and ideals". When they arrive on Greek territory, they refer to the "marble columns" as marks to identify the new territory they are going to occupy. Their itinerary started in the East and they are dreaming of going *westward*. But this first stop in Greece is still in the East; a provisory stop, which will push them in a different direction according to the vagaries of history and politics. The woman will go back to the East (exiled to Tashkent and Siberia); the man will go West. Later, the woman will try to find a way to move towards the West (to find him), while he will try to find a way to travel towards the East (in order to find her).

That is to say, Angelopoulos' last films articulate, mobilize and dismantle the hegemonic conception of the nation as fostered by the apparatus of the nation-state through an appeal to a sense of Angelopoulos' cultural conception that is antagonistic to the national imaginary. Benedict Anderson believes that "a nation is a community socially constructed, imagined by the people who perceive themselves as part of that group" (Anderson, 1991, p. 224).

The intimacy of the form of the media used for the production and circulation of a sense of (antagonistic) cultural nationalism is appropriate: Angelopoulos' cinema, in particular, has played a central role in the re-construction of the New Greek identity in the years following the junta. The suggestion that Angelopoulos' cinema has participated in the construction and negotiation of a sense of nation and nationalism in post-dictatorship Greece must also address "the question of national cinema" (Rafailides in Stathi, 2010), because the concept of national cinema privileges ideas of coherence and unity and stable cultural meanings associated with the uniqueness of a given nation.

Taking up this suggestion opens up another line of argument and this has to do with the problematization of a Greek national cinema, particularly since Angelopoulos' cinema has been unproblematically labelled an international cinema with characteristics of specific national identities presented as ecumenical identities. This has served to mark out linguistic and cultural differences by putting different languages in the same context. The regionalization of cinematic forms through linguistic differentiation served not only to marginalize the heterogeneity of Greek cinema and affirm cinema's special location as paradigmatic of Greek national cinema, but also to crystallize the post-politics imagining of the Greek nation under the umbrage of a Greek identity expanded beyond the Greek territory (Stathi, 2010).

This view has circulated, even though Angelopoulos' cinema has been particularly concerned with the idea of the nation, most overtly and powerfully during the period that witnessed the strategic use of cinema for political purposes between 1970-1980 and later, when a more existential and ideological purpose appears in his films between 1987-1998. Angelopoulos did not support any form of national commonality but problematized the official version of the nation.

Such a political position, one that strongly affirms Angelopoulos' films as a separatist discourse and as antithetical to the idea of a limited nation, was taken up and played out through cinema in order to set up an alternative version and vision of the nation; to break up established center-periphery relations. It is this rupturing that calls for a conception of Angelopoulos' cinema as a transnational cinema and not simply as a regional cinema in European reality.

Angelopoulos' cinema, particularly the period after the so-called "voyage and boundaries" period between 1991-2004, seeks to offer a critical survey of the various ways in which "Greece" and "Greekness" are negotiated in his cinema, making the argument that, over time, there has been a shift from a pan-historical construction of the nation, that was part of the anti-national cinema, to the call for a communally centered, closed, ethno-nation, premised on a discourse of Greek cultural evolutionism.

In arguing that Angelopoulos' cinema, particularly after his so-called "Trilogy of History" since the late 1970s to the present, be conceptualized as a transnational cinema, the argument draws attention to the ways in which cinematic form and style of cinema itself has been strategically employed to articulate and engender an interruptive notion of the nation. It also reflects the big transformations in the country and the violent change of identity due to the alienation and melancholy provoked by the vagaries of history and society. To this end, we wish to suggest that it would be productive to conceive of Angelopoulos' last *Trilogy* as a transnational cinematic form through its powerful commitment to intervening in the established center-periphery relations that inform the construction of Greekness and of the nation and the inter-nationality-regionality of the whole country. But the nation in Angelopoulos obviously extends beyond the borders of the state. Greekness begins in a mythical as well as in a historical time, and it extends all over the globe, beyond time and space.

Identity's Odyssey: Metamorphosis and Katabasis

Angelopoulos, however, works on a different aspect of identity and belonging, demonstrating that the *strictu sensu* nationality is destined to fail; suddenly, his art proves incapable of controlling, depicting, substantiating or embodying (literally) the bodies which, in the film, become impalpable, like ghosts: the artist is unable to perceive the world which dreamed of granting oneness and harmony. But there is a worse aspect: in an ever-turbulent history, the content of the art itself disappears, the shape of the art is definitely fragmented. Beyond the mangled body and the collapse of Marxist ideology there is a thread for representation itself.

In *Ulysses' Gaze*, there is a distinctive the scene in which a weeping A. recites the poem of "identity" [my own term]. "When I return, it will be with another man's clothes. Another man's name." (Angelopoulos, 1995). A. presents the poem of the pain of loss as a synthesis of fragments of the last verses of the *Odyssey*, as a spontaneous creation, like a contemporary Orpheus who weaves again, in his absolute solitude, the primordial poetic *logos*.

Here, the loss of identity seems to be shaped in death. However, I strongly believe that an issue of major importance concerning the artist's motivation and the particular way in which the artist perceives his vocation is of loss – it would not be an exaggeration to state that almost all serious literature and art can be interpreted as a desperate attempt to create the illusion of immortality through the dual function of the work of art as medicine and as poison. Thus, Angelopoulos uses the words which describe the image of the beloved figure in the most erotic poetry in Mediterranean culture: the poem of recognition of the beloved woman's body, when the warrior returns home. The experience of war (of being "elsewhere") changes the essence of existence while conserving feelings as memories (Stathi, 2012, p. 586).

Angelopoulos' *Ulysses' Gaze* follows not only the myth (Orpheus) by presenting the artistic expression as resistance to certain death, but also the journey of a Ulyssean and, consequently, Dantean pilgrim up or down the Danube or Evros rivers, in search of the first gaze on the Balkans. A. discovers the darkest heart of the war in the saddest artistic expression, while at the same time he discovers the corrupt heart of European and international politics in the Balkans. In other words, he finds himself, or his other self, suffering the continuous losses of name, family, country, ideology and finally, love: a love which appears four times in the faces of different women in different places, but in all cases on the road homeward, essentially, into the heart of *nostos* and the reacquisition of identity.

In this sense, Angelopoulos depicts the countries in which the story takes place as the setting and backdrop which progressively eliminates the people as human factors. Thus, the Balkans (Albania, Bitola, Skopje, Belgrade, Bucharest, Costanza) in *Ulysses' Gaze*, and Thessaloniki, Odessa, Siberia, Tashkent and New York, Toronto and Berlin in *Trilogy* (Weeping Meadow and The Dust of Time) becomes a metaphysical battlefield devoid of all recognizable humanity, into which the wandering artist enters at his peril.

The striking thing about both the films of the *Trilogy* is that, however overtly critical they are of the historical aspects of the twentieth century, they can still be – and often are – interpreted as meta-historical texts, the historical imagination of twentieth century. Thus, in discovering the self, the characters will also fulfill their epic *telos*, their national and global destiny dispersed throughout the globe.

Evidence suggests that Angelopoulos' narratives about the Balkans, Europe, Russia or Greece of the Diaspora (especially to America) really address problems of Western identity. Frantz Fanon's thesis on the "native intellectual" rejects such discourse altogether:

> […] at the moment that the native intellectual comes in touch again with his people, this artificial sentinel is turned into dust. All the Mediterranean values – the triumph of the human individual of clarity and of beauty – become lifeless, colourless knick-knacks […] those values which seemed to uplift the soul are revealed as worthless, simply because they have nothing to do with the concrete conflict in which the people is engaged. (Fanon, 1965, p. 38)

This passage offers one way of escaping the Mediterranean myth of *katabasis* which has so powerfully shaped relations between the nations of West and East, North and South. However, Angelopoulos chooses a different route: he does not reject Greco-Roman myth and Western ideas, but he supports accommodation and hybridization. He employs the *katabatic* myth (Ulysses, Orpheus) on a broader scale, to describe the migration *westward* of his three protagonists in *The Dust of Time*: a musician, an ideologist, and a woman (Spyros, Jacob and Eleni). Angelopoulos thus narrates the story through the woman's point of view; Eleni is the lost love of Spyros, and Jacob is the person who helps her to survive in the hell of history. By deciding to accompany Eleni back home (through his identity) from the heart of the gulag, Jacob loses both Eleni and his identity. Jacob, the Jewish friend/lover remains in a status of seeking an identity. His identity is indissolubly connected to Eleni's decision. He will follow her, assuming the identity Eleni chooses every time. His identity is completely lost; he is "lost" within the various identities, nationalities and homelands: "Once you had said, Eleni, that for you there is no return. Now that's true only for me. I won't cry at the Wall of Tears ... Bon voyage, little Eleni!" (Angelopoulos, 2009, p. 96)

Toward the end of the film, Eleni and Spyros admit that the end of their journey is to go back to the river where their love started. What remains current is only the idea that crossing frontiers in order to reach the final destination radically changes the self, which is forced to accept this cruel destiny. Berlin really is their center and at the same time the periphery of all the previous places in which they have lived and felt vital. It is their center, because it represents the necessary passage to the real homecoming which will complete their love. On the other hand, for Jacob the two stages (New York and Berlin) are his center and his exile.

At the same time that the three protagonists are drawn westward, America is being drawn to the East (Word War II, the Vietnam War). Paradoxically, it is the intersection of opposing quests for selfhood that makes them go back to Europe and the beginning of the story: the river. Angelopoulos thus reangles history to accommodate his heroes of Greek descent. It is just before the collapse of the dividing lines between the West and East (the fall the Berlin Wall) and the triumphant unification of the world: the water Eleni "brings" with her is the unifying but painful force.

> The river... The man takes her hand. Water drips from her hand. Eleni brings it slowly up to her chest still smiling at Spyros. She closes her eyes. A strange peace spreads over her face. (Angelopoulos, 2009, p. 100)

This second attempt to come back to the East does not function as the obsessive Other from whose rejection the self is dependent; on the contrary, West and East flow together to form an ambiguous, paradoxical identity. Press this idea further, and we find that Angelopoulos is refashioning America in the image of another epoch, a lost place in the mist. So Angelopoulos reverses the expected spatial co-ordinates of the infernal journey by sending his Eastern characters in search of a West that's promised, but also unreal. The film's central conceit that the journey originated in Odessa and Greece may be nostalgic, but locating the start of the infernal journey in the East is historically defensible.

Angelopoulos also multiplies the contenders for selfhood so that one person's journey collides with another's, producing strange alliances and explosive mismatches. Every character in this film is in a way Orphic, in that they all lose their heart's desire, and they all search in an underworld for a new sense of self. Myth is not an outwardly imposed symbolic structure, but rather an image of the world each character participates in creating dialogically.

In Angelopoulos' fictional cosmos, human beings live precariously poised over calamity. There seems to be no escape from this process. Spyros says, in *Dust of Time*:

> I was on tour with an orchestra in the northern states when I learnt of your arrest. It made me sick! … Since then I've been searching for you… I kept crossing borders, changing trains, stations, passing checkpoints. I answered with another man's name, another man's life." (Angelopoulos, 2009, p. 24-25)

In Angelopoulos' estimation, we are all disoriented to an extent; we have all been subject to calamitous change. The human condition is to be disoriented, in the sense of being oriented towards Hades or death. The question is how to respond to trauma and loss: does one submit to metamorphosis or resist? Does one embrace change, or remain true to a reality which may now only exist in the mind? Blandly universal as this problem sounds, it is radical in the way it manoeuvres a Western reader into universalizing an Eastern migrant's situation, as if the East has been definitely lost. The film seems to work best on this "as if" basis, that is, by conjuring Western viewers into thinking of themselves as lost Easterners.

Angelopoulos' protagonists unquestionably undergo a series of transformations, so *Trilogy* is a metamorphic story. When Alexis and Eleni complete their journey to the center of the film's cosmos, in Berlin they have to continue to search for the transmogrifying "River". With great deliberation, Spyros abandons the fantasy of his normal and conventional life (without love), where his music is just a job, and follows Eleni, to Toronto at first and to Europe later. Angelopoulos' narrative begins with a disaster: the end of the war in Greece finds Eleni on the road to exile in the Soviet Union and Spyros on a journey in search of her somewhere in Northeast Europe.

The metamorphic world-view shares many of the characteristics of the carnivalesque (e.g., the scenes of Jacob in Berlin, as well as the shots surrounding his suicide, or the dance scenes in the previous part of the trilogy – The *Weeping*

Meadow), an element which transforms heroes, but particularly Jacob, from a mortal failed lover to a symbol of a collective body that has failed to accomplish its desires. As Bakhtin argues,

> Taking sheer delight in the Heraclitian flux, metamorphosis understands the human body not as the mortal husk of an individual bound to suffering, and articled to an end, but as the collective great body of the people [...]. (Bakhtin in Emerson and Morson, 1990, p. 93)

After Eleni's death, Spyros only dreams of having the capacity "to step into the same river again" through metamorphosis/metempshychosis (reincarnation). He transforms Eleni into the young Eleni and in this way he can start a new journey back to the origins – the East (Odessa), where the story began.

But as the end of *Dust of Time* demonstrates, the assumption of indifference can only function as a shield against trauma temporarily. In her East/place of exile, Eleni wrote Spyros a letter every day, which sounds like the content of a repetitive dream. In the end, this is the only link connecting her with her beloved and her origins:

> Siberia, 27 April, 1953. I live in a town the locals call "lost" ... in an infinite expanse of nothingness. They sent me here after three weeks of isolation and interrogation ... I write to you so I can talk to you. I know that my letters will never reach you. But I'll leave them on the last passing train, carrying them along on the icy steppe, journeying to find you in your cell ... (Angelopoulos, 2009, p. 30-31)

In this paragraph of Eleni's letter, we are in presented with a description which gives way to an infernal sense of reality, in multiple layers, one over the other. It reflects, in substance and tone, a historical moment. But in the longer view, we are still in a post-war, post-disaster world. The way we respond to calamity touches the same raw nerves, and is likely to produce an excessive, over-determined response, unless we remain aware of the connections to the past. By the end of the film, Spyros, in front of Eleni's dead body, tries to bring her back in a kind of metamorphosis which can be perceived as a "revelation" on a human scale. He says: "Eleni.../ Wake up... Get up... Eleni.../ Give me your hand" (Angelopoulos, 2009, p. 100). And when he moves his hand towards Eleni, another hand, the one of little Eleni, reaches over the dead body of Eleni to meet Spyros' hand. This is a shape beyond metamorphosis; this is a step towards a new transformation of the narrative itself; a narrative which looks towards the inchoate East, where Spyros dreams to return. This triple Western migration of Spyros, Eleni and Jacob and the double Eastern remigration of Spyros and Eleni illustrate what a metamorphic change of identity could mean to us in the present historical context.

The idea of the eternal return sets its seal on every type of displacement a human being can feel in this world: territorial, cultural, economical, ethical, ideological, etc. Thus, the concept of nationality is abstracted or abolished and exists only as an *anamnesis* which moves the steps of his characters both towards an evolution and a retrospection to the past. This notion of evolution arises from a circular conception of time, present in the cosmological being which is the core-theme of Nietzsche's philosophy: the eternal return, where time is perceived as a continuous repetition, the human being is a form which expresses the inner anxieties of the universe and in that sense it feels like a citizen of that universe.

[T]ime is infinite, but the things in time, the concrete bodies, are finite. [...] Now, however long a time may pass, according to the eternal laws governing the combinations of this eternal play of repetition, all configurations which have previously existed on this earth must yet meet, attract, repulse, kiss, and corrupt each other again... (Kaufmann, 1959, p. 376)

Despite the fact that the idea of the eternal return could lead to an extreme form of nihilism, Angelopoulos seeks a way out from the world's nonsense and idiocy through the dream of utopia (Kolovos, 2001, p. 37) and through the research of new values, well harmonized with the universal movement of things. However, Angelopoulos is profoundly aware of the fact that the time of utopia always lies outside history's circle.

BIBLIOGRAPHY

Anderson, B. R. *Imagined Communities: Reflections on the Origin and Spread of Nationalism*. London: Verso. 1991

Angelopoulos, Th. *The Dust of Time: The Third Wing* (*I skoni tou chronou. To trito ftero*), Athens: Militos, 2009.

Angelopoulos, Th. "Rigas Feraios Map". *Balkan Rewiew* 4 (1995), p. 13-17.

Bosniak, L. "The State of Citizenship: Citizenship Denationalized". *Indiana Journal of Global Law Studies* 7.2 (2000), p. 447-510.

Carter, E. / Donald, J. / Squires, J. (eds.). *Space and Place: Theories of Identity and Location*. London: Lawrence and Wishart, 1993.

Delanty, G. / Rumford, C. *Rethinking Europe: Social Theory And The Implications of Europeanization*. London: Routledge, 2005.

D'Lugo, M. "Authorship, globalization and the new identity of Latin American cinema". In: Gunerate, A. / Dissanayake, W. (eds). *Rethinking Third Cinema*. New York and London: Routledge, 2003, p. 103-125.

Emerson, C. / Morson, G. S. *Mikhail Bakhtin: Creation of a Prosaics*. Stanford, CA: Stanford University Press, 1990.

Fanon, F. *The Wretched of the Earth*. London: MacGibbon and Kee, 1965.

Hansen, R. / Weil, P. "Introduction: Citizenship, Immigration and Nationality: Towards a Convergence in Europe?". In: Hansen, R. / Weil, P. (eds.). *Towards a European Nationality*. New York: Palgrave, 2001, p. 1-23.

Herzfeld, M. "Spatial Cleansing: Monumental Vacuity and the Idea of the West". *Journal of Material Culture* 11 (2006), p. 127–149.

Herzfeld, M. "The Absent Presence: Discourses of Crypto-Colonialism". *South Atlantic Quarterly* 101 (2002), p. 899-926.

Hobsbawm, E. J. *Nations and Nationalism since 1780: Programme, Myth, Reality*. Cambridge: Cambridge University Press, 1990.

Jacobson, D. *Rights Across Borders: Immigration and the Decline of Citizenship*. Baltimore, MD: Johns Hopkins Press, 1996.

Isin, Engin F. (ed.). *Democracy, Citizenship and the Global City*. London and New York: Routledge, 2000.

Kaufmann, W. *Nietzsche; Philosopher, Psychologist, Antichrist*. New York: Penguin, 1959.

King, R. "Introduction: an Essay on Mediterraneanism". In: King, R. / Proudfoot, L. / Smith, B. (eds.). *The Mediterranean: Environment and Society*. London: Arnold Press, 1997.

Kolovos, N. "I anazitisi tis outopias ston Angelopoulo" (Searching for Utopia in Angelopoulos' films). In: Stathi, I. (ed). *The End of ideology and the Tracing of a New Utopia, in Th. Angelopoulos Films*. Athens: Thessaloniki Film Festival, 2001, p. 36-45.

Mazower, M. "Minorities and the League of Nations in Interwar Europe". *Daedalus* 126.2 (1997), p. 47-63.

Massey, D. / Jess P. *A Place in the World? – Places, Cultures and Globalization*. Oxford: Oxford University Press, 1997.

Morley, D. / Robin, K. *Spaces of Identity: Global Media, Electronic Landscapes and Cultural Boundaries*. London: Routledge, 1995.

Nussbaum, M. C. *Cultivating Humanity: A Classical Defense of Reform in Liberal Education*. Cambridge, MA: Cambridge University Press, 1997.

Polanyi, K. *The Great Transformation*. New York: Rinehart, 1944.

Rancière, J. "L'historicité du cinéma". In: Baecque, A. / Delage, C. (eds.). *De l'histoire au cinéma*. Paris: Editions Complexe, 1998, p. 45-60.

Ribas, M. N. *The Mediterranean in the Age of Globalization. Migration, welfare and borders*. New Brunwick: Transaction, 2005.

Roberts, M. "*Baraka*: World Cinema and the Global Culture Industry". *Cinema Journal* 37.3 (1998), p. 62-82.

Sassen, S. *De-Nationalization*. Princeton, NJ: Princeton University Press, 2002.

Sassen, S. "Towards post-national and denationalized citizenship". In: Isin, E. / Turner, B. (eds). *Handbook of Citizenship Studies*, London: Sage, 2002, p. 277-291

Soysal, Y. N. *Limits of Citizenship: Migrants and Postnational Membership in Europe*, Chicago: University of Chicago Press, 1994.

Stathi, I. "Geography as Utopia. From the Rigas Pheraios Map to the Division and Establishment of Borders in the Balkans. An Intercultural Itinerary through the Geography of Ulysses' Gaze". Proceedings of the Conference: "Studying, Modeling and Sense Making of Planet Earth", University of the Aegean, 2008, URL: http://www.geo.aegean.gr/earth-conference2008/papers/papers/C02ID121.pdf (13.5.2012).

Stathi, I. "Critical Theory and Aesthetics in Greek Cinema between 1960s and 1980s". Proceedings of the XVI International Film Studies Conference "In the Very Beginning and at the Very End", Forum Udine, 2010, p. 583-592.

Stathi, I. "*Eros* and *Thanatos* in Theo Angelopoulos' *Trilogy*". In: *Journalism and Mass Communication* (forthcoming).

Stathi, I. "Synora ke ypervasi ton orion sti synchroni kinonia. To synoro os katofli ke perasma ston kinimatografo" (Borders and limits overstepping. The border as threshold and passage in cinema), Proceedings of the conference "Social Sciences Today", Athens: Sakkoulas, 2007, p. 280-299.

Turner, B. S. "Cosmopolitan Virtue: loyalty and the city". In: Isin, E. (ed.). *Democracy, Citizenship and the Global City*. London and New York: Routledge, 2000, p. 129-148.

Tzanelli, R. / Yar, M. "Paradoxes of Belonging: Migration, exclusion and transnational rights in the Mediterranean". *Development* 0 (2009), p. 1-6.

Vertovec, S. "Conceiving and researching transnationalism". *Ethnic and Racial Studies* 22.1 (1999), p. 447-462.

Wendell, F. / Sheats, R. / Sheats, P. H. *Citizenship Education Through The Social Studies: A Philosophy and a Program*. New York City: Row, Peterson and Company, 1936.

Another vision: Memories of the Civil War in Coproductions of Recent (Spanish?) Cinema

Juan Carlos Ibáñez

Varios días, el mundo, camarada,
el mundo está español hasta la muerte.
C. Vallejo.

Perhaps today it may be noticed as a proven fact what a few years ago was only formulated as a hypothesis. In a "post-literate" world, wrote the pioneer Robert Rosenstone, it is possible for "visual culture to again change the nature of our relationship with the past" (1995, p. 43). The evidence should be stressed, however, that contemporary visual culture is not imposed by purely formal or technical criteria, but by factors related to the economic and political structure of our social reality. One of them, no doubt, is that which imposes on communication processes a flow of dialectics between the global and the local. Today any local image of the past tends to be re-framed in global imaginary, and vice versa: a new way to build film stories "for the world" (like the gender named "world music"), can be adopted and properly recycled by national or regional narratives to elaborate identity discourses. Coproductions, authentic "counter-narratives" as Manuel Palacio defines them, "reflect the multicultural and hybrid character which today the world has", and become a true "mixture of identities that can erase national boundaries and take an unexpected place in the official narratives of the nation state, an unprecedented and ambivalent space between the image of us and the other" (Palacio, 1999, p. 232). This paper takes this idea to analyze the Spanish coproductions about the Civil War written and filmed by foreign artists.

Beyond the propaganda films that were shot during the war itself, the catalogue of international productions and coproductions about the Spanish war is extensive and varied. Only in the early sixties, to mention a specific period, there are fictions as suggestive as the Franco-American *Behold a Pale Horse* (*Y llegó el día de la venganza*), directed by Fred Zinnemann in 1964, or the French *La guerre est finie (La guerra ha terminado*, Alain Resnais, 1966), and interesting documentaries, such as the Mexican *En el balcón vacío* (Jomi García Ascot, 1961), dedicated to the Spaniard who died in exile, or the most famous *Mourir à Madrid* (*Morir en Madrid*, 1963) by Frederic Rossif. One should remember that these movies were banned by Franco's censors and were not released in Spain, but certainly reveal the existence of a line of representation on the civil war, conceived as a historical event of global significance, evolving marginally into the Spanish film culture itself. At that time, films with different and contradictory approaches as *La paz empieza nunca* (León Klimovsky, 1960), *La caza* (*The Hunt*, Carlos Saura, 1966) or *¿Por qué morir en Madrid?* (Eduardo Manzanos, 1966), which share a concern for domestic and local issues in their narrative approach, arrive at the "25 Years of Peace" scenario in Spain which is proudly announced by Franco. In order to delimit the object of the study, our work has to limit itself to the analysis of Spanish coproductions of fiction in the last decade, an unexplored territory so far, which can provide clues to the development of the various ways in which films approach recent Spanish history.

But before turning to the analysis of the films, it is worth explaining briefly the ways the paradigms on the representations of civil war that become visible in the Spanish cinema of recent years shift (Ibáñez, 2010, p. 83-120). During the transition, Spanish films about the Civil War express values related to a scenario of social reconciliation. They are defined from general democratic values, which do not establish a direct relationship with ideological or political presuppositions inherited from the past or with specific or particularly dramatic events of a traumatic history. A history intended to be left behind or at least not to be vindicated or touched upon, as public opinion was under a real threat of a new military-led uprising. The depiction of experiences, feelings and close memories, the emotions, in short, win the game in the canon of representation of the heroic or epic recreation of the war. This model, called by Jose Enrique Monterde as "cinema of identification" or "cinema of recognition" (1989, p. 45-63), will experience its first transgressions in the early nineties with films like *Vacas*/Beiak (*Cows*, Julio Medem, 1992) or *Land and Freedom* (*Tierra y libertad*, Ken Loach, 1995), but it will be due to the progressive advance of the Conservatives in the Spanish political scene that the discussions on historical memory will spread.

In this framework, there are two films that break ties with the transitional paradigm representing the Civil War: *Silencio Roto* (*Broken Silence*, 2001), by Montxo Armendariz, and the Spanish-Mexican coproduction *El espinazo del diablo* (*The Devil's Backbone*, 2001), written and directed by the Mexican Guillermo del Toro (again a Spanish and a jointly produced film, as in the case of *Vacas* and *Tierra y libertad*). Both are released in the same year which was the first in the second term legislature of the Partido Popular. Armendariz and del Toro go along the way already explored by Medem and Loach, so the narrative interest is not centered on the rearguard, but on the very scenario of the commitment and struggle, expressed as a battle for the defense of freedom. The representation of the immediate post-war period as an extension of the war, as a period in which the victors subdue and annihilate the vanquished, is the approach directly related to the debate about historical memory, and so it is shown in later films, like *El lápiz del carpintero* (*The Carpenter's Pencil*, Antxon Reixa, 2003), *El laberinto del fauno* (*Pan's Labyrinth*, Guillermo del Toro, 2006), *Las trece rosas* (*13 Roses*, Emilio Martínez-Lázaro, 2007), *Los girasoles ciegos* (*The Blind Sunflowers*, José Luis Cuerda, 2008), *La buena nueva* (*The Good News*, Helena Taberna, 2008) or *La voz dormida* (*The Sleeping Voice*, Benito Zambrano, 2011). From here on, as the historian Julián Casanova has written, from the "general reflection on how that tragedy was possible, current films have passed onto the battle for memory, the fight against indifference as a form of social forgetting" (Casanova, 2008). Let's see now how "Spanish" films written and directed by foreign filmmakers contribute to the consolidation of this new paradigm, and to which extent they also propose alternatives and complementary strategies of representation.

El laberinto del fauno: Historical Memories and Passion for the Form

At the end of the nineties, Mexican writer and director Guillermo del Toro plans to make a filmic trilogy about the Spanish Civil War. The above mentioned *El espinazo del diablo* and *El laberinto del fauno* are parts of this ambitious project, which develops with difficulty because of many assignments from Hollywood, like *Blade II* (2002) or *Hellboy* (2004). It is interrupted due to the impossibility of writing the last script, entitled *3993*, which is set in the Asturian coalfields. But the spark which lights the imagination of the Mexican film-maker is not precisely linked to the Spanish political juncture of those years, but to the tales that he has heard a thousand times from Spaniards in exile about the rupture of a great dream, that of the liberal-republican utopia:

> For me, in Mexico, in my adolescence, it became a war of importance for the whole world, not only for Spain. My country and my life were profoundly affected by the emigration of Spanish refugees, who changed the culture and the arts for the better. Mexico and Spain have a strong link in this Civil War, but it was interesting for me how, in some manner, it became the foreword and prologue (during the post-war period) of the Second World War. I think that it can be respectfully used to create fantasy fables and parables that not only concern Spain, but the whole world (Del Toro, 2006).

El laberinto del fauno, a Spanish-Mexican joint venture, is the history of Ofelia (Ivana Baquero), a teenager who suffers the traumatic experience of the war. Her mother, Carmen (Ariadna Gil), is going to give birth to a child from her second husband, the wicked captain Vidal (Sergi López). But everything gets complicated when Vidal, who is in charge of Franco's troops which fight the insurrection of the rebels in the north of Aragon, forces Carmen, who is weak, to travel to the camp from where he directs the military operations, putting her life in danger. Aloof from reality and lost in her own dreams and fantasies, Ofelia envisages herself as Moana, the princess of a subterranean world where lies and pain do not exist. A lost paradise, that of childhood (although the war covers it with shadows, unlike the one painted by Alberti in *Marinero en tierra*), to which she wants to return with the help of her mourned father.

In a scenery of vigilance and repression, where a simple gesture or wrong step can provoke death (as can be seen in the sequence of the torture and latter murder of the furtive hunters), Ofelia, like Don Quixote, becomes crazy reading fairy tales. And in her ravings she tries to pass the tests that the faun (Doug Jones) sets for her to allow her to return to her kingdom. What happens, however, is that the relentless captain Vidal does not tolerate the independence or insubordination of anybody, even his own step-daughter Ofelia, who acts as any other rebel. Once convinced of this evidence, it is no wonder that he wants to eliminate her, as he aims to exterminate anyone who does not fit in a "clean and new" Spain, in his own words. When the doctor (Alex Angulo), another rebel, decides to end the suffering of a tortured partisan, Vidal demands an explanation, because he cannot understand his daring:

"Only people like you can obey for the sake of obedience, without thinking about it, captain". These are, of course, his last words. At the end, it is not only the harmonious realm desired by Ofelia which is linked to the republican utopia, it is also the way by which you reach that realm (free imagination, reading, the Republic of letters). "These people", as Vidal says, "sustain a wrong idea: that we all are equal". "But there is a great difference", he adds, "because the war ended and we won it. And if to make us all aware of this we have to kill all those sons-of-bitches, then we will kill them and that's all. We are all here willingly".

Ofelia of Guillermo del Toro, as it happens with the children of *El espinazo del diablo*, with the militant girls of *Las trece rosas*, or even with Andreu and Nuria of *Pa Negre* (*Black Bread*, Agustí Villaronga, 2010), break the models of previous boys and girls in the history of Spanish cinema, shown as mute witnesses of an epoch —passive victims of the war—, or as icons of the perverted and rarefied climate of a long post-war period: Isabel and Ana of *El espíritu de la colmena* (*The Spirit of the Beehive*, Víctor Erice, 1973), Luisito and Angélica of *La prima Angélica* (*Cousin Angelica*, Carlos Saura, 1974), Ana of *Cría Cuervos* (Carlos Saura, 1975), the children of *Las largas vacaciones del 36* (*Long Vacations of 36*, Jaime Camino, 1976), Quico of *La guerra de papá* (*Daddy's War*, Antonio Mercero, 1977), José and Valentina of *Crónica del alba* (*Valentine*, Antonio Betancor, 1982), Estrella of *El sur* (*The South*, Víctor Erice, 1983), Luisito and Manolita of *Las bicicletas son para el verano* (*Bicycles are for the Summer*, Jaime Chavarri, 1984), Nieves and Quirce of *Los santos inocentes* (*The Holy Innocents*, Mario Camus, 1984), Gustavete of *¡Ay, Carmela!* (Carlos Saura, 1990) or Moncho of *La lengua de las mariposas* (*Butterfly's Tongue*, José Luis Cuerda, 1998), among many others. Violating this transitional pattern, Ofelia rebels, acts and creates a fantastic universe which del Toro utilizes to captivate the spectator, seizing him in a strong merry-go-round of visual and auditory sensations.

As if it were a post-modern and trans-national re-reading of the materials which form the seminal *El espíritu de la colmena*, with which it has some points of contact, there is a vindication of the pleasure of telling tales and at the same time of thinking about the ideological and cognitive impact of tales in our lives. However, unlike what happens in the seventies, we find in *El laberinto del fauno* a purpose, not so naïve as it may seem, to vindicate the forcefulness of literary fables which have gone through a media blender, with the structure of the comic as a basic pattern. There is an effort to establish well defined limits between good and evil, or to place the punishment of the villain in the climax of the fiction. And there is also a willingness of not hiding anything, to let everything be seen, to underline the structure of the narrative, to make the materials and the very fabric of the tale transparent. Of a story which is presented since the beginning as meta-narrative. Because it does not hide the fact that it is based on other tales nor does it spare a justification of the *raison d'etre* of the tale told. In the final sequence, del Toro reveals the keys of his narrative contrivance to the spectator, and he explains it as a desperate resource of reason, as a defence mechanism which reacts to the trauma of the subdued, cornered and forced conscience (with a precise fade-out, that of the opera-like image of Ofelia transforming herself into Moana, the spectator can leave behind the unbearable reality of fiction to plunge, as Ofelia herself, in the inalienable universe of dreams).

With these elements, the Mexican film maker separates himself from the typical Spanish approach, to demonstrate that the description in naturalistic form is not the only way to foster the critical views of the spectators or to activate processes which lead them to be interested in a specific period of history. In his case, the keys of the plot are used to augment the communicative potential which emerges from the cinematographic show, in the line of the pioneer approaches like that of David W. Griffith, Abel Gance or Sergei M. Eisenstein, or with contemporary formal models, inspired in the works of Francis Ford Coppola, Steven Spielberg, Ridley Scott, Terry Gilliam or Luc Besson, among others. It is true that *El laberinto del fauno* does not aspire to become a historic film, but at least, with his passion for form and the spectacular nature of images, it serves the purpose of compelling the spectator to exercise his historical memory. First of all, it settles the film in a specific place and time: Spain in 1944, the moment when the old XIV Corps of the Republican Army gets ready to start the so called "Reconquest Operation of Spain", to link the last breath of the Spanish Resistance to the military defeat of fascism and Nazism in Europe.

Secondly, from the first *flashback*, he forces the spectator to identify himself with the female protagonists of the film, the dreamer Ofelia and the courageous Mercedes (Maribel Verdú). Feminine characters, as in *Silencio roto* or *Las trece rosas,* who are testimony and homage to those women who fought fascism after the Republican defeat, risking their lives. As the Mexican film maker states, his film "proposes imagination not as evasion, but as a form of understanding our place in the world and articulating our position in it" (Del Toro, 2006). The hyper-realistic stylization of the Mexican is far from the disenchanted and sour Spanish tradition of considering things (*Juan Soldado*, Fernando Fernán Gómez, 1973; *La vaquilla [The Heifer]*, Luis García Berlanga, 1985), but reality is never far, although it may seem so. *El laberinto del fauno* is, in fact, a film which crudely deals with the violence of the conflict, as well as with the effectiveness of illusion and faith in our convictions as a basic principle of resistance. "Ofelia, magic does not exist. Nor for you, nor for me nor for anyone", says the conservative and conformist Carmen to her daughter. But Ofelia understands, in spite of everything, that she has to face a world devoid of imagination and freedom. An attitude that makes her princess-heroine of that particular realm where realities and dreams cross. And in that epical and transcendental space, as the off- voice of the narrator tells us at the end of the film, is where she leaves "small footsteps of her passing through the world, only visible for he who knows where to look".

La mujer del anarquista: Identity and Spaces of Memory

La mujer del anarquista (*The Anarchist's Wife*, Marie Noëlle and Peter Sehr, 2008) is a romantic drama about the story of Manuela (María Valverde), a young girl from Madrid, from a good family, married to the lawyer and political activist Justo Calderón (Juan Diego Botto). After working during the first year of the war as a radio speaker, Justo thinks that his place is at the front and joins the army to fight in the Ebro battle. Then will come the long road to exile, the internment in French concentration camps, his joining the Résistance, his capture and later deportation to the hell of Mauthausen. Freed by allied troops, he returns to the south of France and joins a cell which helps the Spanish guerrilla. Meanwhile, in Madrid, Manuela loses contact with her husband and endures all sorts of humiliations and troubles. The murder of her brother and the death of her minor son bring her to the verge of mental insanity. But she sticks to her love for Justo and only thinks about seeing him again. A dream which comes true after twelve years of separation of the couple.

At a first glance, this German-French-Spanish coproduction starts from a frame known by the Spanish for decades, where topics abound: sentimental drama, visions of the rearguard, cruelty and fatuity of war, the impact of the conflict in liberal families of both sides, which do not have anything in common with the barbaric situation unleashed by uncontrolled extremists, etc. Perhaps this is the reason because of which Jordi Costa, film critic of *El País*, defines the film without any subtlety as an unsuccessful "exercise in style", which does not stand over the hemp of boring and Manichean films done on the Civil War (Costa, 2009). But if we put aside the film prejudices to focus on the film from a cultural and sociological perspective, we will immediately find that there are details of great interest in *La mujer del anarquista*. The first thing that can be observed is a peculiar narrative design. Ultimately, it is Paloma (Irene Visedo), Manuela's daughter, who tells us from her point of view the history of her parents, so the film can and should also be interpreted as a story of initiation into life, Paloma's own (in two aspects: emotional and intellectual).

From the perspective of lovesick Manuela, the search and rescue of Justo is a question of survival, because she has realized that she cannot live without him. For his daughter, Paloma, however, to live again with a fatherly figure is a challenge, because she is forced to judge the man, unknown to her, who left them, depriving them of his protection and company. Thus, the enigmatic and troubled silence in which the father takes refuge when he is rescued (in 1949's France), can not be more than a manifestation of guilt. Paloma, and also the viewer, can come to believe that Justo is a coward and a selfish man, who has been unfaithful to his wife and renounced his ideals to save his skin. But soon the mistakes are cleared, and the figure of Justo, sick, mentally and physically beaten, is redeemed forever on the mythical horizon of the beach of Argelès-sur-Mer. That's when Paloma stops to consider what happened. It is also at this point that Marie Noëlle decides, consciously, to develop a discourse on memory from elements that have nothing to do with the old political parameters of modernity (unlike, for example, Ken Loach, who seeks to resurrect the ghost of the libertarian revolution at the gates of the 21st century). The exaltation of love from the field of ideology (and not as a mere expression of a narrative mold, as an effect of the mechanics of melodrama), implies the vindication of the character of Justo from a more ethical than political position, so what makes Justo a hero is the consistency observed between his ideas and the dignity with which he stays loyal to Manuela ("we were soldiers and they treated us like criminals", says Justo, in a clear parallel with the suspicions that Paloma holds about his enigmatic life in France).

The key which enables Paloma to transmute the image of the father-villain to that of father-hero is the discovery of the fidelity of Justo. In Paloma's eyes rather than a Justo faithful to his own principles, he is a Justo faithful to the commitment made to his own people, which transforms him into a subject of veneration and memory. A revelation that is obvious in the climax of the story, when Paloma looks at the camera to address the audience and states this reality in a performative way, re-knowing Justo as she utters the solemn words "my father". We will not discuss here if Noëlle's look is a response to the hegemonic masculine discourse, or if it is proposed as a way to answer the dominant political discourse, but the truth is that many questions arise when the proposals of *La mujer del anarquista* are ignored arguing that this is a film that does not live up to its claims. At least no one can deny Noëlle and Sehr's film the credit for opening a debate so often overlooked in Spain: the memory as the core of a European identity project in which racism and xenophobia are banished for ever:

> Because it is very important to learn to know each other. Europe can not be built if we do not share, if we do not talk to our neighbors, telling each other the stories that we have in common. For me, the most important thing about this film is the goal of telling these stories, trying to build a European identity (Noëlle, 2011).

Another issue related to this is the issue of the places of memory, which very few current Spanish films about the war have dealt with so intensely as *La mujer del anarquista*. Because Noëlle and Sehr's film hits us, primarily for being a film about the geographical, cultural and political frontiers that divide and separate countries, and from here on, by the example of solidarity that many men and women gave on either side of those borders. Speaking at the program *Versión española*, Noëlle stresses:

> For me it was very important to shoot on the beach at Argelès ("the beach of shame" as called in the press-book of the film). That site, for many Republicans, is the site of humiliation. Because they came to France and had the idea of France as the country of democracy. And when they came they were unarmed (...) and put on that beach, where there was nothing. Not even a hut. They themselves had to build a place to sleep. Many died there. But they never lost courage. This is what fascinates me. (Noëlle, 2011).

The fiction begins and ends at this beach: "I was four when Franco threw the crows of the German Condor Legion on us," remembers the character of Paloma at the beginning of the film, while walking on the sea-shore. And after telling all her history she adds (with the murmur of the waves crashing in the background, the same faced by the refugees seventy years ago): "Mom never returned to Spain. Her homeland is where the man who she loved all her life lies." Before that, the viewer has seen the father acquitted, eventually rescued and missed in a sequence that may be real, but also dreamed or imagined, in which he walks along the beach of Argelès, holding the hands of his beloved Manuela. Defeated by disease, as if trying to conjure up another kind of threat, much more painful than oblivion, he recites the verses by León Felipe:

"Haz un hoyo en la puerta de tu exilio,
planta un árbol,
riégalo con tus lágrimas
y aguarda."

"Make a hole in the door of your exile,
plant a tree,
water it with your tears
and wait."

Encontrarás dragones: Images of the "Other" Spain

The Spanish-American coproduction *Encontrarás dragones* (*There Be Dragons*, Roland Joffé, 2011), written and directed by British director Roland Joffé, twice nominated for Oscars for *The Killing Fields* (*Los gritos del silencio*, 1984) and *The Mission* (*La misión*, 1986), can be described without doubt as a definitely atypical film. Probably it is the first fiction in the last three decades that adopts the perspective of the victors in war, and of course, it is the Spanish film about war as well as religion with a big budget, 25 million euros, which makes it the third most expensive production in Spanish film history, after *Ágora* (Alejandro Amenábar, 2009) and *Planet 51* (Jorge Blanco, 2009). It is also the first time that a work of fiction aims to depict the "official" biography of one of the most influential characters in the recent history of Spain, the Aragonese priest José María Escrivá (Barbastro, 1902-Rome, 1975), founder of the powerful Catholic institution Opus Dei. It is atypical, finally, because the film, contrary to what happens with *El laberinto del fauno* and *La mujer del anarquista*, leaves very few chinks to find any signs of Spanishness in its approach. The production, featuring foreign actors (the American Wes Bentley, the British Charlie Cox, the Ukrainian "Bond girl" Olga Kurylenko and Brazilian Rodrigo Santoro), is designed from the outset with the intention of building a story to the world, capable of influencing public as diverse as the American, Filipino, Turkish, Australian, Polish or Argentine (though in Latin America the footage is shortened and the film becomes a romantic drama, being released a year later under the title *Secretos de pasión* –secrets of passion).

Encontrarás dragones tells the story of Roberto, a Spanish-born writer who lives and works in London, away from the authoritarian Franco's Spain, represented by the figure of his father, the old Judge Manuel Torres. Roberto is commisioned to write a book on the process of canonization of José María Escrivá, upon which some buzz has been generated, and the encounter seems unavoidable since Torres was a friend and class-fellow of Escrivá and certainly can provide his son with firsthand information. During the film we find out what are the reasons for the rift between José María and Manuel and between Roberto and his father. The life of Judge Torres has been marked by bitterness and jealousy, an irrational hatred that leads him to commit murders before and during the war. On the other hand, Torres has never given affection to his motherless child, and has told him nothing about the past. In the end, the miraculous intercession of Escrivá causes repentance in the old and dying Torres and inspires Roberto's compassion. And what's more important: it determines the approach of the book about the founder of Opus Dei. "This is how

I came to find a saint, and found my father", Roberto says in the film, in a way that could be put in reverse and complementary form: that is how I came to Madrid to try talking to my father and I found a saint. Through the character of Robert, and the significant differences that separate him from his father, Joffé wants the viewer to emotionally assimilate the true scope of of Escrivá's thought and to attach it to the social and political realities of his time.

Now, what is that reality? While Marie Noëlle leads us to the French May, Joffé sets an action from which he recalls the events of the war in November 1982. That is, the time when the Socialists come to power in Spain with absolute majority and the country prepares to join the European Union following the media backup received by the organization of the World Cup that year. The attempted coup of February 1981 is left behind, and a period of modernization and standardization of political life starts, after centuries of civil strife. The transition, therefore, is conceived as a stage for dialogue and collective consensus, as a result of a long journey in which the interests of the democratic left converge with the aspirations of Franco-led reforms and openness done since the late fifties by the technocrats of Opus Dei, with Laureano López Rodó in the lead. It may be said, in a sense, that the film takes us back to a time of reconciliation, though at present between the two Spains, cracks once thought forgotten, begin to emerge again.

The memory exercise that triggers *Encontrarás dragones* (with the use of a character who tries to investigate about the past, just as in *Tierra y Libertad* or in *Soldados de Salamina —Soldiers of Salamin—*, David Trueba, 2003), proposes an obviously conservative and revisionist vision of history: social peace threatened by the masses ("all wars begin before the first shots are fired"), and Franco's army revolt as the only possible response to crime and anarchy ("after years of political and social instability, in the summer of 1936 a group of generals led an uprising" that due to the resistance of the revolutionaries, "became a bitter and lengthy civil war"). During the war, the Republican-controlled cities such as Madrid, are transformed into a huge ghetto in which bourgeois, Catholic or anyone who raises suspicion is persecuted and eliminated ruthlessly. In a representative sequence, an old priest, dressed in a cassock, is arrested and executed in the street by a gang of the CNT, but immediately comes Franco's aviation to give the criminals what they deserve. The bombing of cities and the killing of innocent civilians seem to be justified, but Escrivá's character insists that revenge can not solve the problems. From here on, the issue of violence is essential to understand the ideological keys of Joffé's film. In the days following the proclamation of the Second Republic, when the first excesses against the Church take place, Escrivá finds one of his disciples with posters calling for a crusade against the new government. "A crusade? Is it Christian to use the cross to incite hatred and anger?", he complains. "I will not tell you what to think ... but before you rush, before attempting to change the world, we should change ourselves. We together are building something vital. Now, especially now, we must be sowers of peace and joy." Already during the war, and immediately after the murder of Father Lazarus, Escrivá restrains his men and makes an effort to understand the savage behavior of the extremists: "They see us as part of a system that oppresses them, and they despair."

While the army and the Falangists ruthlessly fight the revolutionaries with weapons, Escrivá distances himself from them to build his own "way", which aims to overcome the class struggle through prayer, discipline and the incorporation of workers into the establishment. A philosophy of life, therefore, that displaces to the extreme the oligarchic conception of Judge Manuel Torres, and the revolutionary one represented by anarchists like Olga and Oriol. To achieve that utopia it is necessary "to cross the mountains", beat the "dragons" and the "demons", more internal than external, who encourage fratricidal struggles: the lower passions, the individualism, the lack of discipline or the temptation to be isolated in the ivory tower of religion, avoiding the problems of everyday life. In contrast to the image of the all powerful and controlling Opus Dei, present in films like *The Da Vinci Code*, adapted from the bestseller by Dan Brown (Ron Howard, 2006), or the Spanish *Camino* (Javier Fesser, 2008), Joffé proposes a return to the essence, a return to idealism and the moment of candor of the founding time when José María Escrivá reveals himself as a visionary, as a new Moses to lead His people into a social setting of peace and well-being (the flight to Andorra with his men has a biblical epic flavour that underlines this idea). Heir of two antithetical positions, those of Torres and Oriol, who cross into the fabric of life referred to by the mysterious Abileyza (Geraldine Chaplin), the character of Robert in the film embodies the synthesis of a new redeemed man.

Far from the stereotypes and bold portraits that have been frequent in Spanish cinema from the sixties, *Encontrarás dragones* presents the image of a modern and integrated Church, which cares about civil affairs and proposes alternatives for solving the problems generated by contemporary secular society. It is the image shared by half a million believers who fill St. Peter's Square to see Escrivá proclaimed a saint, as the titles at the end of the film reminds us, and it is also the conviction of citizens who participate in the mass demonstrations convened by the Spanish bishops in recent years. The 340.000 spectators that the film brought to Spanish theaters is worth mentioning. A noteworthy figure if we take into account the impact of emblematic Spanish films of recent years set on the Civil War or in the immediate postwar period, as *Silencio roto* (411.000 spectators), *Soldados de Salamina* (433.000), *Pájaros de papel* (*Paper Birds*, Emilio Aragón, 2010; 339.000), *Pan negro* (438.000 spectators, after two reruns following its huge success in the awards by Catalan and Spanish film academies) or *La voz dormida* (327.000).

With memories in mind of the Spanish war (symbol of the 165 wars that have taken place since, as the character of Robert reminds us), the film presents us with the dilemma of falling again and again into the nets of irrational confrontation and violence, or to opt for fraternal Catholicism conceived in the early twentieth century by Escrivá. "They all faced the same question", we read in the opening titles of the film, "On whose side are you on?" Of course, the choice of the historical period in which the story develops (1911-1939) is not accidental, since the film omits the years of consolidation and expansion of the influence of "the Work" in the world, especially in Franco's Spain, with whom he had deep and very close relations, and in the Vatican, where he installed a long standing member of the institution, Joaquín Navarro-Valls, a communications expert, who, for over twenty years was the voice of John Paul II. Nor is the omission of aspects of the saint's life or their fellow students accidental, which could contradict their political neutrality, as is intended to be reflected in the film. Among them, the enrolment of Álvaro del Portillo – a member of Opus Dei since 1935 and Prelate Escrivá's successor – in the Academy for interim Officers of Engineering, where he obtained the post of second lieutenant ("Alférez Provisional") in 1939, amidst a feeling of euphoria unleashed in Burgos by the warlike deeds of the Caudillo Franco (De la Cierva, 1993, p. 143-158).

So far, a brief analysis that we believe demonstrates how jointly produced fiction, from a transnational creative space, contributes to the construction of a new imagery of the civil war. The memory of the war among Spaniards, the last domestic conflict in a long string of internal strifes, is essential to advance in the consensus on our own national identity. But at the same time, even today, the so-called Spanish war continues referring to the history of the twentieth century. It refers both to the illusions and dreams thwarted by the threat of totalitarian thinking of either sign, as to the desire to forever forget the ghost of internal division and war in Europe (with Picasso's *Guernica* as a universal symbol).

In general terms, the foreign authors add very original themes and approaches in the joint film productions, as it can be seen. Approaches that help to shake the foundations on which the traditional creative streams of Spanish cinema are based. Firstly, they reinforce the myth of the war in Spain in a context that transcends local disputes, to delve into issues that deal with the moral and political lessons that even today continue being extracted from the conflict. Secondly, they propose an epic and spectacular approach, which aims to be consistent with the magnitude of the deeds lived. A tone that is not too common, unfortunately, in Spanish cinema, tempted into seclusion within the limits of drama or psychological melodrama. In the third and last instance, as a logical consequence of the two previous premises, fictions jointly produced and directed by foreign authors are committed to the need for the restoration of very specific ethical values and attitudes. They lay on the table, in other words, the need to define and to militate in an ideological space from which to deal with the vicissitudes and uncertainties of today's world. In any case it is interesting to study how different local and transnational versions of the Civil War are, or how they have helped to shape a new canon about their representation against the common risk of thinking that they are all "Spanish" movies.[1]

BIBLIOGRAPHY

Casanova, J. "Guerra y dictadura en el cine español". *El País* (08.09.2008), URL: http://elpais.com/diario/2008/09/08/opinion/1220824812_850215.html (06.04.2012).

Costa, J. "Un ejercicio de estilo". *El País* (23.09.2012), URL: http://elpais.com/diario/2009/01/23/cine/1232665212_850215.html (06.04.2012).

1 This work has been made possible by the help of the Research Projects "Media co-productions in the European context: Identities and cultural transnationalization processes" (AT2009-0020, Ministry of Science and Innovation, Government of Spain, Integration Actions Program) and "Cinema and Television in Post-Transition Spain (1979-1992)", Ministry of Economy and Competitiveness, Government of Spain (CSO2011-15708-E).

De la Cierva, R. *Los años mentidos. Falsificaciones de la historia de España en el siglo XX*. Madrid: Editorial Fénix, 1993, p. 143-158.

Del Toro, G. "Encuentros digitales". *El mundo.es* (09.10.2006), URL: http://www.elmundo.es/encuentros/invitados/2006/10/2192/ (06.04.2012).

Ibáñez, J. C. "La guerra civil en el cine español de la primera década del siglo XXI". In: Ibáñez, J. C. / Anania, F. (eds.). *Memoria histórica e identidad en cine y televisión*. Sevilla-Zamora: Comunicación Social, 2010, p. 83-120.

Monterde, J. E. "El cine histórico durante la transición política". In: Benet, J. V. (ed.). *Escritos sobre el cine español (1973-1987)*. Valencia: Filmoteca de la Generalitat Valenciana, 1989, p. 45-63.

Noëlle, M. Interview on television, *Versión española* (TVE1), (11.6.2011), URL: http://www.rtve.es/alacarta/videos/version-espanola/version-espanola-mujer-del-anarquista/1126844/ (06.04.2012).

Palacio, M. "Elogio posmoderno de las coproducciones". *Cuadernos de la Academia* 5 (1999), p. 221-235.

Rosenstone, R. A. *Visions of the past. The Challenge of Film to Our Idea of History*. Cambridge (Mass.): Harvard University Press, 1995.

A French Novel transformed into a German Movie: Michel Houellebecq's *Les particules élémentaires* and Oskar Roehler's *Elementarteilchen*

Matthias Hausmann

Introduction

In 2002, Mexican cinema experienced one of the biggest scandals in its history: The movie *El crimen del padre Amaro*, directed by Carlos Carrera and with a screenplay by Vicente Leñero, caused uproar in the Mexican Catholic church and conservative sectors of Mexican society. A large polemic had already started prior to the premiere and there were several intents to prohibit the exhibition of this movie that depicts the sexual relationship between a priest and a young girl that finally dies after a failed abortion. The scandal was closely linked to the fact that *El crimen del padre Amaro* is a specific kind of adaptation of a literary text: The movie is based on the homonymous novel of the Portuguese realist Eça de Queiroz (1875/1880), but the adaptation transposes the action from the Portuguese 19th century to contemporary Mexico and adds current controversial issues of the Catholic church, such as financial ties between drug cartels and the clergy, to the original plot.[1]

It is obvious that a transposition of a 19th century European plot to current Central America reality leads to great changes. We will try to demonstrate in this article, however, that even a seemingly completely different sort of adaptation without any big chronological or spatial differences can also lead to significant modifications solely by placing the setting from one country into another: We will compare the novel *Les particules élémentaires* (1998) by the current best-known French author Michel Houellebecq with its first – and so far only – filmic adaptation, which was directed by the German Oskar Roehler under the title *Elementarteilchen* (2006). The title remains thus unchanged (being the literal translation of the French title, which was also used for the German translation of the novel) and also the time of the diegesis is nearly the same: the novel's plot begins in 1998, the one of the film in 2005, so that in both cases the action within the works is almost simultaneous to their release.

Nevertheless, the movie transposes the plot from France to Germany and this transposition to a neighboring country leads to considerable differences between the two artworks that underscore how different national cultural contexts still are today within the European Union. Thus, this article may prove a counterpoint to other contributions in this volume and show that despite the often

1 For a summary of the scandal as well as an analysis of the novel's adaptation and the changes made by the director and the screenwriter see Hausmann, 2014.

evoked *europudding*[2], national traditions in film production remain strong, and that the differing cultural contexts within Europe may lead to substantial changes in adapted models.

Our article aims to demonstrate and discuss some of the most important changes Roehler introduced in his movie due to the German setting. Moreover, the following lines also intend to introduce the reader to the filmic adaptations of Michel Houellebecq's novels. Despite the major success of his books, these films are still not very well-known and can add interesting facts to our argumentation since only one movie is set in Germany, whereas the other two films are French and do not change the setting of the original plot.

For these reasons, the first chapter of our contribution will deal with the relation between Houellebecq and cinema and the three feature films based on novels by him in general, before we will focus on *Elementarteilchen* in particular. The most significant changes between novel and movie will be analyzed and possible reasons for these changes discussed; finally, the conclusion will inform about the reception of Roehler's cultural adaptation in Germany and France.

Michel Houellebecq and Cinema

When in 2010 Michel Houellebecq's latest novel, *La carte et le territoire*, was published, critics were unanimous in their celebration of this text that also won the Prix Goncourt. This success formed a sharp contrast to Houellebecq's project prior to this novel, his film *La possibilité d'une île* (2008). For this movie he adapted his own novel from 2005 and worked for the first time as a director of a feature-length film. Throughout the European press this movie was regarded as a disaster. In France, the reviewer of *Le monde* spoke of the movie as a "défilé d'images sans vie, montées sans rythme, sans rien." (Douin, 2008)[3] A review of the German *taz* also arrived at an unrelenting judgement: "Michel Houellebecq verfilmt seinen Endzeitroman *Die Möglichkeit einer Insel* und scheitert an sich selbst." (Müller, 2011) Finally, the English *Independent* wrote with black humour: "As a novelist, Michel Houellebecq has long been the enfant terrible of French literature. As a film director, according to initial reactions to his first movie, he is simply terrible." (Lichfield, 2008)

Taking up this last statement and judging by his movie adaptation one is tempted to say that Houellebecq, although a very gifted writer (despite all the polemics about his works), is not also a gifted director. Contrary cases of artists equally talented in both fields are probably rare, an important current example being Lucía Puenzo. The young Argentinean excels as a writer and as a director of adaptations of her own works, like *The fish child* – probably because she is well aware that the two media differ significantly and have their respective possibilities: "[Lo literario y

2 For the concept of *europudding* see besides other contributions the articles of Manuel Palacio (p. 39 f.) and Concepción Cascajosa (p. 51) in this volume.

3 A general overview of the French critiques can be found in a release of *La Dernière Heure*, which concludes: "La critique en France a démoli dans son ensemble le film de l'écrivain polémique Michel Houellebecq *La possibilité d'une île*." (http://www.dhnet.be/cinetele/cinema/article/222676/le-film-de-houellebecq-ereinte-par-la-critique-en-france.html).

el cine] son lenguajes muy distintos." (Lerer, 2009)[4] Houellebecq seems to lack this awareness and does not seem to realise all of film's potential, as he states, for example: "Es ist unmöglich, im Kino ironisch zu sein." (Gärtner, 2008, p. 15) This misjudgement of the possibilities of cinema might explain in part the failure of his movie. At the same time this misjudgement is surprising, because Houellebecq has had a long and intense relation with film. In his "unauthorized" biography Denis Demonpion writes: "Houellebecq a toujours rêvé d'être cinéaste. C'était même sa seule aspiration avant ses essais en poésie et la gloire littéraire." (2005, 14)[5] Because of this aspiration Houellebecq attended, after his studies at the Institut national d'agronomie, an institution for film-studies for two years, the Ecole nationale Louis-Lumière. During the studies there, when he still wore his original name Michel Thomas, he realized his first two short films *Cristal de souffrance* and *Déséquilibres*, the last of which being a first adaptation of a literary work before his experiment with his own novel. *Déséquilibres* is a short film version of a story by the Belgian author Raymond Jean Marie De Kremer (Jean Ray) and contains a scene about the killing of a canary bird, which is interesting as dead canaries are a recurrent element in the work of Houellebecq, which underlines a certain continuity between his first films and his novels.

Some years later, in 1992, Houellebecq wrote in a bitter letter to his mother: "Avant de mourir, il te reste quelques années pour essayer de rattraper tes mauvaises actions. Voici, en résumé, ce que tu dois faire : 1. Téléphoner, en insistant, à toute personne pouvant m'aider à faire aboutir mes projets dans le domaine du cinéma. [...]." (Ibid, 169). This letter demonstrates that cinema remained important for Houellebecq, and his continuous interest was also demonstrated by a third short movie, *La rivière,* that he directed in 2001.[6]

Before this last short film so far, Houellebecq participated as a co-screenwriter in the first adaptation made of one of his novels: *Extension du domaine de la lutte*, which was in 1999 transposed to the cinema screen by Philippe Harel, who also performed the protagonist's role. This movie, which adds an additional narrative instance to the novel's structure, conveys rather well the protagonist's solitude and desperation and was seen as a fairly successful adaptation.[7] It is interesting to note that this first adaptation significantly changes the ending of the plot: Whereas the novel ends in deep desperation of the protagonist, who seems inapt to have any normal relationship with other people, especially women, the movie shows him in a

4 For some aspects of the changes Puenzo introduced in the adaptation of her own novel *El niño pez* for the cinema screen, see Hausmann, 2013.

5 Houellebecq sharply criticized Demonpion's biography and attacked this book in his text "Mourir", which was published online (http://homepage.mac.com/michelhouellebecq/textes/mourir.html). Nevertheless, in some respects this biography seems a more reliable source about the life of this author who is so keen on spreading a certain image of himself – an image also spread by his "official" biography by Dominique Noguez (*Houellebecq, en fait*, Paris: Fayard, 2003) that seems too positively biased. For this reason information provided by Demonpion is used here.

6 For all of his short movies Houellebecq also wrote the screenplays. For further information about the films see the following imdb-site: http://www.imdb.fr/name/nm0396391/?ref_=fn_al_nm_1.

7 Johannes Wetzel (2008) accurately comments: "Philippe Harels Verfilmung von *Ausweitung der Kampfzone* 1999 war ein Achtungserfolg."

last scene taking dancing lessons and dancing with a woman, thus giving the spectator a glimpse of hope. Houellebecq complimented this new ending: "[La fin du film *d'Extension*] est assez réussie." (Haan, 2004, p. 14). In general he was satisfied with the co-operation with Harel, and this collaboration found a repetition in the adaptation of *La possibilité d'une île*. This time Houellebecq himself was the leading person, Harel only supporting him. It is no big surprise that Houellebecq chose this particular novel for his own adaptation, as he regards it as one of his favourite works: "*La possibilité d'une île* est mon chef d'œuvre, sur le plan romanesque tout du moins."[8]

Transposing this book to the cinema by himself also might have been a reaction to the second adaptation of a novel of his, namely of *Les particules élémentaires*, which was brought to the cinema screen by the German director Oskar Roehler. Houellebecq had for a short time himself had the project to make this adaptation, again with Harel, as recalls Philippe Sollers: "Il y avait un projet de film d'Harel, dans lequel [Houellebecq] voulait que je joue mon propre personnage."[9] This project finally failed due to a lack of funding, and later on Houellbecq declared himself rather pleased with the movie by Roehler, stating: "J'avais peur, mais en fait je suis assez content. [...] c'est un film qui a le courage d'être sentimental, ce qui n'est pas facile... Beaucoup de gens critiquent le fait qu'il y ait un happy end, mais en fait la possibilité d'un happy end existe dans le livre." (Treeck, 2011, 384) This citation also shows that Roehler's movie seems to satisfy Houellebecq's desire of a mitigated and more positive cosmos of his works in cinema, which leads us to a closer look at all of the movie adaptations so that later on we can contrast Roehler's version with the two French ones.

It is already interesting that Houellebecq's participation is different in the three cases. In the Roehler movie he is not involved at all, in Harel's movie he is present as a co-screenwriter and finally he is in charge of almost all the production in his own attempt. Despite this differing participation of Houellebecq and the different styles of the respective directors, there are two important aspects that the three versions have in common. First, the long philosophical, historical and sociological passages that are so important in Houellebecq's novels pose a great problem for all of the movie adaptations; none of them have found convincing strategies to convey these thoughts. Secondly, and perhaps even more importantly, the movies mitigate the novels' contents. The scenes of sex and violence are significantly reduced, and above all, the endings are by far more positive than in the respective models, as we have already commented in the case of Harel's *Extension du domaine de la lutte*. This is also true for the other two movies that have a much more conciliatory ending than the narrative prose works, which we will examine in more detail for Roehler's version. It can be added that Houellebecq's last book, *La carte et le territoire*, ends with an evocation of a "sentiment de desolation [...] qui s'empare de nous" (Houellebecq, 2010, p. 428), which describes rather appropriately the cosmos of Houellebecq's novels – all the movie versions, however, try to convey a more positive feeling for the spectators.

---

8 Houellebecq, "Mourir" (see note 5).

9 Cited by Demonpion, 2005, p. 244 f. Here Demonpion also recounts how this project finally collapsed.

Such mitigated versions of Houellebecq's works do not only exist in cinema, but there has also been a German theatre adaptation of *Les particules élémentaires* that reduces the negative elements significantly: Uwe Eric Laufenberg's adaptation for the stage that was performed in the Cuvilliés Theatre in Munich in 2002 softened the source material considerably (Dössel, 2002, p. 14). This theatre version is only one of various, for, besides the three feature films, there have been several attempts to transpose Houellebecq's works also to other media. This is especially true for his first novel *Extension du domaine de la lutte,* which has given birth to repeated adaptations, for example various plays performed in Paris, Avignon, and Switzerland.[10] Very interesting for us is the fact that there is also a TV adaptation of this book: *Udvidelse af kampzonen,* which was realized by Jens Albinus in 2002 for Danish television. Moreover, the German director Martin Zylka realized a radio drama based on *Extension du domaine de la lutte* in 2000, which was followed by an extensive radio drama of *Les particules élémentaires* by Leonhard Koppelmann in 2001.[11] This emphasizes the great interest in Houellebecq's works in Germany, which is one of the reasons why Roehler chose to adapt *Les particules élémentaires*.

To end this section about the relationship between Houellebecq and cinema, it could be added that a movie adaptation of *La carte et le territoire* certainly will only be a matter of time, seeing as how all of Houellebecq's novels (except *Plateforme,* which can be considered his weakest work) have given way to movie versions. *La carte et le territoire* even seems especially appropriate for a transposition to another medium as it contains strong intermediality thanks to its protagonist Jed, who works as a painter and photographer. Furthermore, the novel stages reflections about the differences between media with a clear allusion to film.[12] Such aspects of intermediality are by far not so prominent in *Les particules élémentaires* with one important exception: Bruno writes a film script while in the mental asylum he will stay in for the rest of his life.[13] From this film in the diegetic universe of the novel we will come now to the film that Oskar Roehler made of the novel.

Oskar Roehler's Movie *Elementarteilchen*: Romanticization and Melodramatization

Roehler's film *Elementarteilchen* had its premiere at the Berlinale of 2006, where it was awarded a Silver Bear for Best Actor for Moritz Bleibtreu. The premiere at the Berlinale seems to be no coincidence, for the movie is an exclusively German project – produced, directed, and performed by a sort of Who is Who of the

10 Besides others there has been a theatre adaptation of *Extension du domaine de la lutte* realized by the German director Helena Waldham in Lucerne. There has also been a play based on *Plateforme* (realised by the Dutch theatre director Johan Simons in 2008 and performed in Strasbourg) and other adaptations of his works that cannot all be mentioned in the framework of this article.

11 For a short description of this radio version, see Treeck, 2011, p. 380.

12 The figure "Houellebecq" differentiates between the "monde comme narration", including film, novels and music, and the "monde comme juxtaposition", including poetry and painting (Houellebecq, 2010, p. 258 f.).

13 Cf. Houellebecq, 1998, p. 321: "J'ai écrit un scenario de film paradisiaque sur le thème de la Jérusalem nouvelle."

German film business. The producer Bernd Eichinger was, until his death, one of Germany's most influential film producers, being for a long time head of the largest German film production enterprise, Constantin Film.[14]

As director for this project, Eichinger chose Oskar Roehler, who is often considered one of the leading filmmakers of unified Germany (Abel, 2010, p. 75). It was not surprising that Roehler was interested in Houellebecq's novel, since literature has been an important and frequent inspiration for his work, as he stated in an interview: "Ich habe eher literarische Vorbilder, ich könnte jetzt auch keinen Regisseur nennen, vielleicht außer David Lynch […]."[15] That there were probably further reasons for him to pick up Houellebecq's novel will be discussed in the next chapter.

Roehler and Eichinger selected some of the most popular German actors for the various roles; this was made possible with a budget of six million euros, which is very high for a German production. The role of Bruno is played by Moritz Bleibtreu, who had already performed the protagonist's role in Roehler's last movie before *Elementarteilchen*, *Agnes und seine Brüder* (2004). He played Bruno's role very convincingly, graphically conveying the desperation regarding all the (often erotic) failures in his life. The role of Bruno's brother is taken on by Christian Ulmen, who persuasively transports the unworldliness of his character. The roles of the two girlfriends of the male protagonists are performed by two of the best-known German actresses: Franka Potente is Michael's fiancée Annabelle and Martina Gedeck is Christiane, Bruno's lover. Even the roles of secondary characters are performed by well-known actors such as Corinna Harfouch as the psychologist and Nina Hoss as the mother of Bruno and Michael. The array of stars in this movie might be best indicated by the role of Bruno's father, which is performed by Uwe Ochsenknecht, in a scene that is secondary in the novel and does not add much to the story in the movie, either, but seems more or less introduced only for the purpose of having another German acting star in the movie to boast.[16]

This accumulation of German movie stars was also used for publicity purposes in Germany, as shows the cover of the DVD, one half of which is covered by the names of the actors. Additionally, it shows the pretension to match the classic status of this novel with an equally significant film. More important for our purpose is the fact that this well-known German crew already betrays the objective to transpose the action to a German setting. Before analyzing this German cultural setting in more detail it is interesting to show some general aspects of the movie.

As usually in his films, Roehler was also the scriptwriter and he retained the main structure of the novel's plot around Michel and Bruno that is staged in the pre-

---

14 This company has produced some of Germany's greatest film successes of the recent years, namely *Der Name der Rose*, *Das Parfum* or *Der Schuh des Manitu*.

15 Michael Althen, Andreas Kilb und Peter Körte, "'Wir sind noch nicht gut genug in der Spitze'. Filmregisseure auf der Berlinale", in: faz.net (9.2.2006), URL: http://www.faz.net/aktuell/feuilleton/kino/filmregisseure-auf-der-berlinale-wir-sind-noch-nicht-gut-genug-in-der-spitze-1303623.html. It can be added that meanwhile, Roehler has also begun to write, publishing in 2011 his first novel *Herkunft*, which demonstrates his literary interests. Furthermore, this fist novel contains important autobiographical elements, a parallel to his movie Elementarteilchen as will be shown later on.

16 A review in the important *Frankfurter Allgemeine Zeitung* stresses this alignment of German stars stating: „Ein Allstar-Team des deutschen Films spielt in Oskar Roehlers *Elementarteilchen*“ (Althen, 2006, p. 41).

sent time. However, he eliminated the important framework of this plot: the gaze of the new, transformed mankind from the future (2079) back to our time is not taken up in the movie. There is no indication, not even in the written epilogue that closes the movie, about this new mankind created according to the discoveries made by Michael.[17]

This is a considerable change compared to the novel which has two notable consequences. First, this simplified structure without the future framework leads to an almost complete removal of the novel's philosophical and ethical aspects. Particularly by leaving out the future dimension, Roehler lets the opportunity pass away to discuss the possibilities and problems of human engineering (cf. also Mueller, 2010, p. 2 and 9). Furthermore, most of the important elements of the novel's (anti-)utopian meaning are therefore absent in the movie, which is already a major drawback of Roehler's film. This forms a parallel, however, to the two other movie adaptations made so far, because these, likewise, eliminate much of the theoretical and ethical potential of the novels they adapt.

Secondly, by cutting off the future framework, the narrators of the story are no longer the *néo-humains* as in the novel, which has some considerable consequences concerning *how* the plot around the two half-brothers Michel and Bruno is narrated. Similar to the novel, the history of the two brothers is shown in constant switches from one to the other and in matters of the general action, the plot is, for the most part, retained. However, this is not true for the style and certain important details, which significantly change the character of the whole adaptation, which centres on the two love stories of the protagonists with Annabelle and Christiane respectively. Within these love stories many aspects are mitigated; this forms another parallel with the two other movie adaptations. The sex scenes are much toned down, and probably even more remarkable is the fact that some of the most cruel events are omitted or are merely insinuated, which is particularly true for the abject crimes committed by David di Meola: in the novel, they form a long passage that is difficult to bear, but in the movie, they are hardly talked of.

Furthermore, some highly problematic aspects of the relationships between the characters in the novel are not included in the movie. In Houellebecq's book, for example, Christiane is frightened by her son, underscoring a collapse of all stable human relationships; this fear of her own child is not transferred to the movie. Another example is the relationship between Mich(a)el[18] and Annabelle: in the novel, Annabelle wants to get pregnant so that Michel will not leave her to go to Ireland (and therefore has selfish motives for her pregnancy, which also shows her deep

---

17 This epilogue recounts that Michael won the Nobel Prize and that Bruno was probably happy in the asylum, which is another significant change of the novel in which Michel commits suicide and Bruno has a rather bleak existence in the asylum. This is another element of the romanticization of the movie which we will comment on later on.

18 The protagonists' names are slightly Germanized in the movie: Bruno's Christian name remains unchanged and his family name is Germanized (Clément becomes Klement). Michel becomes Michael (whereas his family name Djerzinski is guarded), which can be regarded as a minor change, but one should however recall that by naming his hero Michel, Houellebecq gives him his own name, thus evoking a parallel to his own life which is strengthened by certain autobiographical details nearing his life to that of his character and thus this change made by Roehler should not be underestimated.

desperation), whereas in the movie she gets pregnant by accident; thus a romantic aspect occurs that is not at all present in the novel.

This leads us to an important point of our analysis: Roehler's movie undertakes a romanticization and melodramatization of the plot around Bruno and Michael which is diametrically opposed to the novel's clinical style. *Les particules élémentaires* are narrated in an extremely sober manner, which is characteristic for Houellebecq's novels in general. The French author's style is very prosaic and it is highly interesting to combine this observation with the following commentary of the narrator in Houellebecq's first novel *Extension du domaine de la lutte*: "La forme romanesque n'est pas conçue pour peindre l'indifférence, ni le néant ; il faudrait inventer une articulation plus plate, plus concise et plus morne." (Houellebecq, 1994, p. 42) This sentence, often quoted by literary critics who analyze Houellebecq's works,[19] describes his style very well: he intends to write with "une articulation plate", just because he describes the indifference of the life of the Western people at the end of the 20th century also evoked in the citation. So his prose works are narrated in a style that stresses objectivity, omits concentration on deep human feelings and can be characterized as "flat": "Le 'plat' (re)devient 'style'" (Célestin, 2007, p. 356) in his novels.

In Roehler's movie, on the other hand, we find a romanticization and a melodramatization,[20] for which further examples will now be given. The romanticization is particularly palpable in the handling of the relationship between Michael and Annabelle. Their re-encounter in the novel is a mere coincidence, whereas Roehler makes his Michael visit Annabelle's home to see her again, so that from the beginning of their new relationship there are more feelings in the movie. Moreover, this relationship accounts for much of the movie's time, whereas it does not take up a lot of space in the novel, where Michel and Annabelle only come together at the end of the second part and Annabelle already dies at the middle of the third part. Furthermore, in the movie, every aspect of their relationship is given a romantic significance: For instance, in the novel, Michel has a meaningless and bleak sexual encounter before he meets Annabelle again (Houellebecq, 1998, p. 158), whereas in the movie, Annabelle introduces him to sex.

Besides this romanticization, elements of melodrama find their way into the movie, which can be shown with special insistence in the case of Christiane's death: In the novel her suicide is not narrated, but the reader is only told in a highly laconic way that she was found dead: "On avait retrouvé la fauteuil roulant désarticulé, près des boîtes aux lettres, en bas de la dernière vole des marches. Elle avait le visage tuméfié et le cou brisé." (Houellebecq, 1998, p. 309). This is transposed in a highly melodramatic scene in the movie: Christiane is shown climbing on the veranda of her apartment's balcony and letting herself fall down – and at this precise moment

19 Amongst others, the studies by Pöppel (2006, p. 72), Noguez (2003, p. 108) and Célestin (207, p. 350) quote this sentence to speak of Houellbecq's clinical style.

20 A malicious critic could point out certain vicinity between Roehler's style and the script Bruno writes in the asylum. As Bruno tells his brother some details of this script it becomes clear that it is about a utopian society in which only women and dogs have survived a biological catastrophe and in which ridiculously melodramatic and romantic actions take place, so Roehler's style, though much more earnest of course, in some respects resembles the script written by the novel's anti-hero.

Bruno finally calls her, a call that could have prevented the suicide had it come a minute earlier. The melodramatic aspect is still heightened by the fact that Bruno instinctively knows that something bad has happened and he hastens to Christiane's home with a taxi, but arrives only to see her battered on the floor. This melodramatic orchestration forms a stark contrast to the novel's clinical style.[21] This hard laconic style is also used in the novel for recounting the suicide of Bruno's first girlfriend Annick, which is left out completely in the movie.

To highlight the melodramatic aspects of the movie it is helpful to use the classic study of Peter Brooks about the "melodramatic imagination"; this seems even more appropriate, as Brooks emphasizes that cinema is "the contemporary form that most relayed and supplanted melodrama" (1995, p. 14). Brooks' ideas may not only be applied fruitfully to the "hyperbolic situation" (Brooks, 1995, p. 25) of Christiane's death, but also to another highly remarkable change in Roehler's movie: The most positive character of the novel and the film alike and maybe the most positive figure in the entire cosmos of Houellebecq's works,[22] Annabelle, does not die in the movie version. This "angelic person" (Haan, 2004, p. 24) survives in the version of Roehler, which is typical for the aesthetics of melodrama according to Brookes who highlights the "*reward* of virtue" as one of its central elements (Brooks, 1995, 27 (italics in the original)). Such rewards do not exist in the cold universe described in Houellebecq's novels, where the death of Annabelle (and her bitter fate before the event) explicitly underline that no one is lucky in current society.[23]

It is interesting to combine this observed melodramatization and romanticization in the movie which forms such a stark contrast to the novel's neutral style with the elimination of the future mankind as the narrators; for this style in the novel is not only a deliberate choice of Houellebecq as explained above, but can also be interpreted in an intradiegetic manner by the fact that the story is narrated by the genetically transformed new humans who lack typically human feelings. This lack of feelings makes them ideal narrators in Houellebecq's sense, for they can recount the indifference of current society with "une articulation plus plate, plus concise et plus morne" as was demanded by the narrator of *Extension du domaine de la lutte*. This can be seen very well by their cold style with which they recount the events of Bruno's and Michel's lives. The movie on the contrary is narrated in a highly melodramatic manner which would be completely improbable for future mankind, and this weakens the novel's proposition considerably.

---

21 It is highly remarkable, but cannot be treated in more detail in the framework of this article, that the clinical style of the novel that only evokes the dead Christiane with her destroyed wheel-chair causes a much greater impression on the reader than the explicit scene in the movie.

22 Cf. the commentary of Martin de Haan who states in an interview with Houellebecq that Annabelle is "sans doute ton personnage le plus angélique: on a l'impression qu'elle est hors de portée, presque inhumaine" (Haan, 2004, p. 24).

23 Houellebecq also stresses that there are no punishments either for his characters – they simply die (Haan, 2004, p. 15: "Il n'y a jamais de punition dans mes livres. En général, les gens qui meurent expient rien, ils meurent, c'est tout."). This is a fundamental contrast to the melodrama in which moral implications are central as Brooks shows constantly in his study – this moral dimension does not exist in Houellebecq's cosmos, what makes the melodramatization of his novel by Roehler so problematic.

This look at the missing framework leads us to the movie's ending that we want to discuss a bit more in detail, because it possibly best shows the changes introduced by Roehler and Eichinger. Their movie stages a happy ending: Michael and Annabelle are a happy couple and one day they visit Bruno and take him to a lake, and the last scene shows the three of them, and also Christiane who accompanies Bruno mentally, sitting beside the lake. It seems that all of them have made peace with their lives and will face a positive future. This is the complete opposite of the end of the characters' story in the novel, in which Bruno unemotionally vegetates in the asylum (Houellebecq, 1998, p. 366: "[Bruno] n'attendait plus rien de la succession des jours.") and all the other protagonists commit suicide. Houellebecq stresses explicitly that personal happiness can only be temporary in our society and that the love stories that Bruno and Michel experience with their two girlfriends will necessarily end in a negative way. This is expressed unequivocally in two sentences that can be regarded as variants of a leitmotif of the novel and that are programmatically placed at the beginning of chapters: "Au milieu du suicide occidental, il était clair qu'ils n'avaient aucune chance." / "Naturellement, là non plus, il n'y avait pas d'issue." (Houellebecq, 1998, p. 295 and 303 respectively). These sentences show without a doubt that there is no hope for the two couples and therefore foreshadow the ending, namely one "which entails a complete denunciation of human nature in general." (Mueller, 2010, p. 9).

Roehler radically changes this ending in his movie because he was unwilling to accept Houellebecq's version, as he openly admits: "Das war ein Ende, das man so nicht hinnehmen kann." (Körte, 2006, p. 23).[24] Christian van Treeck comments accurately that this ending also destroys the sense of the novel's title that Roehler has kept, but which is not really adequate for the movie's storyline: "les quatre protagonistes n'apparaissent plus ici comme des 'particules élémentaires' mais plutôt comme des 'molécules' – plus précisément deux molécules à deux atomes. [...] Au fond, les modifications effectuées sont telles que le titre *Les Particules élémentaires* n'a plus beaucoup de sens.'" (Treeck, 2011, p. 376)[25]

It must be stressed again, however, that the deaths of the characters do not conclude the novel, which ends with a commentary from the néo-humains. The existence of these new human beings that have already almost completely replaced the "old" mankind in 2079, the time from which the plot is narrated, is one decisive reason for the ambiguity that characterizes Houellebecq's entire novel. Ambiguity is in general very important for Houellebecq's works and this is particularly striking in this future framework of *Les particules élémentaires* that is so difficult to classify as either positive utopia or negative dystopia.[26]

---

24 Peter Körte shows in this article as well clearly that the producer Eichinger strongly supported a much more positive ending, which will be commented again at the end of this article.

25 However, it should be added that Marco Abel gives another interpretation, stressing that it is a deliberately exaggerated ending that should call the attention of the spectator to this improbability (Abel, 2010, p. 96). Although this is possible, it seems that Abel underestimates the romanticization of Roehler's movie in general that prepares for such an ending.

26 The question whether the depicted future is utopian or rather anti-utopian is debated with vehemence in the scientific community; for recent and exhaustive reflections about the (anti-) utopian dimensions in Houellebecq's works see Kian-Harald Karimi, 2012. In Roehler's movie the ambiguity between a utopian and an anti-utopian dimension is further weakened by the fact that the important discussion about Huxley's *Brave New World*, which is a central part of

This deliberate ambiguity is lost in the movie version and this is a direct result of using a melodramatic mode, for melodrama does not allow ambiguity as has been shown by Brooks, who stresses that a fundamental element of melodrama's aesthetics is "a refusal of nuance and the insistence on dealing in pure, integral concepts." (1995, p. 40). Closely linked with this aspect and caused by the same reason is the loss of irony in the movie, for irony is not possible within the melodrama, as Brooks points out using the case of Flaubert and his "radically ironic" stance that destroys melodrama's forces (1995, p. 198). This disappearance of irony also has major consequences for the adaptation, for in Houellebecq's novels there is a lot of irony, as he denounces our current Western society with "grands coups d'ironie" (Rabosseau, 2007, p. 45). This irony completes, and partly also subverts, the clinical report of the future people and contributes a lot to the novels' ambiguity. This irony is not found in Roehler's movie either, but it is also interesting that Houellebecq himself did not transfer the ironic elements of his novels to the screen, as he is of the opinion that irony is not possible in cinema (see his citation above). That underscores that Houellebecq has developed a very adequate literary style to convey his worldview as has been shown; nevertheless he has not been able to find a cinematic equivalent for this style, which is a major difference to Lucía Puenzo and the few writer-directors who excel in film and literature alike (another example would be Alain Robbe-Grillet). This is also the main reason why Houellebecq's own adaptation failed. However, neither did even the experienced director Roehler find an equivalent for this particular houellebecquien style, but he opted for a conventional cinematic style; this already destroys a lot of Houellebecq's intentions and the ambiguity of his novel, as is accurately pointed out by Gabriele Mueller: "Roehler's decision [...] to utilize narrative conventions of the melodrama rather than finding a formal equivalent to the radicalism proposed in the novel may account for some of the disappointment expressed by the film's reviewers, and it contributes to the oversimplification of the conflict." (Mueller, 2010, p. 10)[27]

Aspects of and Reasons for the German Cultural Adaptation of the Novel in Roehler's Film

In her interesting analysis of Roehler's film, Gabriele Mueller also states: "Apart from transplanting the main characters, half-brothers Michael and Bruno, from France to Germany and from changing the ending, the film remains relatively close to the plot of its literary source." It seems, though, that she underestimates the consequences of this "transplantation of the main characters [...] to Germany", because this leads to some significant changes that will be discussed in this chapter.

Before, one can ask oneself why Roehler transplants the action to his home country in the first place. It is important to highlight that Houellebecq treats a subject in

the novel (and placed in its exact middle), is turned into a simple conversation of young Bruno and Michael without deep insights.

27 This is also an indication that Roehler's film is rather an expression of popular culture that – in the words of Brooks (1995, p. 12) – "is attempting less, risking less, is more conventional and less self-conscious" than the highbrow art Houellebecq's novel belongs to.

Les particules élémentaires, as in his other novels, that is explicitly not national.[28] His novel is by no means limited to France, but discusses general problems of all the Western societies at the end of the 20th century, especially its individualization and alienation. This universal dimension becomes obvious right from the beginning, as the novel's first sentence tells us that Michel "vécut la plus grande partie de sa vie en Europe occidentale, durant la seconde moitié du XXe siècle" (Houellebecq, 1998, p. 9, our accentuation).[29] This universal dimension, which disrupts any national dimension, is further emphasized by the fact that Houellebecq evokes in *Les particules élémentaires* the future of the whole of mankind; this becomes even clearer when one takes a closer look at *La possibilité d'une île* which can in some respects be seen as a continuation of *Les particules élémentaires*, for it shows the future of the néo-humains created at the end of this novel and this is a world-wide future. This supra-national tendency would have been an ideal theme for a European co-production, and even more so as co-productions are highly in vogue, as a lot of the other contributions of this volume illustrate. The novel would have been a perfect basis for a filmic adaptation across borders, but nevertheless Eichinger[30] and Roehler opted for a deliberately national production,[31] as can already be seen by the cast. This specific case of a transposition of a theme concerning the whole of Western society to a national context therefore stresses that the often evoked tendencies of a Europeanization of cinema and *europudding* should not be overestimated. Even more important for us is the fact that the national production also led to a transposition to a specific German cultural context, which changes important aspects of the novel; maybe already the cutting-off of the future framework can be seen in the light of these aspects as this considerably lessens the universal tendency.

Much more interesting for the transposition to a German context than the Germanized names (see note 18) seems the fact that this transposition already starts with the movie's epigraph, for Roehler begins his film with the following citation from Einstein: "Man muss die Welt nicht verstehen, man muss sich in ihr nur zurechtfinden". This epigraph that cannot be found anywhere in the novel is indicative of several aspects. First, Einstein appears this way as a central scientific figure for the plot, which is not the case in the novel. There, the most important scientist is Niels Bohr, whose theories are treated in long passages. These scientific passages were of great importance for Houellebecq who did not commit any faults concerning their presentation (Schober, 2001, p. 204) and who was indignant that these passages were not considered by the critique as he had hoped for (Prill, 2005, p. 63).

28 This is a significant difference to the initially cited novel of Queiroz and its filmic transposition, as Queiroz' novel clearly examines the situation of a certain nation, describing the problems of Portuguese society in the 19th century, and therefore a transposition to another country is quite consequent to examine a similar situation there at another time.

29 Cf. also the passage cited above in which the unhappy ending of Annabelle's and Michel's relationship is anticipated: "Au milieu du suicide occidental, il était clair qu'ils n'avaient aucune chance." (our accentuation).

30 In the case of Eichinger this is even more surprising, for his company Constantin Film realized in the same year 2006 another literary adaptation in a co-production: *Das Parfum* (after the novel of Patrick Süskind); see also our remarks at the end of this article.

31 Of course it could be argued as well that by transferring the plot to another national context, the producer and the director show that Houellebecq's observations are as precise for the German as for the French context, but it seems that this was not their main intention.

Moreover, Bohr is very important for the structure of the novel, which is another reason why it begins with lengthy reflections about him, whereas the name of Einstein is mentioned only once (Houellebecq, 1998, p. 22 f.). Bohr is presented as "le veritable fondateur de la mécanique quantique" and it is added that the results of his works "invalidaient dans une large mésure les catégories antérieures de l'espace, de la causalité et du temps" (ibid.). This is of importance for Houellebecq's novel as he tries to show that the modern societies also have destroyed all previous prevailing categories. The analogy is made perfectly clear in a later passage, in which Bruno's life is associated with the findings of modern physics:

> De même que l'installation d'une préparation expérimentale et le choix d'un ou plusieurs observables permettent d'assigner à un système atomique un comportement donné – tantôt corpuscule, tantôt ondulatoire –, de même Bruno pouvait apparaître comme un individu, mais d'un autre point de vue il n'était que l'élément passif du déploiement d'un mouvement historique. (Houellebecq, 1998, 221)[32]

This idea of the elementary particles that are at the same time wave and particle can be traced back to the theories of Bohr who for this reason is central for the novel's basic idea, its title, and its structure (Schober, 2001, p. 184). That is why his substitution by Einstein in the movie does not convey Houellebecq's thoughts.[33] In a broader perspective, this change also prepares for the film's ending in which the retained title of the novel has lost much of its sense, as shown above by the quotation of van Treeck. Furthermore, also the epigraph underlines that the philosophical dimension of the novel will not be found in the film, for the focus is on "finding one's way along" ("sich zurechtfinden") and not "understanding" ("verstehen"), thus stressing that the (love) life of the protagonists is at the centre.

This quotation of a German scientist initiates a cultural transposition that is consequently continued in the following first scene. Directly after the Einstein-epigraph, the German setting is made clear by showing Michael writing a letter that informs the reader not only of the date of the action (14.5.2005), but also the place: Berlin. Even more important is the fact that Michael unmistakably evokes a central figure of German culture in his letter, for he writes that he wants to find, "was die Welt im Innersten zusammenhält" (*Elementarteilchen*, 00:01:09). This well-known citation of Goethe's *Faust* presents Michael as a typical German scientist; and that, after briefly thinking, he erases this Goethean part of the sentence and substitutes it by the word "Elementarem", which is shortly followed by "Elementarteilchen", can be seen as a meta-commentary of the film's director/scriptwriter Roehler that there is a strong German substrate lying beneath his adaptation of the French novel whose title is thus given – lying on a hidden German subtext.

This allusion to *Faust* is immediately picked up again in the scene that – after the brief interlude of Michael's farewell cocktail – follows the formulation of the letter and shows a conversation between Michael and his boss. Here, Roehler combines

32 The stressing of an experimental situation that can be observed throughout the novel's structure shows that there are many parallels between Houellebecq and Zola – for these parallels, see above all the article of Sandrine Rabosseau (2007).

33 During the farewell cocktail another scientist compares Michael to Niels Bohr, but this single mentioning of Bohr's name – moreover in an absolutely secondary scene – does not convey at all the importance of the Danish physicist in the novel.

two conversations of Houellbecq's Michel with his boss, one of which only takes place rather late in the novel (in the first chapter of the last part, p. 331-339). This late conversation is mainly used by Roehler but with strong changes that point out his intended parallels with *Faust*, for the boss in the film stresses twice that the "Wissensdrang" (00:03:13 and 03:29) is one of Michael's characteristics, whereas in the novel he speaks about "le desire de connaissance" more in relation with himself. Thus, in the movie, the idea of an obsessive striving for knowledge is clearly linked to Michael, further strengthening the Faustean aspect with which he is presented. That this passage is furthermore placed from the end of the novel to the beginning of the movie forms of course another parallel with *Faust*; for his striving for knowledge and the sentence of "was die Welt zusammenhält" can also be found right at the beginning of Goethe's work. Moreover, with this early presentation of Michael as a scientist with a Faustean attitude, the protagonist is deeply anchored in a German context and the spectators are at once prepared for a plot that is essentially German.

So the film's epigraph and its first two scenes clearly manifest a transposition to a German cosmos, and this is continued throughout the movie. Here, we only want to give one more significant example: In the novel, Bruno, who always wants to publish texts of his own, has two short conversations with Philippe Sollers as representative of the large French publishing house Gallimard (Houellebecq, 1998, p. 229 f. and p. 241-243). This is fused in the movie into one conversation and now with a person from the German publishing company Rowohlt (*Elementarteilchen*, 00:12:50-00:14:22). Probably Rowohlt was chosen because Houellebecq's German translations of *Extension du domaine de la lutte* and *Plateforme* were published there, as well as the paperback version of *Elementarteilchen*. This substitution of a French publishing company by a German one is of course not particularly significant, but the conversation between Bruno and the representative is in so far highly interesting as it manifests a sort of cultural censorship that again highlights the transposition to Germany: Whereas some contemptuous racist remarks of Bruno about "Neger" are cited unchanged in the movie, another part of one of Bruno's manuscripts is left out. This passage deals with Jews (Houellebecq, 1998, p. 242) and one can suppose that this was considered too delicate for a German movie. This omission is to be viewed in the context of cultural changes of narrative or filmic models that Tanja Weber has studied recently using examples of transpositions of foreign TV-series to a German market; she shows that such eliminations of potentially problematic scenes because of historical or social aspects are not uncommon in adapting aesthetic works to the new target market (Weber, 2012, p. 107 f.).[34] Many more examples can be found for the transposition to a German cultural context that cannot all be analyzed within the framework of this article, but emphasize that the movie goes far beyond a simple renaming of the characters. One can there-

34 Such a cultural censorship had already taken place in the conversation between Michael and his boss analyzed above, for a wicked remark against the Islam that can be found in the second conversation between Michel and his boss in the novel (Houellebecq, 1998, p. 336: "L'Islam – de loin la plus bête, la plus fausse et la plus obscurantiste de toutes les religions") is not taken up in the movie, which seems logical for a German film, where such remarks seem hardly acceptable. Of course these censorships also contribute to the mitigation of the movie version in comparison to the novel.

fore speak of a "cultural adaptation" that Roehler makes out of Houellebecq's novel.[35]

It seems interesting to discuss possible reasons for this "cultural localization" in Germany. One of them seems to lie in the personality and aesthetic interest of the director and scriptwriter Oskar Roehler. Already his first movie (*Gentlemen*, 1995) was an adaptation of a foreign novel that was transposed to a German setting, namely *American Psycho*. So it seems a typical procedure for Roehler to relocate adaptations into his native country. In the case of Houellebecq's novel there was an important additional reason, for Roehler had a strong personal interest to make this movie: It is well known that Houellebecq integrated many aspects of his own youth into the history of Michel and Bruno (Prill, 2005, p. 59 f.), and Roehler also saw many important parallels to his own life. He openly admits that he was so intrigued by *Les particules élémentaires* because he found his own personal story within the novel, having been abandoned by his mother and growing up with his grandparents (*Elementarteilchen*, Extras: Interview with Osker Roehler, 00:05-00:55).[36]

Roehler's films have always been coined by personal themes, which is not only obvious in his best-known film *Die Unberührbare*, which portrays his mother, but also in his latest one, *Quellen des Lebens*. For this movie he has adapted his first and so far only (autobiographical) novel *Herkunft* (see note 15). So he has also brought a literary work of his own to the screen like Houellebecq has done with *La possibilité d'une île*.[37] More important for our subject is the fact that this latest movie also shows that Roehler's perpetual autobiographical interest is interlaced with a thematic constant, which a German critic accurately sees as his central subject: "Das Modell der dysfunktionalen Familie, das in Facetten immer auf seiner eigenen beruht, zieht sich wie ein roter Faden durch seine Filme." (Steinitz, 2013, p. 12) This is also at the heart of *Agnes und seine Brüder*, the movie released just before *Elementarteilchen*, in which Roehler treated the following topic in his own words: "Der Film soll zeigen, daß unsere Gesellschaft und ihre Keimzelle, die Familie, trotz guten Willens einfach nicht mehr funktioniert. Darum geht's. Daß aber auch das Single-Dasein keine Alternative ist." (Abel, 2010, p. 75).[38] These failures of families and the impossible alternative of a single-existence are of course a central topic of Houellebecq's novel as well, and this shows that there are two – interrelat-

35 The term and idea of a "kulturelle Adaption" ("cultural adaptation") is used in Tanja Weber's recent study which shows how TV series have been adapted to other cultural contexts. Her examples, taken from the last years, underscore that the topic of cultural adaption is important at the moment. The article of Concepción Cascajosa in the present volume also shows effects of such a cultural adaptation, in her case in an English series that was transposed to Spain.

36 Roehler says that Houellebecq has written "genau die gleiche Lebensgeschichte [...], die ich selbst hatte".

37 The critical reception of Roehler's attempt to transpose his own literary work to the screen was not as negative as in Houellbecq's case, but the German critics were far from enthusiastic about this film.

38 Marco Abel's article is especially instructive for a comparison between Roehler's other films and *Elementarteilchen*. Abel develops the interesting category of the "postromance film" that indeed well describes the films made by Roehler, who, in Abel's words, "can be regarded as perhaps the quintessential German postromance director." (2010, p. 78; the concept of "postromance films" is explained in more detail on p. 77)

ed – reasons why Roehler had such a strong desire to make a movie out of the French novel: his biographic and thematic interests came together.

It is important to add that the discussions about family values, without a doubt a theme existing in all modern countries, have in Roehler's films always a certain particularly German dimension, which heavily confronts the '68ers and their children, the '78ers. This conflict is at the heart of Roehler's films: "[I]t is this antagonism between the 68ers and their children that Roehler's work almost obsessively dramatizes." (Abel, 2010, p. 78) He sees himself as a victim of the generation of the '68 movement and shows the problems the '78ers have in building functioning relationships, so he takes up the main topic treated in Houellebecq's novel, but from a German perspective. This German dimension has a further nuance, which is pointed out convincingly by Gabriele Mueller: "[W]ithin the German context, the debate highlights an additional dimension [...] a critical assessment of the 1968 generation also involves an interrogation of their values, in particular in comparison to those of the grandparent generation who had been socialized during the Nazi regime." (2010, p. 13)

Elementarteilchen shows the universal theme of the failing modern family in its specifically German occurrence. This is why the transposition of the French plot to Germany seems a natural consequence for Roehler, because this gives him not only the opportunity to narrate a story that has a biographical proximity to him and deals with his thematic obsession, but also highlights a particular German debate of the last years that has been central for him right from the beginning of his career as a director.[39]

Conclusion

Our observations have shown that the German movie *Elementarteilchen* features many significant changes in comparison to Houellebecq's French novel. Oskar Roehler worked on the script for his movie for three years, which indicates that these changes are well thought-out.[40] Apart from a certain mitigation of the novel's crudest scenes, which forms a parallel to the other two movie adaptions so far that also softened the novels' plots, these changes can be mainly summed up as a melodramaticization and romanticization on the one hand, and a cultural adaptation to a German cosmos on the other. Whereas the second aspect seems to have its causes in Roehler's personal interest in the topic which was also of considerable interest for a specific German debate at the time, the choice of a conventional cinematic style that almost completely eliminates the stylistic choices made by Houellebecq in his novel is probably largely due to Eichinger's economic concerns, since he wanted to produce a film that was able to "appeal to as broad an audience

39 Roehler started his career just when this debate became more and more important as has been shown by Marco Abel: "Roehler began making films at the very moment when a sociopolitical debate in Germany focused on the relationship between family values and what Germans call *Single-Dasein* (single-existence)" (2010, p. 78).

40 Cf. also the commentary in the German *Frankfurter Allgemeine Zeitung*, which underlines that he took great efforts to adapt the novel to the screen: "Roehler hat sich, mit Unterbrechungen, drei Jahre mit dem Drehbuch gequält" (Körte, 2006, p. 23).

as possible" (Mueller, 2010, p.13).[41] These economic considerations also might have fostered a transposition to a German cosmos, as the main target market for the film was Germany. This seems to be accentuated by the fact that such an array of German stars constituted the movie's cast. These well-known German actors were probably also the main reason for the movie's success with audiences in Germany, where more than 800,000 spectators saw the movie and where it headed the box-office for some time, which is achieved by a German production rather seldom.[42]

It should be noted, though, that the movie's success was rather limited to Germany, for in other countries the results were quite disappointing. For example in Austria, which is also German-speaking, only 35,000 spectators saw the movie, which could also be an indication that the marked cultural adaptation to Germany was not approved of in its neighboring country. This seems even more plausible, as in Switzerland only 9,000 spectators saw the movie. Of course, it is particularly interesting to have a look at the spectator numbers in France: There, only 50,000 spectators saw the movie, which is a frustrating result for a film based on a French source. This becomes even more evident when placed in a broader context, as has been done by Christian van Treeck, who comments: "Si on compare ce chiffre à celui atteint par une autre adaptation allemande, *Le Parfum*, produite par le même Bernd Eichinger, laquelle a été vue cette même année 2006 par plus de 900.000 Français, on mesure à quel point le succès des *Particules élémentaires* allemandes a été limité en France." (Treeck, 2011, p. 382)

This result is a conspicuous parallel with *El crimen del padre Amaro*, the movie with which we began this article and which only had great success in Mexico, the country to which its plot was transferred; it did not succeed at all in Portugal, the country the novelistic model is set in (Hausmann 2014). These two cases seem to indicate that cultural adaptations can significantly contribute to success in the respective producing country but seem to prevent great successes in other countries, for which co-productions seem more auspicious. In this respect the comparison with *Das Parfum* addressed by van Treeck is particularly striking as this movie was a co-production between Germany and France and was successful in both countries alike.

After this look at the audiences' reaction, a last consideration should be given to the critics' reaction to this filmic adaptation of Houellebecq's novel. In this respect, there are no big differences to spot between Germany and France, as has also been pointed out by van Treeck: "les réceptions critiques en France et en Allemagne ont été assez comparables, du moins dans leur tendance globale." (2011, p. 382). This might be explained partly by the fact that the cultural changes introduced by

41 See especially Mueller's note concerning this quotation: "an important factor influencing stylistic decisions was certainly the involvement of producer Bernd Eichinger [...] to whom commercial considerations are as important as artistic ones." (2010, p. 18). In the Interviews on the German DVD version (*Elementarteilchen*, Extras: Interview with Osker Roehler, 04:45-04:58) Roehler also points out that for Eichinger a certain lightness always is important to let the spectators come to terms more easily with the novel's bitter themes – such a lightness essentially contradicts Houellebecq's style and accounts for some of the changes analyzed.

42 The numbers of the spectators are taken from the Lumière database (http://lumiere.obs.coe.int/web/film_info/?id=25777). It should be added that *Elementarteilchen* was very successful in Germany, but far from spectacular: The comedy *Der Schuh des Manitu*, the most successful German film in Germany so far, reached more than 11,7 million spectators.

Roehler passed rather unnoticed and did not play a role in the reviews of his movie. These reviews were by far not as annihilating as the critique for Houellebecq's *La possibilité d'une île* cited above, but Marco Abel is right to speak of a "predominantly negative critical reception of this film in Germany" (2010, p. 97). A representative example of these critiques is a review of the *Frankfurter Allgemeine Zeitung*, whose author drew this conclusion: "Was zählt, ist einzig, ob *Elementarteilchen*, der Film, überzeugt. […] Es ist das Privileg der Kritikerin, ohne Rücksicht aufs Geschäft zu sagen: Nein." (Lueken, 2006, p. 41) Many critics focused on the mitigation of the novel's critical potential, for which they mostly incriminated Eichinger, as can be seen in the following commentary on a major German movie critics page: "Wer gehofft hatte, Oskar Roehler möge subversiven Wind durch Bernd Eichingers Kinoschmiede Constantin Film […] blasen, wird enttäuscht sein. Der Trick funktioniert genau andersherum." (Schultz, 2006) A final comment, a review in the German newspaper *Die Welt*, can furthermore illustrate the short-lasting success of *Elementarteilchen* even in Germany: "*Elementarteilchen* in der Regie von Oskar Roehler wurde trotz Starbesetzung schnell vergessen." (Wetzel, 2008)

Even if the movie was indeed rather quickly forgotten, *Elementarteilchen* is in so far an interesting example for the current European film market as it shows that an overly transnational view of today's cinema seems exaggerated. There are currently many discussions about the question if something like a „national cinema" still exists in a period of time in which co-productions have become so important, but Roehler's version of one of the most successful and controversial French novels of the last years indicates that a strong national element is still to be found in many recent films and can lead to important changes in adaptations of literary models, changes that go far beyond ordinary modifications of a text transferred to the screen.

BIBLIOGRAPHY

PRIMARY SOURCES

Houellebecq, M. *La Carte et le territoire*. Paris: Flammarion, 2010.

Houellebecq, M. *La possibilité d'une île*. Paris: Fayard, 2005.

Houellebecq, M. „Mourir" [2005], URL: http://homepage.mac.com/michelhouellebecq/textes/mourir.html (05.05.2011).

Houellebecq, M. *Les particules élémentaires*. Paris: Flammarion, 1998.

Houellebecq, M. *Extension du domaine de la lutte*. Paris: J'ai lu, 1994.

SECONDARY SOURCES

Abel, M. "Failing to Connect: Itinerations of Desire in Oskar Roehler's Post-Romance Films". *New German Critique* 37.1 (2010), p. 75-98.

Althen, M. “Die sexuelle Revolution frißt ihre Kinder”. *Frankfurter Allgemeine Zeitung* (13.02.2006), p. 41.

Célestin, R. “Du style, du plat, de Proust et de Houellebecq”. In: Clément, L. M. / Wesemael, S. (eds.). *Michel Houellebecq sous la loupe*. Amsterdam: Rodopi, 2007, p. 345-356.

Demonpion, D. *Houellebecq, non autorisé: enquête sur un phénomène*. Paris: Maren Sell, 2005.

Dössel, C. “Ausweidung der Kampfzone”. *Süddeutsche Zeitung* (27.5.2002), p. 14.

Douin, J.-L. “*La Possibilité d'une île* : l’impossibilité d’un film”. *Le monde* (9.9.2008), URL: http://www.lemonde.fr/cinema/article/2008/09/09/la-possibilite-d-une-ile-l-impossibilite-d-un-film10931733476.html (17.04.2013).

Gärtner, B. “Sex ist sentimental. Michel Houellebecq über sein Regiedebüt, unschöne Genitalien und sinnlosen Urlaub“. *Süddeutsche Zeitung* (18.8.2008), p. 15.

Haan, M. “Entretien avec Michel Houellebecq”. In: Wesemael, S. (ed.). *Michel Houellebecq*. Amsterdam: Rodopi, 2004, p. 9-27.

Hausmann, M. “Historia de un escándalo: Anticlericalismo y melodrama en *El crimen del padre Amaro*”. In: Schmidt-Welle, F. / Wehr, C. (eds.). *Construcciones de la nación en el cine mexicano del pasado al presente. Formas históricas y procedimientos cinematográficos*. Madrid: Vervuert, 2014 (in print).

Hausmann, M. “*El niño pez* de Lucía Puenzo: ¿Lo indígena como elemento mítico y vivificante dentro de la vida deshumanizada de las grandes ciudades latinoamericanas?”. In: Gimeno Ugalde, E. / Poe, K. (eds.). *Representación de lo indígena en el cine contemporáneo de América Latina: lenguas, culturas, tradiciones y mitos*. San José 2013 (in print).

Karimi, K.-H. “‘*Nous n’étions que des machines conscientes*’ – Von der Unausweichlichkeit des Utopischen in Romanen Michel Houellebecqs”. In: Hahn, K. / Hausmann, M. (eds.). *Visionen des Urbanen: (Anti-)Utopische Stadtentwürfe in der französischen Wort- und Bildkunst*. Heidelberg: Winter, 2012, p. 205-229.

Körte, P. “Oskar Roehler: Der Elementarteilchenbeschleuniger”. *Frankfurter Allgemeine Sonntagszeitung* (05.02.2006), p. 23.

Lerer, D. “Me interesan las emociones”. *Clarín* (6.2.2009), URL: http://edant.clarin.com/diario/2009/02/06/espectaculos/c-00701.htm (16.04.2013).

Lichfield, J. “Houellebecq’s first venture into movies ends in farce”. *The Independent* (12.8.2008), URL: http://www.independent.co.uk/news/world/europe/houellebecqs-first-venture-into-movies-ends-in-farce-891515.html (15.04.2013).

Lueken, V. “Das Drama der männlichen Sexualität: *Elementarteilchen*”. *Frankfurter Allgemeine Zeitung* (22.02.2006), p. 41.

Müller, J. “Das Ende ist nah”. *taz* (06.07.2011), URL: http://www.taz.de/!73896/ (15.04.2013).

Mueller, G. “Surviving Ourselves: Mothers, Clones, and the Legacy of 1968 in *Blueprint* (2003) and *The Elementary Particles* (2006)”. *German Politics & Society* 28 (2010), p. 1-18.

Noguez, D. *Houellebecq, en fait*. Paris: Fayard, 2003.

Pöppel, H. “Das Klonen von Menschen in den Zeiten des Menschenparks: Utopie und Anti-Utopie bei Joao Ubaldo Ribeiro (*O sorriso do lagarto*) und Michel Houellebecq (*Les particules élémentaires*)”. *ABP. Jahrbuch zur portugiesischsprachigen Welt: Lusophone Literaturen und Kulturen im Kontakt* 2006, p. 63-75.

Prill, U. “Die Ausweitung der Literatur-Zone. Michel Houellebecqs *Particules élémentaires* zwischen Quantenphysik und Romantik”. In: Leeker, J. / Leeker, E. (eds.). *Text – Interpretation – Vergleich*. Berlin: Erich Schmidt, 2005, p. 58-67.

Rabosseau, S. “Houellebecq ou le renouveau du roman expérimental”. In: Clément, L. M. / Wesemael, S. (eds.). *Michel Houellebecq sous la loupe*. Amsterdam: Rodopi, 2007, p. 43-51.

Schober, R. "Weltsicht und Realismus in Michel Houellebecqs utopischem Roman *Les particules élémentaires*". *Romanistische Zeitschrift für Literaturgeschichte* 25 (2001), p. 177-211.

Schultz, S. M. "*Elementarteilchen*". *critic.de* (16.02.2006), URL: http://www.critic.de/film/elementarteilchen-440/ (15.04.2013).

Steinitz, D. "Zurück zu den Quellen". *Süddeutsche Zeitung* (19.2.2013), p. 12.

Treeck, C. "L'adaptation cinématographique des *Particules élémentaires* et ses réceptions française et allemande". In: Clément, M. L. / Wesemael, S. (eds.). *Michel Houellebecq à la Une*. Amsterdam: Rodopi, 2011, p. 373-387.

Weber, T. *Kultivierung in Serie. Kulturelle Adaptionsstrategien von fiktionalen Fernsehserien*. Marburg: Schüren, 2012.

Wetzel, J. "Houellebecq scheitert mit seiner Verfilmung". *Die Welt* (12.9.2008), URL: http://www.welt.de/kultur/article2431282/Houellebecq-scheitert-mit-seiner-Verfilmung.html (16.04.2013).

FILMOGRAPHY

El crimen del padre Amaro (2002). Dir. Carlos Carrera. Mexico: Columbia Tristar.

Elementarteilchen (2006). Dir. Oskar Roehler. Germany: Constantin Film.

Extension du domaine de la lutte (2002). Dir. Philippe Harel. France: StudioCanal.

La possibilité d'une île (2009). Dir. Michel Houellebecq. France: BAC.

THE EUROPEAN GLOBAL

Transnational Scandinavia? Scandinavian Film Culture in a European and Global Context

Ib Bondebjerg and Eva Novrup Redvall

Cinema has always been both a very national and a very global form of cultural expression. Images often travel more easily and faster across borders than literature and other cultural forms, but since 1945 the global trends in cinema have been remarkably stable in the sense that the consumption of films has been dominated by American films and by national films in most European countries, whereas the distribution and consumption of films from other European countries has been rather limited. The figures vary from country to country, but the general structural pattern is clear. In 2008 for instance, the average percentage of films in EU27 shows an American share of sold tickets of 63.9% and a total European share (both on the domestic market and in other European countries) of 27.8% (Lumiere Database, 2008).

The total cinema admissions for 2008 were 925 million tickets, out of which the US took 591 million. In addition to the dominance by American films, 6,5% of the European films are in fact EU/American co-productions, which means that the US is involved in a further 60 million admissions. The remaining world cinema is almost invisible, accounting for less than 2% in Europe. The actual EU share of total cinema admissions this year was thus only a mere 256 million tickets. The EU is an insignificant player in this context and, furthermore, most of the 27.8% can be broken down to figures showing that non-national European films is down to 6-8%. The exchange of films between the European markets is not impressive, despite years of co-production and EU support for films. When we examine markets and audience figures it becomes clear that there is a very limited European film culture. What we have is a family of film cultures with some regional and bilateral cooperation and interaction.

Into this generally gloomy picture of a weak European film culture comes the Scandinavian film culture, perhaps dominated by a 'myth' of being a film and television culture with a strong affinity between the three countries (Denmark, Sweden and Norway) and a tradition of collaboration. The idea of a strong affinity is supported by the fact that Scandinavia has a common film policy with similarly structured national Film Institutes, a strong public service television sector and an institutionalised tradition of collaboration through for instance the Nordic Film & TV Fund (NFTF) and Nordvision. Maybe the feeling of belonging to a Scandinavian culture can also be found in a cultural, historical and social alikeness identified as the Scandinavian welfare state. We have to ask ourselves, however, if this perceived affinity is a myth or a reality, and whether or not it is reflected in the way in which the Scandinavian countries produce film and television and in the transnational distribution across borders.

In this article we analyze how there are many similarities in the cultural policy and production frameworks of the three Scandinavian countries, facilitating transnational production of both film and television. However, looking at the over all patterns of distribution and tracking the life of individual titles it becomes evident that in spite of the many similarities between the three countries, Scandinavian films do not fare very well in the neighbouring countries, whereas Scandinavian television drama is doing much better, both in Scandinavia and globally. The numbers for film show how the primary markets for Scandinavian films outside each of their national territories are most often outside of Scandinavia, since the local audiences do not seem to find an attraction in films from Scandinavia as such. Even established art house auteurs have a hard time finding audiences in the co-producing, Scandinavian countries, as we will discuss at the end of the article, focusing on the films by Norwegian director Bent Hamer and Swedish director Roy Andersson as two examples of art house auteurs with international acclaim rather than regional audiences.

The article concludes that while the transnational co-production culture between the Scandinavian countries is of great importance for getting films made in a rather small and fragmented production culture, much more could be done to improve transnational co-distribution strategies and the over-all images of Scandinavian films in the neighbouring countries. As the impressive numbers for e.g. Danish television drama series have shown for a number of years, there is not a resistance as such to watching productions in each other's languages, but the move from the sofa to the cinemas seems hard for the vast majority of the audiences.

The article concludes by arguing for the value of moving beyond only understanding film culture as box office numbers in the cinemas, since the major circulation of films takes place on television and already also on other platforms. One has to take these new viewing patterns into account if one wants to discuss a Scandinavian film culture as such and to develop fruitful transnational strategies in European cinema more generally.

The article is based on data collected for the Scandinavian Think Tank on films, markets, audiences and film policy, organized by the European Think Tank on Film and Film Policy in Copenhagen in December 2010 (Bondebjerg and Redvall 2011; Redvall and Gubbins 2011). The data covers the period 2002-2006, because it takes time to get data on transnational film consumption. This means that some of the tendencies may have changed after 2007, which in fact is the case with especially Norway. As the Think Tank clearly showed, there is a great need in the Scandinavian industry to try to understand the current changes in markets, new platforms and changing audience preferences from both a national and a transnational perspective. And – as became evident – the traditions of regional co-production among Scandinavian players are much stronger than the audience enthusiasm for regional fare, challenging the myth of the natural affinities between the three countries.

The Cultural Diversity Model: Scandinavian Film Policy and Support Principles

The national film cultures in Scandinavia share many similarities and there is a long tradition for cooperation. As a whole, however, there are also numerous obvious differences based on the size of the population of the three countries and different historical traditions and developments, one of the most striking of these perhaps being the fact that Norway has a very regionalized public cinema sector and until 2001 also had a state owned production company. That said, the Scandinavian film and TV culture is historically one of the European regions with the strongest public service television tradition and with a cinema culture and cinema policy dominated by a culturally oriented 'soft' subsidy system and much less of the kind of 'tough' economic oriented subsidy system based on loans, tax incentives or automatic market support systems with film audience performance and thus commercial success as central criteria than we find in other parts of Europe (Finney 1996). Generally, the dominance of cultural support criteria has shifted towards a stronger emphasis on also market oriented support criteria, and today Denmark, Norway and Sweden combine a film commissioner scheme with market oriented support schemes (Bondebjerg 2005a). In Denmark, this dual focus on supporting both artistic and commercial fare together with the impact of teachings at the National Film School of Denmark educating the majority of new talent for the industry has been highlighted as an important reason for the emergence of what has been termed The New Danish Cinema (Hjort 2005; Redvall 2010). While the more detailed structure of support systems or state institutions like film schools vary to some degree, the global challenges have been met with much the same response in all three Scandinavian countries, where one can note a common increase in co-production, both on a European level and through the Nordic Film & TV Fund (NFTF), an important partner in the building of transnational, Scandinavian connections. An example of NFTF's importance is the socalled High Five initiative in 2010-2012 where NFTF received around € 1m from the globalisation fund of the Nordic Council for Ministers to improve the Scandinavian and international distribution of films.

Another contributing factor to the shared structures amongst the Scandinavian countries is a very strong and still dominant public service television tradition with a monopoly status that remained until the late 1980s, whereby a dual system of commercial and public service television (in line with the main European tendency) was established. Not only were the public service channels important as a platform for showing Scandinavian films, they also served as co-producing partners. The development of a Scandinavian TV drama tradition with a rather spectacular success from the 1960s and onwards, and with a modern revival after the 1990s in both Sweden and Denmark, has also been of great importance. The production of TV drama has been based on the idea of creative collaboration between the film and TV industry (Redvall 2012). This so-called crossover between the industries has been important for not only improving the quality of Danish television drama, but also for the careers of many later successful film directors like Niels Arden Oplev, Ole Christian Madsen or Per Fly having the opportunity to gain production experience as episode directors of drama series between directing feature films (as discussed by Oplev, Madsen, Fly and others in Hjort, Jørholt and Redvall 2010).

Seen in a global perspective, and compared to trends in major European countries, public support and the soft culturally oriented policies and subsidy systems dominate. Nevertheless, the national systems in Scandinavia can be characterized as *a cultural diversity model*, since it is neither just a soft cultural support for the sake of art, culture and creativity, nor a tough market oriented model based on stimulus to the film sector that automatically creates diversity. The way this cultural diversity model is implemented in the different Scandinavian countries varies – but the common ground is also obvious. The problem with this otherwise rather successful model is that such a model tends to create weak production structures (a fragmented culture of small unstable companies) and that the motivation and structures for marketing and distribution can be severely undermined. Since the 1990s the deregulation of the Scandinavian TV system and the increased competition on both the national and the global market has also contributed to new elements in the traditionally soft culture oriented systems. Not least because there has been an increase in a not always uncomplicated collaboration on feature films with TV and many new initiatives to professionalize support for development and production, for distribution and for internationalization of film production and distribution.

Even though Norway (just as Iceland) is not a member of the European Union, the country joined both the Eurimages programme in 1988 and the later film and media programmes. All three Scandinavian countries are thus completely integrated in the developing of a transnational co-production and co-distribution film culture in Europe and the emerging transnational film and media policy. As we will move on to discuss, the European dimension of film distribution and income from Europe has become a quite significant element in the modern Scandinavian film culture, and for certain films and directors these are even much more important than the national cinema incomes and audiences.

National Production Cultures – Global Challenges

Since the breakdown of the classical film culture in Scandinavia from the 1960s and onwards, the production structure of the Scandinavian film sector has undergone major changes, moving away from a market driven culture with big companies dominating, towards a much more diverse and fragmented structure based on public support, with very few big and strong production companies and a lot of small and rather unstable production companies (Bondebjerg 2005b). In Denmark, the period between 1995-2001 was dominated by two big companies only (Nordisk and Zentropa), producing 37.2% of the total number of films in this period, a number of medium sized companies (Grasten, Nimbus, Metronome, M&M, Thura) producing 26.5% of the films, that is 63.7% for the big and medium sized companies together. A very large number of companies (41 companies in total) produced the remaining 36.3% of films, but many of these production companies during these seven years only produced between 1-4 films and many of them just 1 or 2 films (Bondebjerg 2003: 180).

The situation hasn't changed a lot since then, and many of the same companies are still in operation. The most remarkable change in Denmark is that the biggest and most innovative company, Zentropa, and the oldest and most established (and traditional), Nordisk Film, merged in 2009, thus creating a very large and powerful company in a Scandinavian context. The second important trend to observe is also related to Zentropa, which in 2011 had established international branches and sister-companies in 13 countries (Belgium, Estonia, Finland, France, Germany, Italy, Lithuania, Holland, Norway, Poland, Spain, Sweden and the UK). Following the globalisation of Scandinavian cinema, production companies of this size are thus starting to become European-global players. If we shift our focus to only examine the Danish productions between 2002-2010 we find that 52 companies were behind the 214 films made in this period, while the share of distribution is very unevenly dispersed.

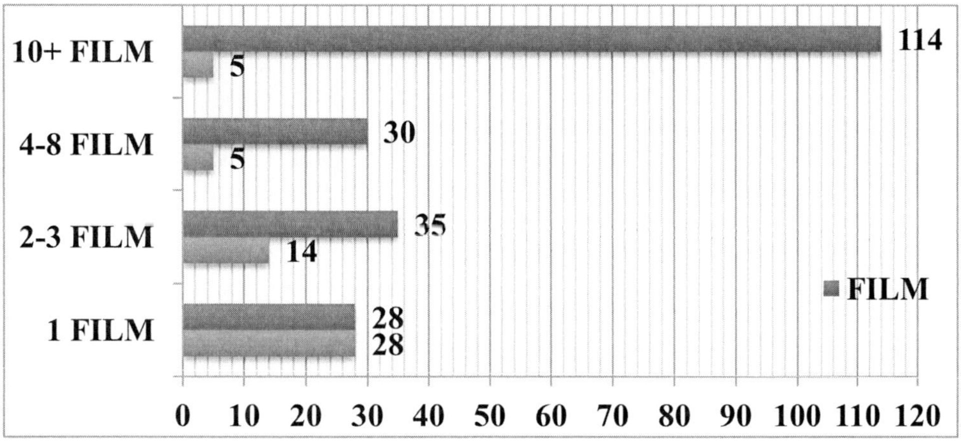

Figure 1: Number of production companies in Denmark 2002-2010 and number of films produced. 52 companies have produced 207 films.

An examination of the main companies behind the production of films in Denmark, Norway and Sweden between 2002-2006 confirms the fragmentation of the production sector. In Sweden, there were around 125 production companies in existence between 2002-2006, but only 13 of these companies produced four or more films during this five-year period, and the two biggest production companies, Sonet Film AB and Memfis Film AB, only made eight films each. However, the data from these years show that, compared to Sweden, Denmark maintains a stronger division between the two big companies, some medium sized companies and a larger group of very small companies. Sweden has no large-sized companies, instead the production landscape consists of medium sized companies as well as a large group of very small companies. Norway proves to be a similar case, where only Maipo Film and Nordisk Film can be counted as medium size companies. In Norway, more than 95 companies produced films during this period, but as in Sweden and Denmark most of them only made one or two films each. Denmark is thus the only country in Scandinavia with any large production companies.

Generally, the numbers show that indeed very few Scandinavian film companies, even in Denmark, reach a critical mass that could be deemed necessary to meet a greater global challenge and serve as hubs for creative international alliances and co-production agreements. Few companies have managed, like the Danish Zentropa, to develop a broad international strategy. However, the statistics from this period also show that size is not everything: the success of films produced by large companies compared with those by small companies aren't direct proof that a large company with a sizable output is more likely to produce hits. Some smaller companies seem to manage success with only a few films. However, larger companies do have the ability to both streamline production for large scale mainstream films as well as for smaller and more experimental/innovative films.

Transnational Patterns of Co-Production and Distribution

As discussed by many scholars, co-production is an obvious strategy to pursue for small, national cinemas in an incresingly international market (e.g. Sklaan 1996; Jäckel 1996; Bergfelder 2000; Brandstrup and Redvall 2005; Givskov 2011), and co-production has become increasingly important for Scandinavian film culture as a whole in the past twenty years. In this regard, both the Nordic and European dimension of this internationalisation plays an important role. As mentioned previously, Nordic co-productions are facilitated by the existence of a regional institution like Nordic Film & TV Fund and the hitherto strong tradition of collaboration between public service television channels. However, the total figures for the production and distribution of films from Denmark, Norway and Sweden show that the number of and the importance of co-productions is not reflected convincingly in the distribution of films in Scandinavia. Many films that have Nordic partners do not receive wide distribution in Scandinavia, not even in the co-producing countries, and many films that are not co-produced get a better distribution and better admission figures than those co-produced. Co-production probably is an important factor for the internationalisation of films, but other elements such as genre, star quality and distribution play a central role.

Moreover, the figures show that when it comes to audiences, European distribution and television distribution holds much more importance than the Scandinavian cinema sector. There is no doubt that the relatively low priority given to distribution and marketing in the European film culture, when compared with the American film culture, plays a part. In Scandinavia, the average distribution and marketing share of the public film funding is low, and often the private sector doesn't have the power or will to make a difference. The average budget for distribution and audience activities in the Scandinavian Film Institues is just 10-12% of the total budget and most private production and distribution companies cannot afford a really high scale international distribution. Compared to the budget for Anglo-American films, film distribution in Europe in general is not a strong area.

Furthermore, initiatives to promote Scandinavian films are rare and, as in the rest of Europe, the synergy between even closely related national film cultures has not been developed to its full potential, although NFTF has obviously tried to encourage and support Scandinavian production and collaboration and to develop strategies for distribution on the international markets. One recent example of this is *The High Five* at the Toronto Film Festival in 2009 and 2010 where NFTF and the Nordic Council branded Scandinavian film through a presentation of both upcoming

Scandinavian film projects and already completed films. This was a coordinated Scandinavian event and a promotion aimed at launching Scandinavian films more efficiently internationally by giving support to foreign distributors of the selected films. Initiatives of this kind are rare, however, both in Scandinavia and the rest of Europe, and if this region is small on a global scale, the individual Scandinavian nation states carry even less weight.

While co-production is on the rise, is is worth noting that the majority of films in the three countries from 2002-2006 are not co-produced. In Denmark, the figure is 34 co-productions out of 110 films produced, in Sweden it is 53 out of 174 and in Norway it is 17 out of 72. Despite Europeanisation and globalisation, production structures still to a large degree remain national. National support for minor co-productions must be added to these figures, but international collaborations are not dominant, although in e.g. Denmark these have been increasing since 2010.

Moreover, a different picture emerges of the structure of co-production if we take a closer look at the countries and regions with which Scandinavia collaborates. The two big countries here are clearly Denmark and Sweden with 77 and 91 partners from other countries involved in co-production. Norway in this period must be characterised as a rather closed, national film culture with only 25 noted co-production partners, but this must also be seen on the background of fewer feature films in this period. Furthermore, there is a clear tendency towards both a much stronger Scandinavian and European profile in Denmark and Sweden than in Norway, whereas the rest of the world plays a more minor role with regard to co-production. As an example, Danish films have made use of 36 co-production partners from Scandinavia, 36 partners from EU and only five from the rest of the world, and in addition Denmark is involved with 40 other Scandinavian film productions, most of them Swedish. Swedish films have even more partners from Scandinavia, mostly Danish, but as the only one of the three countries Sweden also has extended to co-production with Finland. The co-production partners found in the EU and rest of the world partners are on the other hand a much smaller number than in Denmark.

Scandinavian Cinema and Globalisation

While the Scandinavian film culture does collaborate with international partners and has directors like Lars von Trier shooting major, international productions on local ground, a number of other Scandinavian directors have also made films abroad in the past years (examples from 2011 being e.g. Lone Scherfig (*One Day*), Nicolas Winding Refn (*Drive*), Daniel Espinosa (*Safe House*), Tomas Alfredsson (*Tinker, Tailor, Soldier, Spy*). The Scandinavian film culture can in many ways be said to be globalised, both in terms of directly international films and in terms of national films and co-productions and their transnational distribution. Looking at the top 10 films from Scandinavia 2002-2006, based on total cinema admissions, one can clearly see an international picture emerge. Figure 2 shows how the admissions in Scandinavia of these 10 films (7.364.334) are almost equalled by the European-global admission (6.899.168). For a large number of films, the European-global share carries more weight than both the national and the Scandinavian share.

While most of the titles are more mainstream fare, a more art house production like Lars von Trier's *Dogville* is also on the list. However, the numbers for *Dogville* show how both the national and Nordic ticket sale for the film is insignificant compared to the international box office. While some of the more mainstream Swedish hits like *Så som i himmelen* (*As It Is in Heaven*), *Ondskan* (*Evil*) or *Grabben i graven bredvid* (*The Guy in the Grave Next Door*) have an impressive amount of admissions on the domestic market, *Dogville* is an example of the importance of the international rather than the national market for the more upmarket, art house titles. Even for a film by a national star director like Lars von Trier and with a major international star like Nicole Kidman in the lead, the national and Scandinavian distribution is not as impressive as the broader European distribution. What becomes apparent is an example of a more widespread tendency, where some directors achieve an international art cinema success that isn't matched at the national market as we will discuss with regard to the films by Bent Hamer and Roy Andersson.

Film	DK	SE	NO	FI	IS	Scan-total	Rest-EU/US	Total
Såsom i himmelen (SE/DK)	11.920	1.433.655	197.882	23.485	0	1.666.942	1.864.994	3.531.936
Dogville (DK+)	109.759	51.347	23.027	20.419	0	204.552	2.332.957	2.537.509
Kopps (SE/DK)	50.178	770.424	293.740	36.269	561	1.151.172	346.232	1.497.404
Efter brylluppet (DK/GB)	388.010	155.330	30.354	11.773	0	585.467	779.568	1.365.035
Den grimme ælling og mig (DK+)	108.267	0	47.391	9.600	0	165.258	1.053.845	1.219.103
Ondskan (SE/DK)	50.697	959.111	16.500	24.696	0	1.051.004	96.400	1.147.404
Grabben i graven bredvid (SE/NO)	3.425	976.027	49.410	8.359	0	1.037.221	9.121	1.046.342
Masjävlar (SE/DK)	6.885	785.716	26.585	21.563	0	840.749	155.671	996.420
Elsker dig for evigt (DK)	506.493	99.501	51.493	4.482	0	661.969	257.382	919.351
Total	1.235.634	5.231.111	736.382	160.646	561	7.364.334	6.899.168	14.263.502

Figure 2: Top 10 Scandinavian films 2002-2006 including Europe36+US (cinema admissions, Lumiere database 2010).

However, it should be noted that despite the increased globalisation of Scandinavian cinema on the European market there is still a long way to go before any inroads can be made on the American market. No Swedish film was distributed in the US in the period 2002-2006, and for Denmark and Norway there are also only few examples of American distribution. In NFI's *Eksportundersøgelse* ('Export report' 2008), it is documented that the Norwegian film export from 2002-2008 has grown by 23% (NFI 2008: 2), and the total European sale in this period is measured to 3.1 million compared to the 11.9 million tickets sold nationally (or 26% compared to the national sale) (NFI 2008). The report doesn't cover the American/Canadian region, but there are Norwegian films with a minor transatlantic distribution. Bent Hamer's *Salmer fra kjøkkenet* (*Kitchen Stories*) was seen by around 5000 Canadians, and his English language co-production with the US, *Factotum*, had a minor American festival and art cinema distribution.

In Denmark, the structural relationship between the Scandinavian, European and American market is in essence the same as in Sweden, but a few films and directors have developed a more permanent relation with the US-region. An example of this is, of course, Lars von Trier, with *Breaking the Waves* (1996) as the most bestselling Danish film in US/CA (897.193), closely followed by *Dancer in the Dark* (2000) with 755.907 tickets. Lone Scherfig's *Italiensk for begyndere* (*Italian for Beginners*, 2000) had 767.719 admissions. Some of Susanne Bier's films have also established a transatlantic position, not least her latest film *Hævnen* (*In a Better World*) that won an Oscar for best foreign film in 2011 has also had a broader European and some American success. By the end of 2011, the film had made around € 765.000 in the US, and maybe the effect of both the Oscar, the Golden Globe and the European Film Award as best film will have an effect on sales in years to come.

If we examine the bigger picture and measure cinema admissions for Scandinavian films on their own market (HOME), in cinemas of the other Scandinavian countries (SCAN) and in the rest of the EU36 countries a fairly clear picture emerges (see fig. 3 and fig. 4): the national market is by far the most important, with Sweden and Denmark in the lead. The Scandinavian market holds no real sway, and for all three countries the EU market is much more important.

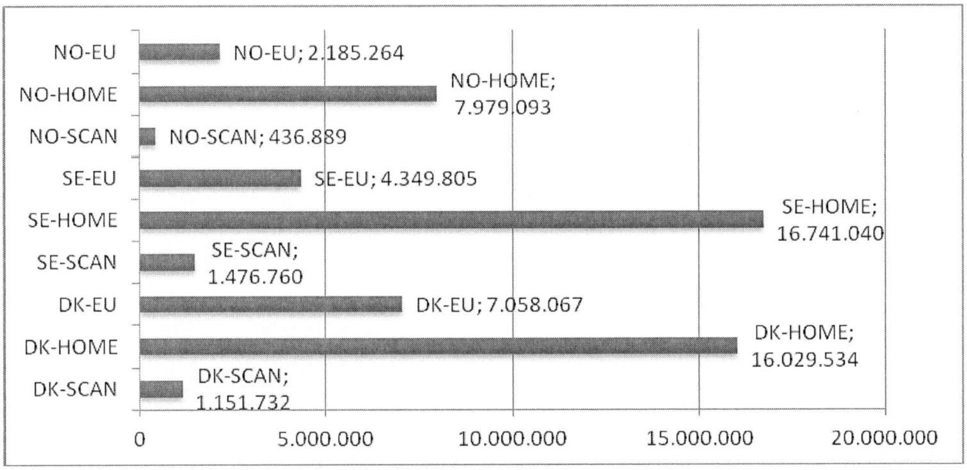

Figure 3: Regional shares in Scandinavia based on cinema admissions 2002-2006 in EU36, absolute numbers. Lumiere database 2010.

If we simplify the data and divide these figures into the Scandinavian films on their own market (DK, NO and SE together) on the other non-national Scandinavian market (SCAN) and EU 36 we get a strong picture of the strength of the national cinema market, the weakness of the non-national Scandinavian market and the rising role of the EU market (see fig. 4)

If we turn our focus towards the television figures for the same three countries, we can observe much higher numbers, since the films are watched by far more people on television. Yet the relationship between the national TV market and the non-national Scandinavian market for these films is no better: the national TV figures dominate, although the TV exchange between Denmark and Sweden is generally better and the share of Swedish films on Norwegian television clearly the highest among the three countries (see fig. 5).

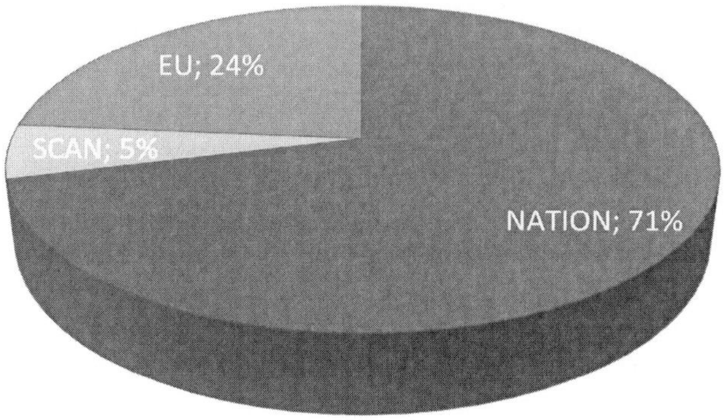

Figure 4: Regional shares for Scandinavian films 2002-2006 based on cinema admissions for Norway, Denmark and Sweden in Scandinavia and EU36

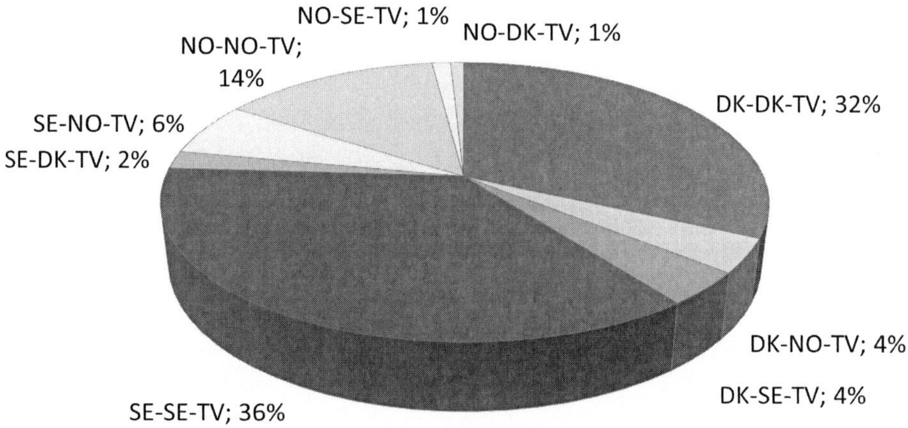

Figure 5: Regional shares for films 2002-2006 on TV in Norway, Denmark and Sweden. We have no TV figures for EU36.

There is no doubt that sales to foreign markets, including Scandinavia, Europe and the rest of the world, is important for a number of films from the Scandinavian countries and that the Scandinavian *auteur* tradition – dating back to world cinema icons like Carl Th. Dreyer and Ingmar Bergman – has contemporary equivalents in e.g. Lars von Trier. A few of the Scandinavian auteurs do in fact have a transnational audience, but the large proportion of Scandinavian films is rarely able to travel, neither in Scandinavia nor in Europe as such.

In a report for The Danish Film institute (DFI 2010), the Danish and Swedish share of films distributed in the European market is estimated to be 8% (4% per country), however, the share of ticket sales is only 2% (1% for each). The biggest shares go to France and the UK. If we examine to what extent sales abroad contribute to a film's total sale, however, both Denmark and Sweden figure with quite high percentages: between 2003-2008, 30% of all tickets sold for Danish films and 23% of all Swedish films were sold abroad, both in the EU and the US. In some cases (Lars von Trier's films are an example), the main sale happens abroad. Seen in a broader perspective, a globalisation and Europeanisation of Scandinavian cinema can therefore be said to have taken place, even if the national market remains the dominant and most important factor for a film's success.

If we shift our focus to cinema only and the general trends between the countries in the Scandinavian market we see both similarities and differences between the three Scandinavian countries, but also structural similarities between Scandinavia and Europe in general. The average pattern of films on national markets in Europe is national films around 20%, American films around 65% with the remainder attributed to the rest of the world, of which Europe accounts for around 7-8%. In Europe as a whole the big five (France, Germany, Italy, UK and Spain) dominate what remains of the European market after the national and the American share. Furthermore, most of the actual share of the European countries is not taken on the European market as such, but on the national markets. As figure 6 shows there is a transnational European film market, but it is very fragmented and dominated by the share that European films take on their own market and the share taken by the five big.

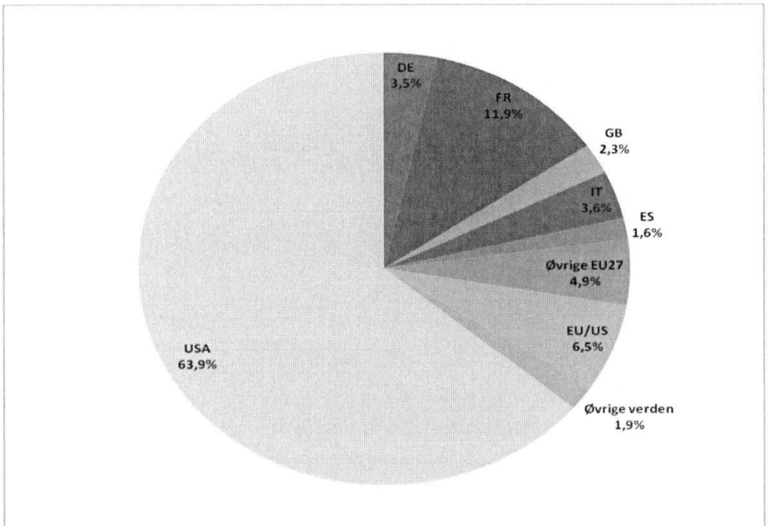

Figure 6: Regional shares of total European cinema market 2008 (Lumiere)

The Scandinavian patterns are just as clear: Denmark and Sweden dominate, both in terms of the number of films produced, the average audience per film and the average share of the Scandinavian market. The Scandinavian market is, however, much smaller than the national market and the European market, and all in all only 30% of Scandinavian films are distributed to the other Scandinavian countries, a figure only slightly higher than the figure for European distribution. As it is clear in fig. 7, the national, Scandinavian films are almost invisible outside of their national borders, only Swedish films in Norway (SE-CIN-NO) pass the 1 million threshold, and – as described later – only the fact that films from these countries fare much better on both national television and the television channels in other European countries creates a Scandinavian film exchange of any significance.

The exchange of films between the Nordic countries doesn't indicate a *natural cultural connection* with an obvious audience interest in films from the nighbouring countries. As fig. 8 illustrates, the national home market and the EU market are much more important for each of the Scandinavian countries than the Scandinavian market. On the other hand it is unlikely that culture in itself is an argument for or against transnational exchange, since American films do so well. As we shall see from the following, Scandinavian television culture seems to fare much better when we examine the presence of Scandinavian television series in other Nordic countries. A clear hypothesis therefore is that the reasons for a lack of a better Scandinavian exchange have to be found in factors related to areas of production and distribution as well as to film genres.

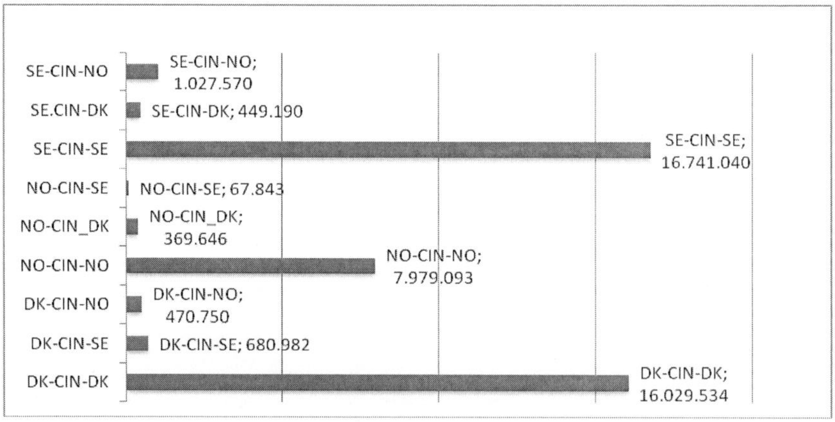

Figure 7: Scandinavian films in domestic cinemas and in cinemas of the other two Scandinavian countries, total amount of sold tickets 2002-2006[1]

What the figures illustrate very clearly is a Scandinavian region that is moving towards a greater transnationalisation of cinema, but which is in fact still very much a cinema dependant on its own national territory, including both cinema, national television and the emerging digital market for films. The internal distribution of films from Scandinavian countries to other Scandinavian countries is not impressive, although some directors and films have a very broad, Scandinavian success. The European transnationalisation is not very big either, although Danish cinema in recent years have improved the European share and certain genres, like crime, have done very well. The role of television is again rather interesting, because just as television drama as such travels much easier that films, both between Scandinavian countries and globally, the Scandinavian tv-channels are relatively better in distributing Scandinavian films to a broader audience.

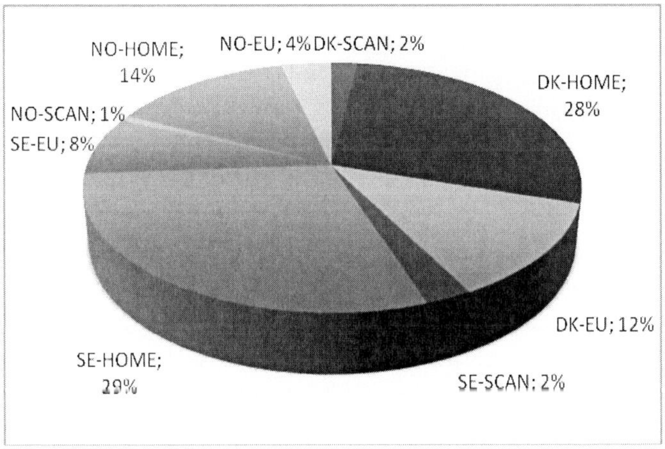

Figure 8: Cinema admissions in Scandinavia, 2002-2006, percentage of national films on the domestic market, Scandinavian market (only NO, SE and DK) and European market, EU36 figures

The Scandinavian Art Cinema and Transnational Cinema

Many observers of European cinema (e.g. Bordwell 1979; Neale 1981; Elsaesser 2005; Bergfelder 2005) have pointed to the art cinema as a strong tradition linked to both the realist drama and more experimental forms of non-narrative cinema. As a genre or aesthetic trend, this kind of cinema seldom reaches a very large audience. Lars von Trier is an example of a European exception to this rule, but overall this is a cinematic form, which often has a much wider distribution internationally than many more national mainstream films – at least in terms of number of countries and regions. The European and Scandinavian art cinema is linked to a tradition of manifestos and movements from the new wave of the 1960s to the Dogma 95 movement, and institutionally they are clearly dependent not just on cultural support and public funding, but also on a growing network of festivals that are international launching sites for this kind of films. However, for Scandinavian filmmakers, as discussed in the case examples below, finding an international audience after winning prestigious festival prizes does not naturally lead to the interest of the national or Scandinavian market. One could be tempted to think that the foreign interest and acclaim would nurture a regional interest, but these things do not go hand in hand.

To go behind the numbers presented in the above, we will briefly exemplify the hardships of Scandinavian art films on their regional markets based on discussions of films by acclaimed directors Bent Hamer and Roy Andersson. In both cases, international acclaim in the international festival circuit has been crucial in establishing their careers, but while the ambitions and budgets have been increasing, the national/regional audiences have been decreasing. However, while the films might not have a big impact at the local box office, they can benefit from a longer life on television and other platforms and are of course also examples of the cultural policy ambition in the Scandinavian support system of ensuring the creation of artistic films and not only commercial productions.

Bent Hamer is an example of a Scandinavian director who has found a wide international audience for his character-driven art house films through successful festival distribution. He made a name for himself with his quirky film *Eggs* (1995) which premiered at the Director's Fortnight in Cannes. *Eggs* was produced by Hamer's own production company Bulbul Films, which he had established in 1994, and since then he has produced his feature films through this company. His second feature film, *En dag til i solen* (*Water Easy Reach*, 1998) about a young Norwegian sailor (Eric Magnusson) stuck in a Spanish port town, didn't enjoy the same kind of success, in spite of being shot predominantly in English and with an international cast.

This changed with *Salmer fra kjøkkenet* (2003), which saw Hamer back in the Director's Fortnight, while the film was the Norwegian submission for the Academy Award for Best Foreign Language Film. *Salmer fra kjøkkenet* was a Norwegian-Swedish co-production with a story perfectly suited for attracting the attention of spectators in both Sweden and Norway. Based on real post-war research on the efficiency of Swedish housewives, the story explored the fictional set up of a Swedish researcher who is sent to a small Norwegian town to live with an aging bachelor to document his kitchen habits. Besides the intriguing and humorous set up of the Swedish researcher trying to silently study the Norwegian man from the top of an umpire's chair in the kitchen, the story also draws upon themes of overcoming post-war Norwegian-Swedish animosity and fostering friendships despite initial differences.

The film sold 85.000 tickets in Norway and a little over 20,000 tickets in both Sweden and Denmark. Thus, the film can hardly be deemed a Scandinavian success. However, the film enjoyed widespread success in Europe, selling 456,062 tickets in EU36 (not including Scandinavian countries) and audiences in especially Germany, Italy and France bought into the story. The film is a good example of the transnational 'success' of Scandinavian art cinema films: not a blockbuster success in quantitative terms, but in more qualitative terms a film that reaches a broad European audience along with critical and festival success.

The European success of *Salmer fra kjøkkenet* was followed by the English language drama *Factotum* (2005), shot in the United States and starring Matt Dillon as the fictional alter-ego of *Factotum*-author Charles Bukowski. *Factotum* was also selected for the Director's Fortnight, but is an example of a Scandinavian director turning his hand to an English-language film only to be deserted by his local audience. Even though Matt Dillon – as well as supporting actresses Lily Taylor and Marisa Tomei – is well known in the Scandinavian countries, the film only attracted 26,284 spectators in Norway, 3,573 in Denmark, 2,253 in Sweden (Lumiere 2010) and sold 321,000 tickets in EU27, making it less popular than Hamer's previous film.

Hamer returned to Norway and his native language with his next feature, *O'Horten* (2007), exploring themes of loneliness and old age. *O'Horten* follows the events on the evening of the retirement of the 67-year-old train engineer Odd Horten. The legendary Danish actress Ghita Nørby plays an important part as the mother of O'Horten, but the film never opened in Danish cinemas. The film was chosen for *Un Certain Regard* in Cannes, but in spite of the festival attention, an international sale to 40 countries, and a good critical reception, the Norwegian audience didn't bite, buying only 35,000 tickets and to date the film has only sold 153,509 in EU27, again with much bigger sales in France and Germany (76,000).

While the film festival circuit and the international critics hail art house directors such as Hamer, local audiences often shrink during the years of their international success. As mentioned, Lars von Trier is another example of a renowned director not selling an impressive amount of tickets in his home country anymore with his English-language productions with foreign actors. Thus, while the high profile art house films are popular with an international audience looking for interesting alternatives to the American fare, the domestic audiences seem to prefer other national films as alternatives to the English-language films.

Another example of an acclaimed Scandinavian art house director is Swedish Roy Andersson whose latest film is *Du levande* (*You, the Living,* 2006). The film was released seven years after its predecessor *Sånger från andra våningen* (*Songs from the Second Floor*, 2000), which in turn was preceded by a hiatus from theatrical features on the director's part of almost twenty-five years. *Du levande* was made in what may be recognised as Andersson's mature style, developed in the years when Andersson supported himself by directing commercials. The director's mature style consists of painstakingly crafted, almost static tableaux shots, containing in depth staging and carefully controlled mise-en-scène on, primarily, cleverly built studio sets. Andersson uses amateur actors, chosen for particular physical traits, rather than any particular acting ability, all with pale faces and instructed to do very little, something they often succeed at after the 40 to 50 takes the director occasionally requires for a particular shot. In all, the exercise creates an icily beautiful, gloomy, existential and somewhat sad stance but with a blend of more theatrical moments mixed in. Paradoxically, humour is a vital part of the overall effect.

After several years of complicated financing – making the film a Swedish-Danish-Norwegian-French-German-Japanese co-production – *Du levande* premiered in the *Un Certain Regard* selection in Cannes in May 2007. After additional festival screenings, where the film failed to pick up any significant awards, it opened in domestic cinemas in September. Notwithstanding, the film continued its round on the festival circuit and eventually won awards at several less prestigious events. *Du levande* was nominated for best film at the European Film Awards and received three prizes, Best Film among them, at the national film awards in Sweden, Guldbaggegalan.

Despite being possibly the most well received and reviewed film of the year in Sweden, *Du levande* only managed to attract an audience of 54,569 in the months following its release. When the film was taken out of distribution at the start of

2009, 71,209 had paid for admission. *Du levande* was picked up in several countries, but achieved little success anywhere. Germany (59,000), France (26,000) and Norway (25,000) appear to be the places in which the film performed best. According to the Lumiere database, the amassed European audience was 277,198.

The production, critical reception and performance of *Du levande* inevitably raises questions about European cinema, film festival practices, the funding system and about the fact that so many critically acclaimed films are unsuccessful in finding a broader audience. The American film historian David Bordwell has discussed the environment in which the kind of film *Du levande* may be said to be representative of the European art film exists. According to Bordwell:

> Few of these subsidized films attract a local audience or overseas distribution, so as purely economic investments they are disastrous. Instead payback shifts to another level. The subsidized film competes to win places in the world's four hundred film festivals, which are hungry for non-mainstream fare of all kinds. If a festival entry wins acclaim, perhaps an award, the sponsoring agency is confirmed in its decision to back the project, with honour flowing to the national culture. (Bordwell 2000: 6)

From a strictly financial point of view, of course Bordwell is right in deeming the films as disastors, but he has a major point in looking for the paybacks on other levels. What we would like to argue in the last part of this article, is how one can hope that the destiny of many art house films might be perceived differently if we do not only focus on cinema as the only important place for exhibition. Transnational audiences today must be found not just in the traditional cinema theatre but on television, VOD and the numerous mobile platforms to which films are moving today.

Looking for the Transnational Audiences

The European Think Tank commissioned a survey of film consumption in Denmark, Norway and Sweden before the Copenhagen Think Tank in 2010. The results tell a story of film consumption, where the cinema is still a strong player, not least in people's mind as the place where films are supposed to be seen and where you get the best quality experience. But the actual habits of the respondents tell another story, a story of films being integrated in a much broader variety of platforms, besides television also DVD sale and rental, VOD and mobile formats.

Country	TV	Cinema	DVD-TV	Computer*	Download
DK	61.9	11.6	24.8	1.6	7.5
SWE	58.8	10.8	25.5	4.6	21.2
NO	58	13.5	25.3	3.2	20.4

Figure 9: Average figures (%) for Scandinavian film consumption, national films.
* Use of computers for film viewing is here divided in two: computer means watching DVDs on your computer or streaming films, whereas downloads is taking films down on your harddisk.

This survey of course tell us what people *think* their consumption is – there is an error margin here – but the figures are overwhelmingly pointing in the same direction in all three countries: cinema is much smaller than TV and DVD-viewing at home, and in at least Sweden and Norway downloading of films is on a sharp upward curve. The age variation behind these figures is even more interesting: in both Norway and Sweden the use of downloads among the 15-40 year group is between 30-40% and even in Denmark the low average figures rise to 15-17% in the younger age groups.

Scandinavians are thus already fully living in a new film culture, a digital, individualized film culture at home or on the move. But this fact is barely registered in the way that current film strategies are developed, but mostly discussed as a scary, dystopian scenario, and the traditional forms of distribution from cinema to the other platforms are still very much following the logic of the traditional, national, cinema oriented mentality and logic.

One can argue, that while the 1980's and 1990's have been marked by the rise of co-production and creating transnational partnerships and collaborations in this regard, what needs to now become the main focus is the challenge of how to reach audiences on all platforms across borders and age groups. Transnational strategies for how to deal with this new media landscape are needed, especially if the niche films or art house auteurs that characterize the international profile of many small national cinemas are to find the audiences needed to staying in production.

Transnational Scandinavia? Concluding Remarks

If one wants to understand the transnational exchange of films between the Scandinavian countries, we would argue that it is necessary to examine the Scandinavian film culture in a context where films are not primarily locked into a national space and can not be seen only from the perspective of the cinema as the only place for film consumption. One needs to look beyond the numbers of admissions in the cinema. In the *new film culture* globalisation exists on many levels, and films can be seen on many platforms, not least by the younger generation. Nevertheless, cinemas are still an important part of the new film culture and will probably remain so in the future. After all, live music or live theatre did not disappear when music and theatre also found new platforms and new media.

It is a fact, that many films not only have an increasing audience internationally, but also that films shown on television (often repeatedly and on different channels) are by far the biggest window for films – at least in terms of numbers of viewers. Moreover, we are entering a new digital era where Video on demand (VOD) and other online formats for film viewing will be crucial for a film's life in a longer time perspective. A film's life in the cinema may be a key and crucial window for the film, but in the long run the film's existence on all the other platforms will represent its actual cultural reach and importance. Thus, one of the main points which this article wishes to highlight is that we need to readjust our image of e.g. the national and Scandinavian cinema to a much broader understanding of the film's actual place within society, and that we need to face the challenges and possibilities of a new film culture with an open mind.

The data presented in this article indicates a Scandinavian film culture that remains too focused on production, on getting the films funded and into production, and less focused on reaching a transnational audience outside the national territory.

Data released by the Nordic Council, following a recent survey, revealed that around 60% of the Nordic citizens feel a special connection to the Nordic region and even supported a federal Nordic union. This fact cannot be seen in patterns of film consumption in Scandinavia. Scandinavia doesn't appear to be a culturally homogenized region where people watch Scandinavian films because they are Scandinavian: most of the films that achieve (even moderate) success in another Scandinavian country must often attribute this to the director, the cast or the genre and story.

However, the current success of e.g. Danish television drama series point to the fact that some works of fiction do repeatedly cross the Scandinavian borders. While British audiences have recently tuned in to Danish series like *Forbrydelsen* (*The Killing*) and *Borgen*, the audiences of the other Scandinavian countries have been faithfully watching the drama series from DR for a number of years. It is worthwhile noting, that this goes for both crime series like *Rejseholdet* (*Unit One*), *Ørnen* (*The Eagle*) or *Forbrydelsen* and for family series like *Krøniken* (*Better Times*) or *Sommer* (*Summer*). While there is currently much talk of successful 'Nordic noir' material and a wave of adaptations of bestselling crime novels, the family series of DR have for a number of years found audiences towards the North while the majority of international attention has been for the crime-oriented material.

The impressive numbers for the drama series in the past years show that there is not a resistance as such to watching productions in the other Scandinavian languages and that not only traditional genre productions, but also broader drama series dealing with historical material (*Krøniken*) or the everyday hardships of a young Danish couple (*Nikolaj and Julie*) can appeal outside of the national realm. Most of the TV series from the public service broadcaster DR are targeted at a mainstream audience, but with the rise of new platforms and new players getting involved in production (like Netflix financing the second season of the Norwegian series *Lilyhammer*) also more niche productions have the opportunity to find audiences on a global scale.

To speak of transnationalisation of film and media industries today thus has to include these developments, and one can argue that it is a grand new time for transnational productions and audiences. However, it is not about finding the big audience in the cinemas, but about finding the many audiences on the many different platforms in the many different countries. It is more about a *subculturalization*, so to speak, but as the drama series are presently showing, this development might prove to be to the benefit of a European film culture under pressure if the industry starts to focus as much on collaborating on complicated issues like distribution and community-building for individual productions as on producing transnationally.

BIBLIOGRAPHY

Bergfelder, T. "The nation vanishes: European co-productions and popular genre formulae in the 1950s and 1960s". In: Hjort, M. / MacKenzie, S. (eds.). *Cinema and Nation*. London: Routledge, 2000, p. 139-152.

Bergfelder, T. "National, transnational or supranational cinema? Rethinking European film studies". *Media, Culture & Society* 27.3 (2005), p. 315-333.
Bondebjerg, I. "Filmen i mediekulturen". In: Jensen, K. B. (ed.). *Dansk Mediehistorie. Bd. 4 1995-2003*. Copenhagen: Samleren, 2003, p. 175-196.
Bondebjerg, I. "The Danish Way: Danish Film Culture in a European and Global Perspective". In: Nestingen, A. / Elkington, T. G. (eds.). *Transnational Cinema in a Global North: Nordic Cinema in Transition*. Detroit: Wayne State University Press, 2005, p. 111-140.
Bondebjerg, I. *Filmen og det moderne*. Copenhagen: Gyldendal, 2005.
Bondebjerg, I. and Redvall, E. N. *A Small Region in a Global North: Patterns in Scandinavian Film & TV Culture*. Copenhagen: Think Tank on European Film and Film Policy, 2011.
Bordwell, D. "The Art Cinema as a Mode of Film Practice". In: Fowler, Catherine (ed.). *European Cinema Reader*. London: Routledge, 2002, p. 94-102.
Bordwell, D. *Planet Hong Kong: Popular Cinema and the Art of Entertainment*. Cambridge, MA: Harvard University Press, 2000.
Brandstrup, P. G. and Redvall, E. N. "Breaking the Borders: Danish Coproductions in the 1990s". In: Nestingen, A. / Elkington, T. G. (eds.). *Transnational Cinema in a Global North: Nordic Cinema in Transition*. Detroit: Wayne State University Press, 2005, p. 141-164.
DFI. *Dansk film: En styrkeposition for den globale markedsføring af Danmark*. Copenhagen: Danish Film Institute, 2010.
Elsaesser, T. *European Cinema: Face to Face With Hollywood*. Amsterdam: Amsterdam University Press, 2005.
Finney, A. *The State of European Cinema*. London: Cassell, 1996.
Givskov, C. *Looking For Europe. Film, Politics and Globalization in Denmark, 1997-2009*. PhD Dissertation. University of Copenhagen, 2011.
Hjort, M. / Jørholt, E. and Redvall, E. N. *Danish Directors 2. Dialogues on the New Danish Fiction Cinema*. Bristol: Intellect Press, 2010.
Hjort, M. *Small Nation, Global Cinema: The New Danish Cinema*. Minneapolis: University of Minnesota Press, 2005.
Jäckel, A. "European Co-production strategies: The case of France and Britain". In: Moran, A. (ed.). *Film Policy: International, National and Regional Perspectives*. London: Routledge, 1996, p. 85-97.
Neale, S. "Art Cinema as Institution". *Screen* 22.1 (1981), p. 11-39
NFI. *Eksportundersøgelse*. Oslo: Norwegian Film Institute, 2008.
Redvall, E. N. "Teaching Screenwriting in a Time of Storytelling Blindness: The Meeting of the Auteur and the Screenwriting Tradition in Danish filmmaking". *Journal of Screenwriting*, 1.1 (2010), p. 59-81.
Redvall, E. N. "Dogmer for TV-Drama. Om brugen af one vision, den dobbelte historie og crossover i DR's søndagsdramatik". *Kosmorama* 248 (2011), p. 180-198.
Redvall, E. N. and Gubbins, M. *Scandinavian Think Tank: On Films, Markets, Audiences and Film Policy*. Copenhagen: Think Tank on European Film and Film Policy, 2011.
Sklan, C. "Peripheral Visions: Regionalism, Nationalism, Internationalism". In: Moran, A. (ed.). *Film Policy: International, National and Regional Perspectives*. London: Routledge, 1996, p. 234-248.

Family Affairs: Coproduction Policies between Spain and Latin America

Alberto Elena

Not long ago Néstor García Canclini mentioned, in a context not very different from today's, that "the only city where in one week you can see five to ten films from different Latin American countries is not Buenos Aires, Bogota, Sao Paulo or Mexico City, but Madrid" (García Canclini, 2008). Of course other Latin American capitals could be cited or Barcelona named instead of Madrid, but that would not change the meaning of the statement. What we cannot be so sure of is whether such an assertion is in fact accurate, since certain additional factors of great relevance must also be examined. It turns out that, in reality, although the film listings in Madrid and Barcelona include many more Latin American films than are usually found in that region's large cities, the only "Latin American" films shown regularly in Spain's commercial circuits are the "Spanish" ones. To put it another way, and simplifying to a certain degree - although not deforming -, the only Latin American cinema shown commercially in Spain nowadays is that which is coproduced by Spain.

The contingent of films coproduced with different Latin American countries between 2001 and 2010 (approximately 300, of which almost 40% were with Argentina) constitute most of the Latin American premiers on Spain's screens. The following figures serve as an illustration: almost 70% of the Latin American films that were shown in Spain during the same period (2001-2010) were coproductions, and the rest mainly got commercial distribution thanks to the prizes and recognition received in the festival circuit (plus the random dose of rarities present in any distribution system) (Elena, 2005a, p. 361-365) (Elena, 2009, p. 294-296) (Elena, 2011, p. 46-48). Naturally, this phenomenon must be contemplated from a certain distance, since this age of extreme globalisation seems to mean that the condition of international visibility of the cinemas of the south depends on whether or not a film is cofinanced by some northern country. But even taking into account the inevitable effects of globalisation, the situation is quite striking. My intention is not to cast doubt, as some have done, on the existence of a certain *national identity* in these increasingly transnational products, but rather to unravel the meaning of these coproductions, their objectives and limitations, their history and future, their politics and poetics, so as to better understand the role they have played, for decades, in the cinemas of the Spanish-speaking world. A role that has changed over time, of course, but that nonetheless probably contains some persistent underlying elements.

Like in many other places and settings, in Spain too the question of coproductions has generated heated debate on occasions (Palacio, 1999) (Hoefert de Turégano, 2004) (Pardo, 2007). From the protests by certain sectors of the profession to the "interference from outside" supposedly found in the shooting of what is officially considered the first coproduction ever made in Spain, *Jack el negro / Captain Blackjack* (Julien Duvivier, 1950) up through the repeated diatribes against "Europudding", the discussions – and the arguments proffered – are heard time and time again, but have no impact whatsoever on the practice itself. European coproductions appeared at the end of the 1940s in the context of a difficult post-war period, and they represented a reasonable industrial effort to reduce Hollywood's hegemonic presence. They largely dominated the audiovisual scene in continental Europe until the mid 1970s, and then again gained new strength at the end of the 1980s thanks to new legal instruments and specific funding sources. Of course Spain did not remain untouched by these developments (67% of the films produced in 1965, a historic high, were international coproductions) and currently, according to the European Audiovisual Observatory, this country's activity is coherent with the practices of other European countries, with coproductions being about 40% of the total of the feature films produced annually (Pardo, 2007, p. 134, 138). The distinguishing feature of the case of Spain is that a large number of these coproductions (practically half) are made with Latin American partners and this, for historic, cultural and ideological reasons, generates a considerable amount of debate which can be more or less specific and, in any case, quite heated.

Although the questions regarding cultural identity and the contours of what might have been (or continue to be) a national cinema are discussed and rediscussed in relation to all coproductions (think, for example, of Amenábar and *Los otros / The Others* [2001] or Rideley Scott's *El reino de los cielos / Kingdom of Heaven* [2005]), never are they as relentless as in the case of Latin America. Because if, in the last analysis, these European coproductions have been, from the outset, a response to an undeniable financial necessity and they are thus viewed basically as a strategy for survival in international markets, in the case of co-productions between Spain and Latin America mention is often made of a kind of empathy, historic debt or moral obligation that inevitably moves the question away from the economic sphere and puts it more into that of a certain *social imaginary.* With no need, then, to invoke the existence of a more deleterious *supranational identity*, it is reasonable to ask ourselves about how the Hispanic community has come to think of and imagine itself and how this preconception has impregnated the different articulations of the now many decades of cinematographic collaboration.

While there may have been previous expressions of a tepid pan-Hispanic will to cooperate in film projects, it was the First Spanish American Film Congress (*Primer Congreso Hispanoamericano de Cinematografía)* held in Madrid in October of 1931 that clearly set the co-ordinates for any possible subsequent action and, especially, that spelled out the ideological considerations that had been simply latent up to that point (García Carrión, 2010). The congress coincided with the change in political regime in Spain and the advent of the Second Republic, but the project had been gestating for a long time and must be understood as something closely linked to the development of the ideology of the *Hispanidad* (Hispanicity) during the Primo de Rivera dictatorship. Although certainly not new – note, for example, that Spain's national celebration had been being held annually on October 12th since 1918 – the *Hispanidad* rhetoric and a certain number of concurrent actions on the political-cultural level would crystallize precisely during the rule of the dictator

Primo de Rivera. Marked by both the emphasis on regeneration found in the discourse of some of the most outstanding intellectuals of the time and by the aspiration announced by the dictator to return Spain to a position of strength and prestige at the international level – which logically involved Spain leading the Latin American countries –, the *Hispanidad* ideology would end up becoming the backbone of Spanish cultural activity during the 1920s.

Ramiro de Maeztu would write "La Hispanidad creó la historia universal y no hay obra en el mundo, fuera del Cristianismo, comparable a la suya" (1931, p. 15)[1]. This statement is a rather blunt synthesis of the lofty motives that legitimated the intellectual, moral and spiritual guardianship of Spain over its former American colonies and the resulting historical mission of the Hispanic peoples. A leading theorist of the ideology of the *Hispanidad* with many supporters on both sides of the Atlantic, Maeztu was also the most influential representative of conservative Hispanism that was becoming an ever stronger element of the dictator's official discourse. Reflecting concerns felt by numerous Spanish intellectuals and politicians about the growing questioning of Spain's 'civilizing presence' in America, and also leading opposition to the Pan-Americanism promoted by the United States (which lacked the aims that a common culture, race and religion gave to the *Hispanidad* ideology), Maeztu produced an effective discourse at the service of a nation in crisis and in need of legitimizing myths.

Defending a kind of Hispanic *Gemeinschaft* thus turned into a political instrument that could possibly help Spain recover a dignified role in the international community, at the fore of a regeneration process in which the motherland, a supposedly prosperous and modern nation, could again lead "la América antes española"[2] (if such an archaic expression can be used here) towards renewed world protagonism. But such a vindication also had considerable worth as a myth for domestic consumption, reinforcing the questioned internal legitimacy of a nation in crisis which by that time had been obliged to send over two million citizens to the lands of America, as modest emigrants. It is in this particular context in which the First Spanish American Film Congress took place. As has been said many times, the event had no aspirations other than to form a Pan-Hispanic front, led by Spain, to better respond to the challenges posed by Hollywood talkies (Gubern, 1995, p. 130). It is not surprising, therefore, that the Congress would adopt an unequivocably protectionist position in its defense of Spanish-language films, but the adoption of a few (modest) fiscal measures did not completely satisfy the expectations of the visionary participants. Although Spain would sign agreements with Mexico, El Salvador, Peru and Chile, in an attempt to counteract the negative image that U.S. productions presented of Latin Americans, and the exchange of films between Spain and Latin America would intensify as the decade progressed, the dreams of a robust Pan-Hispanic market capable of facing up to Hollywood would not come true, either then or in successive revisitations of the project.

Predictably, after Spain's Civil War Franco's regime returned to this popular pro-Spain and Latin America rhetoric, putting it to the service of renewed imperial am-

1 "The Hispanic world gave rise to world history and there is no other creation in the world, other than Christianity, comparable to it."
2 "What was once Spanish America".

bitions and also making it a channel for much yearned-for international presence and, once again, to convince Spaniards themselves of their country's glory and importance (González Calleja and Limón Nevado, 1988). The Falangists had already been talking, even before the conflict, of a desire for empire. Making this wish come true entailed recovering the former protagonism of Spain in Latin America: In fact, the third point in the foundational manifesto of the Spanish Falange is as follows: "España alega su condición de eje espiritual del mundo hispánico como título de preeminencia en las empresas universales."[3] So it is not surprising that the powerful and belligerant Falange sectors were the most vocal proponents of recovering the rhetoric of the *Hispanidad* in post-war Spain. They would also make themselves heard in 1948, when a new Spanish American Film Congress (*Segundo Certamen Hispanoamericano de Cinematografía*) was organised, with the express hope of giving new impetus to cooperation in this area, aware as they were of how little had been achieved since the 1931 event (Tuñón, 2001). With well-intentioned but utopian proposals such as the unification of censorship codes in all Spanish-speaking countries or the supression of dubbing of foreign films, the participants agreed to form the Unión Cinematográfica Hispanoamericana (UCHA), or Spanish American Film Union, the objective of which was to coordinate activities of the member countries with a view to ensuring mutual support and reinforcement of the different national industries, and the promotion – once and for all – of a large Spanish-language film market. As we all know, little or nothing of this would come to pass, but as a by-product of the event a film that can probably be considered the first coproduction between Spain and a Latin American country was made (though it was not recognized as such because this figure did not yet exist in Spanish legislation): *Jalisco canta en Sevilla* (Fernando de Fuentes, 1948).

Exhaustively studied by Marina Díaz López (1999, 2008), *Jalisco canta en Sevilla* was made, it seems, thanks to funds frozen in Spain since the local box-office hit of *Allá en el Rancho Grande* (Fernando de Fuentes, 1936). A typical example of a *transnational romance,* this film inaugurated what would become a series of musical comedies with folkloric overtones and Pan-Hispanic orientation, usually not very rigorous and designed for broad popular consumption on both sides of the Atlantic. But above all, the success of *Jalisco canta en Sevilla* finally demonstrated to Spanish producers, who had made so many epic military stories and cumbersome melodramas, that "salía más a cuenta mostrar cómo un charro del México actual reencontraba a la Madre Patria gracias a la benefica influencia de la copla andaluza"[4] (Rafael de España, 1992, p. 199). That, at least, was the message received by the Galician producer Cesáreo González, who would not take long to embark on an ambitious line of Pan-Hispanic projects, often, although not always, in the form of coproductions. This project would facilitate the arrival in Spain of actors such as María Félix, Luis Sandrini, Pedro Armendáriz and Arturo de Córdova, and of directors such as Miguel Zacarías, Roberto Gavaldón, Tulio Demicheli and Luis Saslavsky (Castro de Paz and Cerdán 2005). Soon copied by other produc-

3 "Spain, in its condition as the spiritual axis of the Hispanic world, is entitled to preeminence in worldwide undertakings."

4 "It was more worth their while to show how a simple man from Mexico was reunited with the motherland thanks to the positive influence of Andalusian folk ballads."

tion companies (CIFESA, Unión Films, Perojo and Balcázar), this coproduction policy – although strictly in the hands of the private sector – had the permanent blessings of the regime and of the audience to such an extent that it would become one of the most characteristic signs of identity of Spanish production in the 1950s and 60s.

A few numbers give an idea of the dimensions of the project and production volume reached: between 1948 and 1975 (the year Franco died) a total of 137 coproductions between Spain and different Latin American countries were filmed, of which approximately 80% were with Mexico and Argentina (twice as many with Mexico as with Argentina, despite the fact that Spain and Mexico did not maintain diplomatic relations during that time) (Elena, 2011, p. 46-48). The strategy of these films was generally to make the most of well-known film stars in a framework of conventional stories which, at least initially, showed a certain cultural (moral, emotional...) continuity in terms of plot and characters, to later branch out to all types of genres and subgenres with no worries other than the strictly financial ones. An article published in 1942 in *Primer Plano* (which strictly followed the official line) had tried to explain the phenomenon of the empathy existing between the Spanish and Latin American cinematographies and their audiences. The author, the influential journalist Nicolás González Ruiz, who was associated with the Catholic sectors of the regime, began by underlining how the success of Latin American films on Spanish screens could not be the result of the technical excellence of these productions nor of the originality of their storylines, since – with all due respect, he said – "these aspects were hardly outstanding". He then mentioned the existence of "a spiritual community" between Spain and "Spanish America" (as he put it) that resulted in a "profound similarity in the primary feelings and the way they are externalized" and accounted for the mutual comprehension between audiences and films. And after condemning the type of conflicts usually appearing in Hollywood films, which were very distant from Hispanic moral and emotional habits, he unabashedly stated:

> Preferiremos ver al gaucho argentino, al minero de Chile o al ranchero de México resolver la cuestión [una infidelidad sentimental] con los 'facones', o en una cabalgada persecutoria en la que los revólveres dibujen sobre el ancho paisaje el humo blanco de la muerte (González Ruiz, 1942, p. 5). [5]

Other writers would put forward less primitive arguments, but the notion of a supranational Pan-Hispanic community was mentioned at the slightest opportunity, while also insistently invoking the old dream of a Spanish-language film market. Both litanies would be the backbone in 1966 of a Third Spanish American Film Congress, this time held in Barcelona. But by that time the nature of Spain's relationship with Latin America was changing a great deal and commercial exchanges (which had multiplied by 1500% between 1960 and 1975) had largely displaced the ideological demands of the *Hispanidad* (González Calleja and Pardo Sanz, 1993, p. 166). And in terms of films, coproductions like *Jalisco canta en Sevilla* and others

5 "We prefer to see an Argentine gaucho or a Chilean miner or a Mexican rancher work out the issue [an infidelity] with knives, or in a wild horseback chase in which revolvers fill the broad landscape with the white smoke of death".

along the same lines had given way, following the dictates of the box office, to titles such as *Misión secreta en el Caribe* (Enrique Eguiluz, 1969), *El retorno de Walpurgis* (Carlos Aured, 1973) and *Tiempos duros para Drácula* (Jorge Darnell, 1975). In any case, there was nothing more significant than the propensity shown by Spanish-Latin American coproductions to follow, in the turbulent years of the transition to democracy, the fashion of *destape*, or liberalization as regards the state of dress of the film's female characters, both in genres cultivated in previous years (adventure, terror, etc.), and also in lighthearted comedies with a certain erotic tone, impassioned dramas and even political flicks. For those who maintain that also in the case of coproductions between Spain and Latin America, rhetorical questions aside, the ultimate motivation has always been economic, this stage of brazen financial operations could represent a valid argument on their behalf.

This is not the place to describe the successive avatars that the Pan-Hispanic cinematographic dream would experience with the arrival of democracy in Spain (particularly, the ambitious coproduction program sponsored by Televisión Española from 1985 to 1995, coinciding with the celebration of the Fifth Centennial of the Discovery of America) (Pérez Estremera, 1994). However, it is important to point out that the dream would be accompanied by new demands and new instruments and would find itself in a substantially different context, in which Latin America no longer fulfilled the ideological role that it had formerly been given by the proponents of the *Hispanidad*, and instead became one of the fundamental vectors of Spain's international policy and an area of top priority in its foreign investment. The context is certainly a new one, and in it the controversial program Ibermedia plays a starring role.

We should begin with what, perhaps because it is so obvious, often goes unsaid. Since the late 1990s, Ibermedia has been engaged, for the first time in the region's history, in an authentic program of transnational coproduction, with governmental support. It is contributing, at least tentatively, to the formation of a common audiovisual space in Latin America (Falicov, 2007) (Moreno Domínguez, 2008) (Álvarez Valencia, 2009) (Villazana, 2009). The program is sufficiently well-known to make giving further details here unnecessary, but it is worth recalling that the program was officially created at the 7th Ibero-American Summit of Heads of State and Government held in 1997 on Margarita Island (Venezuela) with a four-pronged action and support program organized as follows: coproduction; distribution and promotion; project development; and, finally, the training of professionals in the audiovisual industry. Although the details of the program guidelines have changed over the years, as has the number of countries associated with the program, according to initial previsions about 60% of the funds were earmarked to strengthen coproduction, the project's backbone. The other budget items were distributed as follows: 30% for distribution, 5% for project development and 5% for professional training. Another issue altogether is whether the different budget chapters have been respected or remained stable, inasmuch as the tendency has always been to strengthen the production funds (and, to a lesser degee, project development) in detriment mainly to distribution and promotion.

Some authors have lucidly emphasized the historical importance of the Ibermedia Program, while others have put forward severe and well-reasoned critiques of its functioning. For the former, the long-held dreams of cooperation between Spain and Latin America in the area of film have finally taken shape beyond the vacuous rhetoric of the past and, in addition, under a formula that gives full rights (to participate in debates and to vote) to all members (far from any subvention policy seeking to provide directions) (García Canclini, 2008). At the First Congress on Ibero-American Culture held in Mexico in October of 2008, Arturo Ripstein went so far as to say that "programas como Ibermedia han propiciado que se haya filmado una parte importante del buen cine de nuestros países. Que lo hayan acercado a la cultura. La cultura que le da cara, corazón y sentido a un país" (Ripstein, 2008, p. 49) [6]. But for others Ibermedia does nothing but prolong a clearly neocolonial discourse, enabling Spain to benefit from cheap labor and thus economize in its shoots in Latin America, while also broadening the market for its film productions (Villazana, 2009). And although Ripstein also pointed this out ("el apoyo a la cultura [por parte de los estados] no es gratuito ni desinteresado"[7]), these circumstances have generated, in certain circles, an unfavorable opinion of Ibermedia.

It is true, in any event, that Ibermedia is founded on a purely industrial model and gives priority to the economic prospects of the projects beyond any other consideration, and that as a result all alternative proposals are excluded from the outset. The program undeniably exerts pressure on the applicants to make them adapt to market demands and expectations, imposing severe aesthetic limitations in favour of conventional narrative cinema that follows the habitual industry formulas and is destined to be shown in commercial circuits. The fact that, according to certain persistent criticisms, only the large production companies (always the same ones, in general) can gain access to the subsidies, even in not entirely confirmed but very hurtful cases (which need not be mentioned here) of connection with some of the major Hollywood producers, just adds more wood to the fire. Be that as it may, the truth remains; the Ibermedia Program, with all of its defects and shortcomings, has been the lifeline of film production in different countries of the region.

On the other hand, only unmitigated failure can be seen in relation to the objective of developing and strengthening the exhibition markets in Latin America. Certainly, some of the films produced by Ibermedia have had the salubrious effect of broadening the natural boundaries of circulation, and a few of them have even been seen on screens in Europe or the United States. Yet the impact on the region itself cannot be considered significant. Keeping in mind the traditional obsession for the integration of the Ibero-American audiovisual market at the regional level, it does come as a surprise that Ibermedia devotes most of its funds to production but not to guaranteeing better conditions for the circulation of the products, the true Achiles' heel of Spanish-language cinemas. In addition, the hegemonic North American presence in the region's markets, in countries where a network of independent exhibitors really does not exist, means that often it is not even possible to pay out the modest funds assigned annually to distribution and promotion. All differences considered, the situation is reminiscent of what happened with the notable contingent of

6 "Programs such as Ibermedia have propitiated the filming of a large part of the good cinema made in our countries. They have brought filmmaking closer to culture. The culture that gives a face, a voice, a heart and meaning to a country".

7 "[Government] support for culture is neither free nor unselfish".

feature films produced by Televisión Española between 1985 and 1995: of the fifty-odd titles produced through that program, only five or six would be commercially shown in Spain, with the others being condemned to exclusion until – sometimes with an astounding delay – the network itself would finally broadcast them to fill up airtime in the early morning hours (Elena, 2005a, p. 363-365). Far from learning a lesson from that experience, timidness – or simple lack of interest – in dealing with the circulation problems experienced by Ibero-American films in the region is a long-standing weakness.

However that may be, the very existence of Ibermedia invites reflection once again, now from the vantage point of the 21st century, on the nature of Spanish-Latin American coproductions and of the poetics that are found recurrently in them. Because, even at the risk of falling into simplification, as regards the corpus of the several hundred films made over various decades, it is safe to say that the main theme of all of these coproductions has been and continues to be the recomposition of the great, albeit fractured, Hispanic family, a metaphorical, transoceanic and symbolically transhistoric recovery that informs numerous titles filmed in Franco's time and also more recent ones. Although it is not a coproduction, the film *Deliciosamente tontos* (Juan de Orduña, 1943) illustrates perfectly this idea of the necessary fusion of Spaniards and Latin Americans (in this case Cubans) through matrimony, while various of the films from the Joselito saga can be read, in fact, as an allegorical vision of the reconstitution of a great Spanish-Latin American family: in *Bello recuerdo* (Antonio del Amo, 1961), for example, Libertad Lamarque adopts the little Spanish orphan who reminds her of the son she lost in Mexico. Of course there are many variations, such as those that turn to the annals of history and territory to depict, in a transnational setting, reencounters that can only be understood in terms of purely national relationships: the matrimonial alliance between Spaniards from Galicia and Asturias at the height of Spanish immigration to Havana (*Historia de dos aldeas*, Antonio del Amo, 1950) or the reencounters in Spain of Argentine and Uruguayan couples, respectively, in *Nueces para el amor* (Alberto Lecchi, 2000) or the most recent *Paisito* (Ana Díez, 2009). All in all, the key element in these films that I would define as unrepentant allegorical tales is found in the transnational romance they often depict (Díaz López, 1998, 2008) (Gubern, 2009) (Dapena, 2010).

Such is the persistence of Hispanic filmmakers, from *Jalisco canta en Sevilla, Dos charros y una gitana* (Antonio Román, 1957), or *Una cubana en España* (Luis Bayón Herrera, 1951) to the present, in the quasi-obsessive representation of mixed couples that one cannot help but wonder if this particular transnational imaginary perhaps plays a role similar to that played, back in the day, in strictly national terms, by the *foundational fictions* so thoroughly studied by Doris Sommer (1991) in the national literary traditions of Latin America. Only that here the relationships – often leading to marriage – do not serve to bolster the collective dreams of a national community (that period is over and thus no longer needs legitimizing myths) as much as those of a no less imagined transnational community (which is apparently in need of renewed *pseudo-foundational fictions*).

The flow seems to have changed direction and if before it was almost always Latin American men visiting Spain and having a romance with a young *española* (not just the classic examples already cited, but also in the 1960s, with Enrique Guzmán and Palito Ortega as *partenaires* of Rocío Dúrcal in *Acompáñame* and *Amor en el aire*, both by Luis César Amadori, in films that renovated the subgenre for younger audiences), now it is more often Spaniards who travel to Latin America (with Cuba being a favorite destination) and find their soulmate there: *Maité* (Eneko Olasagasti and Carlos Zabala, 1994), *Cuarteto de La Habana* (Fernando Colomo, 1998), etc. Or, a new figure, *female* Latin American immigrants (much more than *male*) arriving in Spain and soon meeting a Spanish lad: *Flores de otro mundo* (Icíar Bollaín, 1999), *I Love You, Baby* (Alfonso Albacete and David Menkes, 2001), *La mujer de mi vida* (Alfonso del Real, 2001), *La novia de Lázaro* (Fernando Merinero, 2002), *Entre Abril y Julio* (Aitor Gaizka, 2002), etc. The perspectives shown in other films, such as *Aunque estés lejos* (Juan Carlos Tabío, 2002), are more complex and try to avoid clichés, while *Los pasos perdidos* (Manane Rodríguez, 2001) intelligently – and perversely – turns the conventions of these transoceanic family melodramas upside-down. But all together they are but a few drops in an ocean of commonplaces (Elena, 2005b, p. 123-125).

The very idea of continuity in the transoceanic family sagas or the transnational romances from the 1940s to present may seem questionable and in fact Kathleen Vernon (2007, p. 187) has set forth some solid arguments against it, but still, I believe it is worth highlighting, insofar as the issue at hand is ultimately the nature of coproductions between Spain and Latin America. Because, curiously enough, the type of coproductions (whether hybrid, mestizo or deeply rooted in national cultures) that some authors describe as having a more complex and enriching perspective, and sometimes even as an indication of a supposed supranational identity, are in many cases (perhaps even the majority) conventional proposals that contribute little or nothing to the matter of identity. They are films that, in reality, tend to underline difference and otherness over the foundation of a curious discourse which frequently has moralistic and even nationalistic overtones, which never presents relationships of true equality between its protagonists, and which, for that matter, tend to show a certain colonial nostalgia that only the old fables of transnational romance seem to be able to bring back to life.

And yet coproductions involving Spain and Latin America are still expected – although no longer from a sense of "moral duty" so dear to Franco's ideologues but rather from a sense of a certain "historical debt" – to have an "extra" that is not required of coproductions between, say, Spain and Finland (Casa de América, 2003, p. 3). What are known as strictly financial coproductions with Latin America have in Spain, if not a bad reputation, at least a reputation as something spurious, as if they were somehow neglecting some intangible obligation. As if they had refused to affirm, once again, the supranational character of the Hispanic community. As if it was necessary to keep on remembering it continuously. As if they had been unable to express an emotional affinity that must not go unmentioned. But just as how in the sphere of European cinematographies some time ago the rhetoric of a possible common culture gave way to more pragmatic industrial and commercial demands, perhaps now the time has come to understand the film relations linking Spain and Latin America in market terms, plain and simple, and to think that even strictly financial coproductions contribute to strengthen the industrial fabric of our cinemas, and of the production, distribution and exhibition networks that, at this point in time, are far from adequate. In short, perhaps any serious and ambitious attempt to take a new look, through film, at the important questions of a supranational Hispanic identity necessarily involves increasing the chances of those films actually being seen in the region and ensuring that every week in Buenos Aires, Bogota, Sao Paulo or Mexico City it is possible to see five, ten or - why not? - even fifteen Latin American films.[8]

BIBLIOGRAPHY

Álvarez Valencia, J. *Programa Ibermedia, 1998-2008. Diez años de apoyo al cine iberoamericano*. Valencia: Fundación para la Investigación del Audiovisual, 2009.

Casa de América, *El puente en imágenes: coproducciones iberoamericanas*. Madrid: Casa de América, 2003.

Castro de Paz, J. L. / Cerdán, J. (eds.). *Suevia Films–Cesáreo González: Treinta años de cine español*. La Coruña: Xunta de Galicia, 2005.

Dapena, G. "Rumbas, Tangos, Boleros and Cuplés: Performing and Crossing Musical Borders in *Una cubana en España* (1951)". *Studies in Hispanic Cinemas* 7.1 (2010), p. 9-21.

Díaz López, M. "Las vías de la Hispanidad en una coproducción hispanomexicana de 1948: *Jalisco canta en Sevilla*". *Cuadernos de la Academia* 5 (1999), p. 141-165.

Díaz López, M. "Connecting Spain and the Americas in the Cold War: the Transnational Careers of Jorge Negrete and Carmen Sevilla". *Studies in Hispanic Cinemas* 5 (2008), p. 25-42.

Elena, A. "Cruce de destinos: intercambios cinematográficos entre España y América Latina". In: Castro de Paz, J. L. / Pérez Perucha, J. / Zunzunegui, S. (eds.). *La nueva memoria: Historias(s) del cine español (1939-2000)*. La Coruña: Vía Láctea Editorial, 2005 (a), p. 332-376.

Elena, A. "Latinoamericanos en el cine español: los nuevos flujos migratorios". *Secuencias. Revista de Historia del Cine* 22 (2005) (b), p. 107-133.

Elena, A: "Medio siglo de coproducciones hispano-mexicanas". In: De la Vega Alfaro, E. / Elena, A. (eds.). *Abismos de pasión. Una historia de las relaciones cinematográficas hispano-mexicanas*. Madrid: Filmoteca Española, 2009, p. 279-303.

Elena, A. "Difusión y circulación del cine argentino en España". In: Ramón Jarne, R. (ed). *Imágenes compartidas: cine argentino-cine español*. Buenos Aires: Centro Cultural de España en Buenos Aires, 2011, p. 29-49.

España, R. de. "España y América: 500 años de historia a través del cine". *Film-Historia* 2.3 (1992), p. 189-219.

Falicov, T. "Programa Ibermedia. Co-Production and the Cultural Politics of Constructing an Ibero-American Audiovisual Space". *Spectator* 27.2 (2007), p. 21-30.

8 This work has been made possible by the help of the Research Projects "Media co-productions in the European context: Identities and cultural transnationalization processes" (AT2009-0020, Ministry of Science and Innovation, Government of Spain, Integration Actions Program) and "Cinema and Television in Post-Transition Spain (1979-1992)", Ministry of Economy and Competitiveness, Government of Spain (CSO2011-15708-E).

García Canclini, N. "Ibermedia y la coproducción cinematográfica transnacional". *La Jornada de Oriente*. Puebla, 8 September 2008. URL: http://www.lajornadadeoriente.com.mx/2008/09/08/puebla/cancli16.php.
García Carrión, M. "Nacionalismo español y proyección hispanoamericanista: el Congreso Hispanoamericano de Cinematografía de 1931". In: *Actas del X Congreso de la Asociación de Historia Contemporánea* (Santander, 16-17 September 2010), URL: http://www.ahistcon.org/docs/Santander/contenido/MESA%201%20PDF/Marta%20Garcia%20Carrion.pdf.
González Calleja, E. / Limón Nevado, F. (eds). *La Hispanidad como instrumento de combate: raza e imperio en la prensa franquista durante la guerra civil española*. Madrid: Consejo Superior de Investigaciones Científicas, 1988.
González Calleja, E. / Pardo Sanz, R. M. "De la solidaridad ideológica a la cooperación interesada (1953-1975)". In: Pérez Herrero, P. / Tabanera, N. (eds.). *España / América Latina: un siglo de políticas culturales*. Madrid: AIETI-Síntesis / Organización de Estados Iberoamericanos, 1993, p. 137-180.
González Ruiz, N. "Del patrimonio común: observaciones sobre el cine hispanoamericano". *Primer Plano* 3/104 (19.10.1942), p. 5.
Gubern, R. "El cine sonoro (1930-1939)". In: Gubern, R. / Monterde, J. E. / Pérez Perucha, J. / Torreiro, C. (eds.). *Historia del cine español*. Madrid: Ediciones Cátedra, 1995, p. 123-179.
Gubern, R. "La exogamia pasional hispanoamericana ilustrada por el cine durante el franquismo". In: de la Vega Alfaro, E. / Elena, A. (eds.). *Abismos de pasión. Una historia de las relaciones cinematográficas hispano-mexicanas*. Madrid: Filmoteca Española, 2009, p. 89-99.
Maeztu, R. de. "La Hispanidad". *Acción Española* 1.1 (15.12.1931), p. 8-16.
Moreno Domínguez, J. M. "Diversidad audiovisual e integración cultural: analizando el programa Ibermedia". *Comunicación y Sociedad* 9 (2008), p. 95-118.
Palacio, M. "Elogio posmoderno de las coproducciones". *Cuadernos de la Academia* 5 (1999), p. 221-235.
Pardo, A. "Coproducciones internacionales españolas: ¿estrategia financiera o expresión multicultural?" *Comunicación y Sociedad* 20.2 (2007), p. 133-173.
Pérez Estremera, M. "Quelques principes, faits et conclusions". *Cinémas d'Amérique Latine* 2 (1994), p. 69-71.
Ripstein, A. "Por un cine peligroso". *Cahiers du cinéma-España* 17 (2008), p. 48-49.
Sommer, D. *Foundational Fictions: The National Romances of Latin America*. Berkeley: University of California Press, 1991.
Tuñón, J. "Relaciones de celuloide. El Primer Certamen Cinematográfico Hispanoamericano. Madrid, 1948". In: Lida, C. (ed.). *México y España en el primer franquismo, 1939-1950. Rupturas formales, relaciones oficiosas*. México: El Colegio de México, 2001, p. 121-161.
Vernon, K. M. "Imperio, identidad y nostalgia: Cuba recuperada en el reciente cine español". In: Berthier, N. / Seguin, J.-C. (eds.). *Cine, nación y nacionalidades en España*. Madrid: Casa de Velázquez, 2007, p. 185-199.
Villazana, L. *Transnational Financial Structures in the Cinema of Latin America. Programa Ibermedia in Study*. Saarbrücken: VDM Verlag Dr. Müller, 2009.

'ACCENTED CO-PRODUCTION': 'GLOCAL' STRATEGIES IN TRANSNATIONAL CUBAN CINEMA

Verena Berger

Transnational Cinema: Co-Productions in Cuba

Daniel Díaz Torres – known mostly for his movies *Alice in Wondertown* (*Alicia en el pueblo de maravillas* 1991), *Love Me and You Will See* (*Quíereme y verás* 1994), *Little Tropikana* (*Kleines Tropikana/Tropicanita* 1998), *Playing Swede* (*Hacerse el sueco* 2001) and *Lisanka* (2010) – is one of the few filmmakers who, despite the economic difficulties in Cuba, is still shooting films regularly since the crisis that began in 1990, with the fall of the Eastern Bloc. His movies *Little Tropikana* and *Playing Swede* emerged from financial collaboration between Cuba, Spain and Germany, and were the first co-productions with this Central European country since the collapse of the German Democratic Republic in 1989: The last German-Cuban co-production dates back to 1964, when the DEFA ("Deutsche Film-Aktiengesellschaft"[1]) and the Instituto Cubano del Arte e Industria Cinematográficos (ICAIC) co-financed Kurt Maetzig's *Prelude 11* (*Preludio 11*) (Muñoz-Aunión, 2010, p. 231).[2]

According to Juan Antonio García Borrero, co-productions have a long tradition in Cuban cinema: Especially with Mexico before the Revolution, after 1959 with many Latin American countries (Cuba being even a promoter of cinematographic production), and since the year 2000, mostly with Spain.[3] In the last two decades, the co-financing of films became more important than ever, due to the economic and political isolation that Cuba has had to face since the dismantling of the Eastern Bloc in 1989 (García Borrero, 2001, p. 14; 2002, p. 200). Faced with the loss of markets in former socialist countries and the tightening of the blockade by the U.S. (*Torricelli Act* 1992; *Helms-Burton Act* 1996), the country plunged into the lack of financial funds. While the most productive phase of the Cuban film industry was recorded between 1981 and 1990[4], the beginning of the so called "Special Period in

1 The DEFA was a cinematographic state organ of the extinct German Democratic Republic.

2 *Little Tropikana* was the result of the collaboration of the ICAIC and the "Bertelsmann Media Group", *Playing Swede* was produced by ICAIC, as well as "Igeldo Komunikazioa", "Impala", Canal +, TVE and "Kinowelt". The protagonist of both films is portrayed by German actor Peter Lohmeyer, who also participated with his own company "Glückauf-Film" in promoting the two projects, as well as in the pre-production of *Playing Swede* (Worthman, 2000).

3 Regarding co-production, the main countries with which Spain collaborates are Argentina and Mexico, accounting for 59.8% during the years 2000 to 2004. Then there are Cuba and Chile with a 22.2%, followed by Uruguay, Brazil and Colombia with a 10.8%, as well as Peru and Venezuela with a 5 % (Caballero, 2006, 17).

4 As Michael Chanan states, the ICAIC, the leading producer in the country, returned approximately 7,7 million USD during the 80s, while in 1993 revenue from sales and distribution of movies, especially in Western Europe, had reduced to just $454.000 USD (2003, p. 480).

Time of Peace" ("Período especial en tiempos de paz") in 1991 struck as a severe crisis that rattled the possibility of making movies. As a result, from the mid-90s, the production of purely Cuban films practically ceased to exists, for, in the eight years following 1995, only two feature films were made without external funding (Hernández Morales, 2007, p. 130).[5] The subsequent lack of economic resources pushed Cuba's cinematographers in search of international capital. This factor was extremely important for the creativity of filmmakers themselves, who sought alternative financial sources by offering cinematographic services to third parties; that is, they would conduct productions for other countries in the Caribbean island, such that would leave a substantial profit margin, allowing them to sustain both domestic productions and co-productions.[6] It was the success of co-productions like *Strawberry and Chocolate* (*Fresa y chocolate*; Cuba/Spain/Mexico 1994) and *Guantanamera* (Cuba/Spain 1995), both made by Tomás Gutiérrez Alea and Juan Carlos Tabío, that enthused Cuban cinema to bet on international relations and co-financing, in order to meet the needs of national cinema itself.

Due to the increasing influence of foreign capital, Cuban filmmakers must currently confront both external dependencies that affect film production, as well as a process of adaptation to the demands of other markets. This creates a dichotomy between the danger of distortion of the characteristics of a national cinema[7] and the expansion of their repertoire. Although he is at the forefront of Cuban co-productions, Daniel Díaz Torres acknowledges the negative sides of the increasing dependence of Cuban cinema on foreign funding. In an interview he affirms:

> A Cuban film that is to be international and please audiences worldwide – I wouldn't know what kind of movie that should be. I think there is a risk of sacrificing movies to the concept of internationalization, and this will take away their soul. This means that they would no longer be perceived as authentic or vital, but as adapted to the needs of the market instead. We run a great risk. (Bremme, 2000, p. 181-182)

As Marvin D'Lugo also states, the move toward co-productions implies that, under the influence of foreign capital, filmmakers "are forced to negotiate their own artistic visions and policies, according to the commercial demand of financial arrangements related to global cinema"[8] (2000, p. 103). When the big screen – as it

---

5 According to Sergio Luis Hernández Morales, one of the two productions may have had external financing, but due to the lack of documentation, it has not been possible to gather any certain accurate data. (2007, p. 130).

6 As a result, Hernández Morales highlights the return to a melodramatic tone on the one side, and on the other, the move towards a *light* cinema, characterized throughout the era of the 90s by simple narrative structures that placed production in a gulf where it was neither "auteur" cinema, nor purely commercial with respect to prevailing co-productions: "It is also symptomatic the fact that of 15 Cuban filmmakers that shot between 1990 and 1995, only 6 could do it again before the century was over, not to mention the five female and male directors that intervened in the film *Mujer transparente* [*Transparent Woman*] (1990), which means that more than 50% of them could not shoot again. Only the aforementioned Daniel Díaz Torres and Fernando Pérez were able to shoot three movies in the decade in which the majority [sic] was not able to find funding for their following projects. This gives us a measure of the crisis through which Cuban cinema is going through, and how difficult it is to adapt to changing times where co-productions prevail" (2007, p. 131).

7 See, amongst others, Higson 2002 [1989]; Hjort / MacKenzie 2000; Crofts 2006.

8 In Spanish: "se encuentran forzados a negociar sus propias visiones artísticas y políticas de acuerdo con la demanda comercial de los arreglos financieros relacionados con el cine global".

often does – becomes a reflection of identities, each movie is an opportunity to rectify prejudices or, contrariwise, to strengthen national stereotypes. In this context, Omar González, current president of the ICAIC, notes that, apart from being now an indisputable necessity, co-productions may jeopardize the concept and understanding of national cinema, since the expectations of other partners' mustn't always comply with the tradition of dedicating films to national identity. These financial co-operations become even more sensitive when the Cuban party can only propose actors and part of the technical crew, or when it becomes merely part of the scenery, as it happened in *Black Tears* (*Lágrimas negras* 1997) by Sonia Herman Dolz, *Who the Hell is Juliette?* (*¿Quién diablos es Juliette?* 1997) by Carlos Marcovich, *Havana Quartet* (*Cuarteto de La Habana* 1998) by Fernando Colomo, *Comandante* (2003) by Oliver Stone, or *Havana Blues* (*Habana Blues* 2005) by Benito Zambrano. At the same time, Cuban directors themselves, particularly younger ones, have hardly any access to material or funds for their own projects (Hoefert de Turegano, 2004, p. 16 ss.).[9] Notwithstanding, according to González, co-productions can also have innovative effects over national cinemas such as the Cuban: The technical and cultural exchange between cinematographies with developmental differences can contribute to and improve the quality of films emerging from co-productions, while breaching into other markets, and confronting international audiences (Sánchez, 2004).

The 'Accented Style' of Co-Production

In his essay "In praise of postmodern co-productions"[10], José Manuel Palacio distinguishes three types of co-financing in contemporary cinema: 1) strictly economic co-productions, which seek a better position in international markets, yet maintain a so called 'national cinema''; 2) co-productions that try to erase the national aspect in search of an international style, and 3) co-productions that "(...) reflect the multinational and hybrid character"[11] of the world today (Palacio, 2002). In the case of co-productions like *Little Tropikana* and *Playing Swede*, which pertain to the latter, the theory of 'Accented Style' is particularly fruitful, because in movies emerging from co-operations, financial factors don't necessarily permeate the narrative and visual levels. According to Hamid Naficy, this 'Accented Style' is the

9 Luciano Castillo offers a detailed description of the conditions of Cuban filmmaking: "The 'art of our time' requires substantial resources; above all, that of international distribution, which amortizes costs and contributes to self-financing. Co-production with a few key European countries became, for Cuba – as for the rest of Latin America – unavoidable: to co-produce or not to produce, that is the un-Shakespearian dichotomy our directors must consider in these globalized times. The services offered by competent ICAIC professionals, known for their effectiveness in conveying what they imagine, and not simply as resources, are exploited as inexpensive labour for the 'directors' of the First World. Washed-up European actors earn higher salaries in these films than the hallowed figures that have only barely been able to make their way into national cinema and are relegated to secondary roles. Being able to shoot for practically nothing compared to the international average has turned Cuban locations into perennial temptation for foreign producers, while at the same time allowing the fees collected to be reinvested in national cinema." (2010, p. 86-87).

10 In Spanish: "Elogio posmoderno de las coproducciones".

11 In Spanish: "(...) reflejan el carácter multinacional e híbrido".

result of the displacement of filmmakers and their experience of exile or diaspora visualized in the screen (2001, p. 10-11). Referring to British linguist David Crystal (1991, p. 2), Naficy transposes the linguistic concept of accent to the movies to develop his theoretical approach:

> If in linguistics accent pertains only to pronunciation, leaving grammar and vocabulary intact, exilic and diasporic accent permeates the film's deep structure: its narrative, visual style, characters, subject matter, theme, and plot. In that sense, the accented style in film functions as both accent and dialect in linguistics. (2001, p. 23)

Hence Naficy notes the emergence of a singular film genre, the 'Accented Cinema', with a cinematic corpus distinguished by it being greatly diverse, multilingual and intercultural, as well as having transnational funding; it also demands, a posteriori, new receptive aptitudes from the audience (2001, p. 18). Most of these films are bi- or even multilingual, multivocal or "multiaccented" (2001, p. 24). Parallel to the 'Accented Style', these films highlight visual elements characteristic to a nation/country (landscapes, photographs, letters, monuments), as well as visual markers of identity (physique, clothing, behavior). Combining the visual, oral, vocal and musical aspects (voices, accents, languages, intonations, music, songs) the 'Accented Cinema' represents a confrontation of individual and collective identities (2001, p. 24).

Parting from Naficy's theory of 'Accented Cinema', we may arrive at a classifying model of co-productions – apart from merely financial co-productions, or such that reproduce successful genres and styles in other film industries or cinematic traditions – into which we may include the category of 'Accented Co-productions'. These are movies whose production is not only characterized by the financial influence of foreign capital, production companies or international directors, but where co-operation has an impact beyond the mere economical aspect, and can be appreciated in the narrative, iconography and sound of the films. The two German-Cuban co-productions *Little Tropikana* and *Playing Swede* are two examples of what we mean by 'Accented Co-productions'. In what follows, we will establish the parameters to define this 'Accented Style' in co-produced films: What factors distinguish them from other co-productions in terms of film narrative, involvement of actors, language and image? What 'accents' do these 'Accented Co-productions' have, and what effect can they have in the configuration of a 'national cinema'?

Little Tropikana and *Playing the Swede*: Film Genre and Narration

Both films by Daniel Díaz Torres are satirical comedies about Cuba's daily reality. In *Little Tropikana*, Amancio, a Cuban cop, investigates – in the best style of noir detectives – the strange death of German tourist Hermann Pangloss, whose body is found on a night of tropical rain, in the garden of a multifamily house; wearing in his back a pair of white wings – an image that evokes the movie *A Very Old Man with Enormous Wings* (*Un señor muy viejo con unas alas enormes* 1988) by Fernando Birri –, and in his hand a bottle of hard liquor. Pangloss stays in Havana to investigate his family history: during World War II his father had sought refuge in Cuba. There he became an antifascist hero deviating German submarines, while falling in love with a Cuban dancer from the legendary "Tropicanita", a little cabaret in the harbor of Havana. After having to abandon the country with their son in the 50s, he ran a bar named "Little Tropikana" on the banks of Lake Titisee in the German Black Forest.

Although most of the story of *Little Tropikana* develops in the 90s, Díaz Torres uses flashbacks at four different temporal levels, to reconstruct the events that lead the spectator through a past filled with mysteries and anecdotes of Nazi spies. In Commissioner Amancio's opinion, Pangloss' death is merely a consequence of him getting drunk at a costume party, and then falling off a rooftop. But Lorenzo, a young police officer and his colleague, begins to investigate a different hypothesis on his own. From then on, the plot of the film becomes an almost surreal story about truth and unreality, and a parody of the detective genre: Horror and fantasy cinema, paired with Lorenzo's ability to make stories up, result in reality merging with the character's imagination.

In *Playing Swede*, a German by the name of Otto Meier alias Björn "plays the Swede"[12] which colloquially means "to pretend not to understand, to play the fool".[13] This time, a German tourist runs from the European police by hiding in the Cuban capital, where he poses as a Swedish Literature professor. He lodges at the house of now ex-commissioner Amancio, a man of rigid moral principles who doesn't precisely like tourists, and whose role in both movies is played by Cuban actor Enrique Molina. During the day, Otto/Björn slowly earns his host's trust, as well as the love of his daughter Alicia. But at night, the fake Swede competes against the very criminals of Havana, robbing bewildered tourists who don't expect such a thing from a foreigner. When the jewels of the Swedish Crown are exposed in Havana, and Otto/Björn intends to steal them disguised as Pippi Longstocking (a character in children's literature created by Swedish writer Astrid Lindgren), the movie doesn't only reach its comic peak, but also exposes his true identity, and closes with a happy ending.

Both *Little Tropikana* and *Playing Swede* are meant for Cuban domestic consumption as well as for an international public. To captivate such diverse audiences, Díaz Torres opts for a commercial approach, and thus creates two movies that oscillate between the lighthearted comedy and the detective genre, the latter being previously nonexistent in Cuban cinema (Castillo, 2010, p. 90). We speak, therefore, of two humorous films with "universal" themes (good and evil, death, love), but at the same time of a cinema with a strong dosage of 'local flavor' (the setting in Havana, the integration of national folklore, the social critique of Cuban life), as well as global (multiculturalism as a theme, stereotypes of Otherness, the integration of European imaginary). Alongside this thematic and formal hybridity, *Little Tropikana* offers elements of Magical Realism, while *Playing Swede* tends rather toward Social Realism. To link the expectations of spectators at a local and global level, Díaz Torres recurs to the theme of mobility – "the mobility of human beings themselves, and the mobility of meanings and meaningful forms through the media" (Hannerz, 1996, p. 19).

---

12 In Spanish: "se hace el sueco".

13 In Spanish: "fingir que no se entiende, pasarse por tonto". Véase la *Real Academia Española* (www.rae.es).

The 'Foreign Gaze' and the 'Local Gaze'

While until 1989 a visit to Cuba was the privilege of few, since the fall of the Eastern Bloc the Caribbean island has become one of the favorite tourist destinations, mostly for Canadians and Europeans. The premiere of Wim Wenders' documentary *Buena Vista Social Club* (1999) surely intensified this boom that Cuba has been experiencing for the past 20 years. Today, tourism is the most important source of income of foreign exchange in one of the last refuges of socialism. As a consequence, since 1989 and the subsequent opening of the country, the subject of tourism, and, with it, the interest in Otherness and the foreigner, are ever so present in Cuban cinema. Examples of this are movies like Fernando Pérez's *Life is to Whistle* (*La vida es silbar* 1998), in which, after a romantic encounter with a tourist, Elpidio, one of the four protagonists, decides to break ties with Cuba, and elope together with his lover in a balloon; Juan Carlos Tabío's *The Waiting List* (*Lista de espera* 2000), a movie in which a Spaniard wants to marry the central character; Fernando Pérez's Madagascar (1995) and Juan Carlos Cremata Malberti's *Nothing More* (*Nada* 2001), two movies in which the protagonists struggle between the dream of departure and their love for Cuba; Humberto Solás's *Honey for Oshún* (*Miel para Oshún* 2001) brings back a Cuban migrant to see the country through the eyes of a foreigner, or Juan Carlos Tabío's *So Far Away* (*Aunque estés lejos* 2002) where an encounter between Spaniards and Cubans serves to treat the subject of exile and return.

Although critics somewhat reproached Díaz Torres, saying that *Little Tropikana* and *Playing Swede* could encourage xenophobia, the director refutes this argument by stating that his aim is precisely the opposite: He wants to dismantle the image of tourists in Cuba that are treated, in his opinion, as "superior beings" (Schaefer, 2000, 12). As satirical comedies about tourism, the two movies distort and ironize the clichés that both Cubans and foreigners cultivate about each other: on the one side, the projection of Cuba as a Caribbean paradise – a paradise at once nostalgic, lost and contradictory in its pre-/anti-capitalism. And, on the other, the image of a foreigner who brings basically money, which is also a necessary evil, but also of someone one who must be wary of his Otherness, just as Amancio's explanations to Silvia, Pangloss's lover in *Little Tropikana*, illustrate:

> The relation to foreigners is a political problem, even more so with a man of this kind, provincial; because the German is in shady businesses with money. He's a fagot and a pervert. And you know that everything is known here. I never liked that guy; most likely his name isn't even Hermann, with his 'I didn't do it' face.[14]

But Díaz Torres does not limit the filmic representation of prejudice to his own countrymen, when he has Pangloss exclaim – as he's filming himself with his own camera – his skeptic description of his first impressions of life in the Caribbean island: "That's what my first day in Cuba was like: Odd people..."[15].

14 In Spanish: "La relación con los extranjeros es un problema político. Y más con un tipo de estos que es de provincia. Es que el alemán anda en negocios turbios con dinero. Es un marica, es un pervertido. Y tú sabes que aquí todo se sabe. Este tipo, que a lo mejor ni Hermann se llama, nunca me cayó bien. Con su carita de que 'yo no fui'".

15 In Spanish: "Así fue mi primer día en Cuba: Gente rara...".

The merit of *Playing Swede* resides in its contrasting the tricky appearance of a country of sun, rhythm and rum with the social reality of the Cuban population, which, faced with economic difficulties, brings characters like Concha, the hostess, to order four Coca-Colas at a dinner she's invited to by Otto/Björn, "because we never know what's yet to happen"[16]. Evidently, she does this because it is a product that is inaccessible to her in her daily life, and the Cuban audience has fun because they'd do the same. At the same time, themes like corruption, misery and, above all, the possibility to touch an abysmal bottom for a handful of dollars is present in the narrative of the film. The movie also denounces the prevailing racism in Cuba: three mulattoes from the cheap apartment complex where Otto/Björn lodges are accused of stealing the Swedish Crown jewels exposed at a museum in Havana. Even though everything indicates that the thief is really the European tourist, in Cuban society an image of black as bad and good as white prevails, therefore, a person from a Nordic country cannot commit crimes.

While in *Little Tropicana* the image of cultural differences still oscillates basically between the exotic and the folkloric, *Playing Swede* presents an intellectual gaze with a strong focus on cultural differences. Díaz Torres, through the figure of Otto/Björn, deconstructs the image of the honest foreigner to the point that even tourists are shocked: "I've been robbed in Barcelona, assaulted in Mexico, but damn, in Cuba, and by a guy that doesn't even speak Spanish… this is already damn much"[17]. Notwithstanding, his physical aspect as a tall blonde serves Otto/Björn to hide in a group of tourists with cameras after assaulting a Cuban citizen in broad daylight. When interviewed by the police, none of the foreigners can identify the nationality of the thief: "a Portuguese", "a Russian", "an Englishman"... Amancio, together with his dog Johnny, is the only one who suspects the "fake Swede". Despite his ambivalent posture and his rejection of Otto/Björn as a host in his house, the Cuban ex-cop imposes a strong regime in his complex, so that "the Swede [won't] get a bad impression from the country"[18]. In this way, the merit of both films by Díaz Torres lies in the representation of a self-reflecting attitude (Naficy, 201, p. 276), regarding what it means to be Cuban and the contrast created between stereotypes of 'the local' and 'the Other'. By exposing clichés in a critical manner, the director successfully evidences the gigantic gap between the socialist dream and reality at the height of crisis during the "Special Period in Time of Peace". From this asymmetry, constructed from his own gaze paired with an external one, this Cuban director manages to effectively integrate in national cinema the impact of a world increasingly determined by international traffic tourism and mobility, with the consequent mixture of cultures, in which, according to James Clifford, "the pure products go crazy" (1988, p. 1-17).

16 In Spanish: "(...) porque uno nunca sabe lo que puede pasar todavía".
17 In Spanish: "A mí me han robado en Barcelona, me han asaltado en México, pero joder, en Cuba, y un tío que ni siquiera habla el español... esto ya es la hostia...".
18 In Spanish: "el sueco [no] se lleve mala impresión del país".

The Accent of a Foreign Actor: Language and Subtitles

Little Tropikana and *Playing Swede* are movies that create and distort the clichés about life in the Caribbean island that motivate foreigners to travel to this country, and also about the foreigners that visit a country in the midst of a political and economic blockade. In both films by Díaz Torres, the performance of German actor Peter Lohmeyer, as Hermann Pangloss in *Little Tropikana* and as Otto/Björn in *Playing Swede*, stands out. The fact that a foreign actor gets to play the leading roles in two Cuban screenplays is particularly striking. Consequently, these co-productions weren't only successful in Cuba, but could also be seen in German-speaking countries – Germany, Switzerland, Austria –, and also helped put Cuban filmmaker Daniel Díaz Torres on the map on both sides of the Atlantic. For all the reasons hitherto stated, co-productions like *Little Tropikana* and *Playing Swede* are key examples of collaborations that go beyond the mere participation of foreign capital, and bring the transnational artistic collaboration to the eyes and ears of the public.

To carry out his roles as an actor in a Cuban movie, Peter Lohmeyer had to learn Spanish, although his performances in Díaz Torres's films weren't his first contact with Spanish-spoken cinema.[19] Before he began shooting, however, he wasn't aware of what the relevant linguistic proficiency would imply, as the actor expresses in an interview:

> In the 1997 Berlinale, Daniel Díaz Torres first invited me to participate in a Cuban movie, back when I couldn't speak a word of Spanish, so I asked him how we would be able to shoot. He answered: You only have to say about five sentences in Spanish. That's it; the rest will be in German and English. When I arrived in Cuba, this Cuban director told me: Something's changed. Now you have five sentences in German and the rest is in Spanish.[20]

While in *Little Tropikana* Lohmeyer, in the leading role of Pangloss, must frequently express himself both in Spanish and in German, as Otto/Björn in *Playing Swede* bilingualism doesn't play an important role; although it is very present in the film when, discovered by Amancio during the theft of the Swedish Crown jewels he exclaims in German: "Damn it! Why does he have to show up now? What is he doing here?"[21] In both films Peter Lohmeyer's German accent is well appreciated, expressly in his difficulty to pronounce the apical 'r', so characteristic to Spanish, when in the role of Pangloss he recounts his first experiences in Cuba: "Gente rara..."[22]. Especially in *Little Tropikana*, the protagonist makes mistakes typical to any Spanish learner, such as "Estoy viviendo a su casa"[23] or "Todo aquí es tan improvisible"[24], when it would be right to say "en su casa" and "imprevisible". His

19 Peter Lohmeyer played the role of migrant and German-Jewish musician Hermann Frisch in Gerardo Herrero's *Frontera sur* (1998), as well as the role of engineer Werfell in Montxo Armendáriz's *Obaba* (2005).

20 See „Interview mit Peter Lohmeyer: Der Cuba Coup", in: URL: http://www.digitalvd.de/interviews/Peter-Lohmeyer-Cuba-Coup.html (03.06.2012).

21 In German: „Verflixt! Warum muss der denn da auftauchen? Was hat er denn da zu suchen?"

22 English translation: "Odd people…".

23 English translation: "I am living to his house" instead of "at his house".

24 English translation: "Everything here is so unpredictable" instead of "unpredictable".

foreignness can also be perceived in several phonetic interferences, such as the wrong pronunciation of the noun "anti-fascista" in Spanish, mixed with the German word "Antifaschist"[25], or of the Spanish verb "registrar"[26] just as the letter "g" is pronounced in German before the vowel "i". These linguistic mistakes confer upon the characters of Hermann Pangloss and Otto/Björn their credibility as foreigners before the Cuban audience.

Another feature is the inclusion of short phrases or words in German, as in the scene in *Little Tropikana* in which Pangloss learns of his mother's past as a cabaret dancer at the Tropicana: "This cannot be true. I can't believe it"[27], or in the scene in which he is shown a film with dancers of the Tropicana cabaret, but the tape tears and Pangloss mutters in German: "Shit"[28]. Generally, the voice in German is left without subtitles for the non-German-speaking audience. But once, Commissioner Amancio asks for a translator to interpret a monologue by the protagonist, recorded in German in his own camera. While the voice of Pangloss is heard saying "It is incredible to love a Cuban woman"[29], the Spanish subtitles offer the wrong translation: "It is incredible to make love to a Cuban woman"[30]. The only character who tries to approach the German language is the young policeman Lorenzo, who in *Little Tropikana* tries to enter "Hermann's world, without knowing the language"[31]. While flipping the pages of a book in German on the history of the German Federal Republic, the camera focuses on the cover of an old book with the title *Hansel and Gretel*, and a woman's voice repeats the German words of the first audio-lesson of a language course.[32]

These facts make both movies 'Accented Co-productions', or, in other words, bi- or multilingual films, in which language use is a factor, at least in the Cuban editions without subtitles, that hinders the understanding of the movie (Naficy, 2001, p. 22 ss.). The lack of subtitles in films like *Little Tropikana* or *Playing Swede* is a frequent practice in movies devoted to the topic of migration, and it is meant to create a sensation of authenticity before the perception of Otherness. As North American theoretician David MacDougall states, subtitles may induce a fake sense of cultural affinity, "(...) since they so unobtrusively and efficiently overcome the difficulties of translation. They may reinforce the impression that it is possible to know others without effort – that the whole world is inherently knowable and accessible" (1998, p. 175). By omitting any subtitle, Díaz Torres isn't only avoiding a possible distraction of or absorption by the Spanish-speaking public who would be reading them, as is noted by another film theoretician Louis Giannetti (1999, p. 233-234), but also, he submerges the spectator into an authentic perception of Otherness when he doesn't understand what the leading characters Hermann Pangloss and Otto/Björn express in some brief sequences.

---

25 English translation: "antifascist".

26 English translation: "to register".

27 In German: „Das kann doch alles nicht wahr sein. Das glaub ich nicht."

28 In German: "Scheiße".

29 In German: "Es ist unglaublich eine Kubanerin zu lieben."

30 In Spanish: "Increíble realizar el amor con una cubana."

31 In Spanish: "el mundo de Hermann, sin conocer el idioma".

32 In *Little Tropikana,* there is also a character named Chrissy, a British national married in Cuba, performed by Luisa Pérez Nieto, who speaks a deficient Spanish with a strong British accent.

Local and Global Iconography

Finally, a determining factor in both co-productions by Díaz Torres is the integration of iconographic diversity. For this aim, and due to the lack of accessibility in Cuba, the director asked Peter Lohmeyer to bring an important part of the required elements from Germany, such as uniforms, Nazi paraphernalia and a full edition of *Pippi Longstocking* (Borchmeyer 2003). This is how *Little Tropikana* and *Playing Swede* successfully face the spectator with strong visual contrasts that intertwine the Cuban, German and Swedish imaginary. From images that in *Little Tropikana* evoke the Black Forrest with cuckoo clocks, dancers in traditional clothing and blonde braids, Nazi soldiers in front of swastika flag, developing a secret drug to turn the Third Reich into a global power, or Pangloss's father in a tassel hat dying to the rhythm of Cuban salsa; the constant evoking of the Central European country with its landscapes, its culture and history, gives this movie a touch of exoticism, since it is a very unusual iconography in Cuban cinema. As for sound-related aspects, the film contrasts traditional German music, the song Lili Marlene hummed by a Cuban in an elevator in Havana with Caribbean music, and integrates stereotypes that a foreign tourist associates with Cuba as a Caribbean island: Rumba dancers, salsa and the rhythm of drums.

In *Playing Swede* the images and stereotypes serve rather as satiric elements, when at the beginning as well as at the end of the film we see an open window in the center of Havana, while outside it is snowing. This irony based on stereotypes finds continuity in the detail that the protagonist Otto/Björn wears a t-shirt from a Swedish football team, and culminates with him giving an anthology of Pippi Longstocking to Alicia. In order to hide his true origin, he wears a Pippi-style mask with two upright braids to perform the theft of the jewels. According to the very director, these factors consecrate the assertion that "appearances deceive"[33] (Río, 2008). By merging in both comedies such diverse imaginaries, the iconography of his films also recurs to the concept of "traveling culture" (Clifford, 1997, p. 36), since they don't only make a theme out of the mobility of people between center/s and periphery/ies, but they also integrate it at an audio-visual level, as the platform for a reception beyond the limits of a national cinema.

'Accented Co-Production' as 'Global Localism'

Little Tropikana and *Playing Swede* are examples of co-productions that, according to José Manuel Palacio's classification, are constructed at a financial level, which is certainly true of the vast majority of these transnational collaborations. What brings these Cuban films to the forefront is that precisely because they are co-productions, they effectively illustrate the process of hybridization and transnationalization that Cuba undergoes since the 90s. An important factor is the dialogue between various national cinemas – in this case Cuban and European –, and the fact that it opens the possibility to a process of reconstruction of typologies ascribed to so-called 'national' characteristics, without questioning the stand of Cu-

33 In Spanish: "las apariencias engañan".

ban cinema as a 'national cinema'. As the theme of both movies, tourism provides the base for an intercultural dialogue that can be treated in 'Accented Co-productions'. By integrating a foreign actor, as well as the use of foreign languages and an iconography that fluctuates between the local, the global and the 'glocal' (Robertson, 1995, p. 28), both films by Díaz Torres approach Robert Stam's thesis, who considers cinema as the ideal artistic medium to express cultural hybridity (2000, p. 37). This is where Hamid Naficy's concept of 'Accented Cinema' lends itself to the theoretical analysis of this kind of co-productions, both at a narrative level, as well as at an audio-visual one. A co-production which is considered transnational is thus not limited to an economical agreement between companies seeking to capture an audience beyond the national. With the urban background of Havana *Little Tropikana* and *Playing Swede* oscillate between the domestic gaze, often incomprehensible to the viewer abroad, and the foreign gaze, alien to the Cuban spectator. Nonetheless, as mediating products, they advocate the reduction, or even the obliteration, of distances; especially *Playing Swede*, which culminates with the wedding of Otto/Björn to Alicia as an integrative factor. The merit as cinematographic production, just as Díaz Torres demonstrates with his accented 'global localism' (Dirlik, 1996, p. 21 ss.), rests in the ambivalence of the construction of collective identity, and the rupture with so-called 'official' stereotypes: "Key to trans nationalism is the recognition of the decline of national sovereignty as a regulatory force in global coexistence" (Ezra/Rowden, 2006, p. 1).

BIBLIOGRAPHY

Borchmeyer, F. (2003). "Nichts ist fiktiver als das Leben selbst". In: *The International Artist Database*, URL: http://www.culturebase.net/artist.php?740 (03.06.2012).

Bremme, B. *MOVIE-mientos. Der lateinamerikanische Film: Streiflichter von unterwegs*. Stuttgart: Schmetterling Verlag, 2000.

Caballero, R. (ed.). *Producción, coproducción e intercambio de cine entre España, América Latina y el Caribe*. Fundación Carolina GeALCI, 2006, URL http://www.fundacioncarolina.es (03.06.2012).

Castillo, L. "Cuban Cinema Beyond Strawberries and Chocolate". In: Russo, Eduardo A. *The Film Edge. Contemporary Filmmaking in Latin America*. Buenos Aires: Teseo, 2010, p. 81-104.

Chanan, M. *Cuban Cinema*. Minneapolis, Minn.: University of Minnesota Press (Cultural Studies of the Americas Series, Vol. 13), 2003.

Clifford, J. "Introduction: The pure products go crazy". In: Ibid. *The predicament of Culture: Twentieth-Century Ethnography, Literature and Art*. Cambridge, Mass.: Harvard University Press, 1988, p. 1-17.

Clifford, J. *Routes. Travel and Translation in the Late Twentieth Century*. Cambridge, Mass.: Harvard University Press, 1997.

Crofts, S. "Reconceptualizing National Cinema/s". In: Willemen, P. / Vitali, V. (eds.). *Theorising National Cinema*. New Brunswick: Rutgers University Press, 2006, p. 44-58.

Crystal, D. *A Dictionary of Linguistics and Phonetics*. New York: Blackwell, 1991.

D'Lugo, M. "The new identity of Latin American Cinema". In: Gunerate, A. R. / Dissanayake, W. (eds.). *Rethinking Third Cinema*. London/New York: Routledge, 2000, p. 103-125.

Dirlik, A. "The Global in the Local". In: Wilson, R. / Dissanayake, W. (eds.). *Global/Local: Cultural Production and the Transnational Imaginary*. Durham/London: Duke University Press, 1996, p. 21-45.

Ezra, E. / Rowden, T. "General Introduction: What is Transnational Cinema?" In: Ibid. (eds.). *Transnational Cinema. The Film Reader*. New York: Routledge, 2006, p. 1-12.

García Borrero, J. A. *Guía crítica del cine cubano de ficción*. La Habana: Editorial Arte y Literatura, 2001.

García Borrero, J. A. *La edad de la herejía*. Santiago de Cuba: Editorial Oriente, 2002.

Giannetti, L. *Understanding Movies*. New Jersey: Prentice Hall, 1999.

Hannerz, U. "The Local and the Global: Continuity and Change". In: Ibid. *Transnational Connections: Culture, People, Places*. London/New York: Routledge, 1996, p. 17-29.

Hernández Morales, S. L. *Cine Cubano. El camino de las coproducciones*. Santiago de Compostela: Universidad de Santiago de Compostela. PhD Tesis 2007. URL: http://bdigital.unipiaget.cv:8080/jspui/handle/123456789/242 (03.06.2012).

Higson, A. "The Concept of National Cinema". In: Williams, A. (ed.). *Film and Nationalism*. New Brunswick: Rutgers University Press, 2002 [1989], p. 52-67.

Hjort, M. / MacKenzie, S. (eds.). *Cinema and Nation*. London/New York: Routledge, 2000.

Hoefert de Turégano, T. "The International Politics of Cinematic Coproduction: Spanish Policy in Latin America". *Film & History: An Interdisciplinary Journal of Film and Television Studies* 34.2 (2004), p. 15-24.

MacDougall, D. *Transcultural Cinema*. Princeton: Princeton University Press, 1998.

Muñoz-Aunión, M. "Viendo las cosas como son *Preludio 11/Operación Cucaña*. Una coproducción del ICAIC y de la DEFA". In: Gremels, A. / Spiller, R. (eds.). *Cuba: La Revolución revis(it)ada*. Tübingen: Narr, 2010, p. 231-240.

Naficy, H. *An Accented Cinema. Exilic and Diasporic Filmmaking*. Princeton, New Jersey: Princeton University Press, 2001.

Palacio, J. M. "Elogio posmoderno de las coproducciones". In: Biblioteca Virtual Miguel de Cervantes (2002), URL: http://www.cervantesvirtual.com/ (03.06.2012).

Río, J. del. "Cine cubano del siglo XXI. Tenue autoría, se imponen los géneros". *Revista Cine Cubano Online* 9 (2008), URL: http://www.cubacine.cult.cu/revistacinecubano/digital09/cap02.htm (03.06.2012).

Robertson, R. "Glocalization: Time-space and homogeneity-heterogeneity". In: Featherstone, M. / Lash, S. / Robertson, R. (eds.), *Global Modernities*. London: Sage, 1995, p. 25-44.

Sánchez, S. "Cubano, latinoamericanista de vocación universal". *La Jiribilla. Revista Digital de Cultura Cubana* (2004), URL: http://www.lajiribilla.co.cu/2004/n151_03.html (03.06.2012).

Schaefer, J. "Von falschen Schweden und getürkter Sozialkritik". *Berliner Zeitung*, Feuilleton (16.12.2012).

Stam, R. "Beyond Third Cinema: the aesthetics of hybridity". In: Gunerate, A. R. / Dissanayake, W. (eds.). *Rethinking Third Cinema*. New York: Routledge, 2000, p. 31-48.

Worthman, M. "Die sich zum Schweden machen". *Die Zeit* 52 (2000), URL: http://zeus.zeit.de/text/archiv/2000/52/200052_kuba.xml (03.06.2012).

BETWEEN BRITAIN AND AUSTRALIA: *ORANGES AND SUNSHINE*

Miya Komori-Glatz

"This was one of the few genuinely 50-50 co-productions in terms of its creative heart. It's a true UK/Australian story."[1] Emile Sherman is better known for his Academy Award-winning, unofficial UK/Australian coproduction, *The King's Speech* (Tom Hooper, 2010)[2]. While this was perhaps the quintessential English movie with Australian characters, actors and filmmakers playing a surprisingly prominent role, Sherman's other film of the same year, *Oranges and Sunshine* (Jim Loach 2010), represents a unique – and much more balanced – collaboration between Britain and Australia. A similarly little-known, yet historically true story, *Oranges and Sunshine* portrays the Nottingham social worker Margaret Humphreys' (Emily Watson) quest to unravel the mystery of the 'Forgotten Children' – child migrants, in many cases 'stolen' from their parents, sent from Britain to populate the large island from the 1920s right up until the late 1960s.

In contrast to *The King's Speech*, however, *Oranges and Sunshine* is both an official UK/Australia co-production, and, as Sherman says, a film that draws deeply on both Britain and Australia in terms of context, setting, production, and impact. This article will begin by outlining the UK-Australia co-production treaty, embedding it in the context of turn-of-the-century British and Australian film economics, and then focus on *Oranges and Sunshine* as a model of co-operation between the two film industries. The various aspects of producing this film will then be analysed to show how the cinematographic background of the cast and crew influenced the final feature.

The UK-Australia Co-Production Treaty

British cinema, despite its important role in the evolution of the industry, has had a rocky relationship with filmmakers from other countries ever since the start of commercial cinema at the beginning of the twentieth century (Street, 1997, p. 5). Consequently, it has enjoyed comparatively strong state support starting in the late 1920s, largely in an attempt to defend it against the strong influence of American productions. In fact, the Cinematographic Films Act, 1927, shared many of the stipulations of today's Cultural Test (which official British co-productions pass automatically), such as being made by a British subject or company, shooting and incurring a certain amount of labour costs within Britain or – notably – the Empire (Street, 1997, p. 7). Incidentally, however, this meant that a number of films classified under the Act as British could in fact be considered co-productions. In particu-

1 www.orangesandsunshine.com.au (under Cast & Crew/Emile Sherman).
2 http://www.kingsspeech.com/index.html

lar, the UK film industry's relationship with the US, which improved due to political pressure during the Second World War and afterwards (Street, 1997, p. 11-15), has varied throughout the decades, with American producers enjoying the benefits of the strong dollar and Britain's funding packages and UK production companies taking advantage of American financing during the good times (Street, 1997, p. 21), and the smaller British industry feeling the threat of its much larger American counterpart at others. Crucially, the UK and the US have never entered into an official co-production arrangement, leaving other countries, and particularly the various forms of the European cultural common market, to provide more reliable sources of funding. The UK was one of the first countries to enter into official co-production agreements, and signed its first with Canada in 1975[3]. By the late 1980s, the Commission of the European Communities' MEDIA 92 EFDO scheme had been developed "to remove the barriers from national markets and to initiate cross-frontier cooperation" (Humphreys, 1996, p. 280). This formed the basis for the European Convention on Cinematographic Co-Production, which Britain signed in 1992, ratified in 1993 and which entered into force in 1994.[4]

Australia's film industry began surprisingly early, boasting several "firsts", such as *The History of the Kelly Gang* (Charles Tait, 1906), a very Australian film from content to form (aspects which will be discussed later in this article), widely claimed to be the world's first feature-length film (Rout, 1999, p. 473; Rayner, 2000, p. 4). Even more so than the British film industry, the burgeoning Australian cinema suffered greatly from the dominance of Hollywood and other American productions, as well as its colonial parent. While it often provided "an exotic backdrop" for British and American films (MacFarlane/Mayer/Bertrand, 1999, p. vii), Australian producers themselves "saw little activity from the 1930s until the late 1960s" (French, 2001, p. 18; see also Rayner, 2000, p. 6). While Australian documentary and newsreels thrived, feature films were barely produced. However, "the revival of the Australian feature film industry in the 1970s coincided with the world-wide surge of interest in film culture and in new ways of considering the production, perception, and reception of film" (MacFarlane/Mayer/Bertrand, 1999, p. vii). As a result, while Australia took longer to seek out co-production agreements due to its late re-entry into cinematographic production, it was relatively quick to enter into its first with France in 1986[5]. This was followed by the UK-Australia co-production treaty, which was signed on 12 June 1990 and entered into force on 27 August[6], just before the treaty with Canada a month later[7]. Perhaps surprisingly, it was also only the second of the UK's eight bilateral treaties still active today[8], and concluded just before Britain's ratification of the European Convention in 1992.

3 http://www.ukfilmcouncil.org.uk/media/pdf/p/9/UK-Canada_consolidated.pdf

4 http://conventions.coe.int/Treaty/Commun/ChercheSig.asp?NT=147&CM=8&DF=02/12/2009&CL=ENG

5 http://www.screenaustralia.gov.au/coproductions/partner_countries/france.aspx

6 The full treaty can be read here: http://www.ukfilmcouncil.org.uk/media/pdf/8/9/UK-Australia_1990.pdf or http://www.sa-minihost.com/coproductions/copro-documents/Treaty_UK.pdf

7 http://www.screenaustralia.gov.au/coproductions/partner_countries/canada.aspx

8 http://www.ukfilmcouncil.org.uk/coproduction

As of September 2011, the total number of official co-productions between the UK and Australia was 38, including one three-way co-production with Canada and 20 feature films, of which one was *Oranges and Sunshine*. It is interesting to note that, while unofficial co-productions and inward investment from the US play a very strong role in the Britain film industry, official co-productions in both the Australia and the UK are, in financial terms, almost equally as important as the respective domestic film production. For example, in the 2010/2011 financial year, the total budget for the 10 domestic (Australian) films amounted to $52m (£34m/€41.5m), of which $50m (£32.98m/€39.89m) was expenditure. The 4 co-productions made in the same period, though not all in co-operation with British producers, represented a slightly higher budget of $67m (£44.2m/€53.47m), with expenditure in Australia of $37m (£24.4m/€29.52m) (Screen Australia, 2011, p. 4). Similarly, official UK co-productions accounted for £32.9m (€39.89m), roughly equivalent to a spend by domestic (i.e. UK only) films of £38.9m (€47.06m) (BFI, 2011, p. 2).

The total budget of UK/Australian co-productions up to 2011 was A$431.6 million (approx. £285.38m/€344.6m), with the contribution of each country ranging from a minimum of 30% to a maximum of 70%.[9] The minimum of 30% investment from each country is stipulated by the Treaty itself (UK-Australia Co-Production Treaty, 1991, Annex (8)). In return, having official co-production status allows the producers to apply for BFI funding and "the benefits of the UK's tax relief system" in the UK[10] as well as production investment from Screen Australia and access to producer offset[11]. Furthermore, official co-production status grants a film British or Australian status, allowing it to take advantage of these benefits without having to pass the British "Cultural Test"[12] or the "significant Australian content test"[13], respectively. These require that a film's subject, story, location, actors and filmmakers as well as a proportion of the various stages and aspects of production can be classified as British and/or Australian (ibid). Additionally, the co-production treaty stipulates that the "performing, technical and craft contribution of each co-producer to a co-production film shall be in reasonable proportion to each of the co-producer's financial participation" (UK-Australia Co-Production Treaty, 1991, Annex (7)).

Oranges and Sunshine

In a brief interview on the film's official website, Camilla Bray, one of the producers from the British side, states: "Because it was such an Australian/British story with Margaret travelling between the two countries we knew from the outset that we were going to make it as a co-production."[14] Bray works for Sixteen Films, a

9 http://www.screenaustralia.gov.au/coproductions/partner_countries/uk_and_northern_ireland.aspx; see also §8 of the Annex of the UK/Australia Co-Production Agreement.
10 http://www.ukfilmcouncil.org.uk/coproduction
11 http://www.sa-minihost.com/coproductions/prod_undertaking.aspx
12 http://www.ukfilmcouncil.org.uk/culturaltest
13 http://www.sa-minihost.com/producer_offset/eligibility_SAC.aspx
14 http://www.orangesandsunshine.com.au (under Cast & Crew/Camilla Bray)

production company formed by Ken Loach, the well-known father of *Oranges and Sunshine*'s director Jim. Emile Sherman's London/Sydney-based production company See-Saw, producers of *The King's Speech*, proved to be the "really solid partner" (ibid) she was looking for to manage production on the other side of the world. "We put together a pretty complex financing structure involving national tax incentives, regional funding in both the UK and Australia, private equity, pre-sales, gap, and equity investment from Screen Australia" (ibid). Sherman adds:

> [W]e shot in South Australia, in Adelaide, and ended up using quite a lot of the Adelaide crew and supporting cast as well. […] Adelaide felt like it was going to be the best environment to be able to capture the time [1980s Perth, Western Australia.] [...] That combined with the crews there, and the fact that the South Australian Film Corporation provided some good support in terms of equity investment made it the right place.[15]

Curiously, this comment reflects the principle of co-production at a regional level, while at a higher level, the film-makers were keen to reflect the financial and creative input from both countries in the final feature. In an interview with an Australian freelance movie critic, director Jim Loach emphasised the importance of filming in the relevant country:

> Obviously there was pressure to do it all in England, or all in Australia, or at least the majority in one or the other. But we were really determined to represent the English scenes in England, and the Australian scenes in Australia, because that it [sic] at the heart of the story.
>
> So we did about 15 days in Nottingham, a couple of days in London, and then we moved everybody over to Adelaide and carried on shooting for 3 weeks, and then moved out to the Flinders Ranges, and finished up there.[16]

In the director's commentary among the extras on the DVD, Loach also explains that they wanted to emphasise the distance – and difference – between England and Australia through the change in the light and the landscape. In particular, Loach wanted to show that "Margaret being at home in this landscape and at odds in the landscape that she discovers and, similarly, the people she meets [are] at odds in the landscape here, although it's their homeland, you know, in Britain" (Oranges and Sunshine, Director's commentary, 0:10:23-0:10:42). Although presumably unintentional, the use of "authentic" Australian and British cast and location in accordance with the co-production treaty's stipulation of sufficient local input from each country did, in fact, support this aim: in their commentary, Loach recalls, "The Australian members of the unit were so cold", with scriptwriter Rona Munro adding, "They couldn't believe it, could they?" (0:04:28-30; 39). Similarly, Emily Watson, who plays Margaret, remembers

> [a]ll the Australian crew were shivering and complaining! It starts getting dark almost after lunch and the light is so completely different from Australia. But I think that realy

15 http://www.orangesandsunshine.com.au (under Cast & Crew/Emile Sherman)

16 http://www.mattsmoviereviews.net/spotlight-interview-oranges-and-sunshine.html (n.d.): An Interview with Oranges and Sunshine Director Jim Loach. Matt's Movie Reviews/Matthew Pejkovic

> reflects the nature of the film, the nature of the story and that sense of dislocation that a person must feel who's constantly travelling between the two – it was tough.[17]

The British actors, in turn, had trouble not only adjusting to Australia's immense heat, but also its troublesome insects:

> Munro: I remember you also saying that the Australian actors were much more relaxed about it than the Brits.
>
> Loach: The flies, yeah. It was incredibly hot when we shot this scene. I mean, I think it was mid-40s, 45 degrees. It was sensationally hot. (1:30:54-1:31:10)

Financing and Location

As already mentioned, location was partly determined by the real story, partly by the physical reality of the locations set twenty years earlier, and partly by the financing. In Humphrey's account of her struggle to help the child migrants, *Empty Cradles*, she acknowledges the considerable support that Nottingham County Council has given to her and the Child Migrants' Trust (Humphreys, 2011, p. 10). Similarly – and in accordance with Loach's desire to use authentic locations the East Midlands Development Agency provided financing for the film through EM Media, amounting to some £125,000. EM Media also secured £25,000 from the National Lottery[18] (through the UK Film Council) with the remaining funding from the UK coming from BBC Films and the British media investment company Ingenious Films Limited.

> The Australian funding component was larger than its UK counterpart [...], with support from Screen Australia, Screen NSW and the SAFC [South Australia Film Corporation]. The Producer Offset was cash-flowed by See-Saw Films' sister company Fulcrum Media Finance.[19]

The ABC (Australian Broadcasting Corporation), whose managing director until 1995, David Hill, was himself a child migrant[20], did not provide any direct financing, although it had previously co-produced a miniseries on the child migrants, *The Leaving of Liverpool* (Michael Jenkins, 1992), with the BBC. However, the ABC did support the project by allowing the film-makers to use their original 1980s Australian studios:

> Loach: God bless the ABC.
> Munro: Giving you a period television studio.
> Loach: And also a period radio station. (Director's commentary, 0:47:23-25)

From a cinematographic point of view, the different locations required very different handling, particularly as Loach and his colleagues felt it was important to stress the geographical and emotional distance between them. "The picture edit was

17 http://www.orangesandsunshine.com.au (under Cast & Crew/Emily Watson)
18 http://www.em-media.org.uk/pages/news/article?C50E4423-B5F7-4BFA-96B9-81C3C24FFB11
19 http://www.encoremagazine.com.au/a-new-hope-oranges-and-sunshine-9068
20 http://www.abc.net.au/queensland/conversations/stories/s1922409.htm

done in the UK and the rest of the post-production in Australia", while Sherman "put together a team of Australian heads of department".[21] This included the DOP Denson Baker, who described the style of the film thus:

> We wanted it to start as an intimate story about this woman who's living her life and then gets launched on this whole involuntary hero's journey, so the film starts to get bigger and more epic as she starts to get embroiled in what we saw as a detective story. So at times we have a bit more of a documentary feel: there's a lot of shooting off the shoulder, a lot of handheld in there. But at other times it'll be more epic, with the occasional crane shot or a little dolly shot. That really takes the audience into the scene and lets them know they're going on a big screen journey. (Russo, 2011, p. 20)

Accordingly, the majority of the scenes filmed in England are enclosed and often intimate: the room where Margaret's Triangle therapy group meets; the archives at St Catherine's House; Margaret's home; in a train or a car; the homes of the mothers. Occasionally the shot opens out to show a street, or the sky, but there are few scenes which do not show buildings or interiors or some sort. In contrast, the scenes filmed in Australia depend much more on the landscape and include several wide shots of the outback and/or the ocean, simultaneously typifying the 'image' of Australia – recalling the (false) promises of a better life for the children, who were often taken from deprived areas, tenements and slums – and drawing on the more epic tendencies of Australian film.

Ross Gibson notes that "the land was represented as the thing that sets Australia apart from the rest of the world" (Gibson, 1999, p. 255). Consequently, the immediately identifiable landscape of outback and ocean features prominently in Australian film and is closely linked to Australian identity. The natural landscape is, in fact, such a marker of cultural identity that four out of the eight lines of the first verse of the Australian national anthem describe the country's natural beauty:

> *Australians all let us rejoice,For we are young and free;*
> *We've golden soil and wealth for toil;Our home is girt by sea;*
> *Our land abounds in nature's gifts*
> *Of beauty rich and rare;*
> *In history's page, let every stage*
> *Advance Australia Fair.*[22]

He continues:

> The country has persisted right up to the present as a mythic cinematic force. By portraying an awesome landscape that simultaneously defines and alienates Australians, film-makers have tried to offer an affirmative, dramatic way to live with the contradictions of our being part of a society that still remembers the estrangement of arriving here even at the same time as we yearn to celebrate a birthright of our arising here. Alienation and powerlessness might define the way we inhabit the country but, in the logic of myth, the grandeur of the setting justifies the continuation of the drama of struggling to create a new culture here. (Gibson, 1999, p. 255-6).

Tara Brabazon also talks about "fetishised outback panoramas" (Brabazon, 2011, p. 148) while Raynor states that:

---

21 http://www.encoremagazine.com.au/a-new-hope-oranges-and-sunshine-9068
22 http://www.dfat.gov.au/facts/nat_anthem.html

> The use of the landscape as an index of nationality [...] epitomises a trend within Australian filmmaking since the revival. The unique Australian environment is foregrounded in numerous productions as the landscape shaping the (masculine) national type, as the primary influence upon the development of national character, and as a distinctive resource or selling point to be used to an aesthetic and commercial advantage. (Rayner, 2000, p. 117)

Thus it is easy to see how the filmmakers' decision to highlight the open ocean and outback landscapes (and light) of the Australian scenes in *Oranges and Sunshine* draws naturally on Australian film tradition, while the British scenes are more concerned with urban settings and the problems that arise from them – council housing, government offices and so on (this will be covered in more detail shortly). In his commentary, Loach explains that water is "a big visual theme for us in this film because obviously [the child migrants] all came on boats" (0:51:29), and many of the key scenes in Australia play out against a backdrop of a sparkling ocean – in many ways truly the visual manifestation of the Australian dream and in stark contrast to cold, grey, urban Nottingham.

While the camerawork and aesthetics of portraying the landscape pay tribute to Australian filmic tradition, however, the uneasiness Gibson perceives is much stronger in *Oranges and Sunshine* than in many Australian films. It is true that they are grappling with the landscape and their identities while trying to come to grips with how the landscape has shaped them. In some cases, such as the boys from Bindoon, a Catholic institution where the migrant children were forced to build the massive neo-Gothic orphanage, making brick and hauling stones by hand, they literally carry the scars of the landscape on their bodies as well as their psyches. When Margaret goes to visit Bindoon with one of the child migrants, Len, in the film, she sees it first from a bird's-eye-view panorama of the beautiful but brutal European building sitting uncomfortably among the dry, dusty environment of the "sunburnt country"[23]. The flashbacks to the horrific tales told to her by the former residents of Bindoon put a very different perspective on the "grandeur of the setting [which] justifies the continuation of the drama of struggling to create a new culture here". Humphreys writes: "This wasn't about giving kids a new start in life. It was a blatant piece of pragmatic social and religious engineering to fill rural Australia with bright, white British stock" (Humphreys, 2011, p. 278).

There is, of course, a certain irony that this echoes Gibson's statement that "it is the White Australian landscape tradition that has sustained the Australian film industry" (Gibson, 1999, p. 255). Incidentally, it is good to note that both Emile Sherman's earlier film *Rabbit-Proof Fence* (Philip Noyce 2002) and the eminent director (*William Shakespeare's Romeo + Juliet* 1996, *Moulin Rouge!* 2001) Baz Luhrmann's latest offering *Australia* (2008) are the beginnings of an attempt to address this somewhat by portraying another generation of 'stolen' children, this time of Aboriginal origin, although that is a topic for another article. Nevertheless, the classic situation of the fish out of water finds an ideal context in the Australian landscape which is so often seen as 'exotic' through White directors' eyes. In *Oranges and Sunshine*, Loach uses many of the topoi typical of the Australian film

23 A popular poetic tribute to Australia by Dorothea MacKellar: http://allpoetry.com/poem/8526595-My_Country-by-Dorothea_Mackellar

tradition to highlight the otherness of the country both for his English characters, like Margaret, and for the migrants who grew up with the landscape but have not learnt to identify with it. The natural surroundings, particularly the ocean, the bush and the light, are shown much more frequently and emphasised with 'epic' wide shots and panoramas. The characters are portrayed as struggling to deal with their environment and to form a sense of self based upon it.

However, the representation and use of the landscape also highlights the collaborative nature of *Oranges and Sunshine* and its combination of Australian and British filmmakers. It can be argued that alongside the 'typically Australian' landscape shots there is a much greater focus on the characters as individuals. Since the migrant children are only half-citizens of the country which has adopted and abused them, this is a very uneasy cohabitation. Thus in contrast to the classic shots of vast, empty landscape typical of Australian film, wide shots of a magnificent ocean or bush are interrupted by a close-up of a character's head in the foreground or a flashback to an interview or a disturbing recollection. The next section will argue that these 'psychological portraits' superimposed on the 'Australian' landscapes are a much more strongly British trait, and that the merging of these creates a "genuinely 50/50 co-production in terms of its creative heart".

Character and Genre

While an in-depth discussion of genre is well beyond the scope of this article[24], director Jim Loach's cinematographic background may help to explain both the choice of material and the handling of it. As the son of the noted British director Ken Loach (*Kes* 1969, *Land and Freedom* 1995), it is perhaps unsurprising that the uncomfortable theme of *Oranges and Sunshine* could be regarded as falling under the broad scope of the 'social realist' genre. A director known for linking "art and left-wing politics" (Leigh, 2002, p. 1), Loach Sr. began making films in the 1960s, in the wake of British New Wave cinema, an era of "kitchen-sink" drama and "cultural authenticity in the period's spirit of sociological enquiry" (Street, 1997, p. 78-80). Though Jim "swore he would never follow his father into film-making"[25], it is hard to deny this influence, particularly as *Oranges and Sunshine* scriptwriter Rona Munro also worked with Ken (*Ladybird, Ladybird* 1994). Like *Oranges and Sunshine*, Ken's films often take the form of "fictional journalism" or "'dramatised documentaries'" (Leigh, 2002, p. 39;40) and follow an individual on a "quest narrative" (Leigh, 2002, p. 143) against a background of social or political troubles. At the time Jim began making *Oranges and Sunshine*, the migrant children were still 'forgotten' and the real Margaret Humphreys was fighting against what seemed to be a massive conspiracy involving not just the British and Australian governments but also the (primarily Catholic) Church and several reputable charitable organisations. Just under a year before the film was released, both the Australian and then

24 See Goldsmith, 2010 and Moran/Vieth, 2006, p. 1-12 for an overview of genre and genre research in Australian film; and Street, 1997, p. 28-113 for an overview of genre in British film.

25 http://www.guardian.co.uk/film/2011/mar/31/jim-loach-oranges-and-sunshine?intcmp=239

the British government issued a formal apology to the child migrants.[26] However, there has been little compensation and, for most of the 'children' who are now in their 40s and 50s, time is running out to be reunited with living parents. Thus, like his father, Jim decided to highlight the very real consequences of a brutal social situation through the story of an individual: "Right at the outset we had a sense of how we were going to approach it: it was very much Margaret's story. It was going to be Margaret the character and seen through her eyes." (Russo 2011)

Finally, Jim's own directorial experience in British soap operas such as *Coronation Street* also indicates an occupation with portraying social issues at a personal level. "One of the characteristics of British television is the way in which the home-produced soaps have undertaken a realist function in their representation of British society," writes Christine Geraghty. In particular,

> [*Coronation Street*]'s story-lines tended to emphasize the drama of human relationships rather than the exemplification of social issues. While problems were placed firmly in a social context, it was the characters who drove the plots and set limits on what stories could be worked through them. (Geraghty, 1995, p. 66)

When asked how the script had evolved, Loach explained:

> It was also quite a challenging scripting process because of course the real events happened over a very long period of time, so we had to find a way of shaping it into a coherent, singular narrative. It was one of those stories that you could go spinning off into all sorts of different areas – you could look at the involvement of the Catholic Church, or you could look at the role of the state in caring for so-called less privileged people. We had to home in on our story.[27]

In contrast, while Tom O'Regan argues that Australian drama has a "tendency to 'social observation' which relies on socially recognizable types, cultural stereotypes which play on recognition" (O'Regan, 1996, quoting Meaghan Morris, p. 226), it is "often less interested in 'psychological characterization' or the 'moral dimension' than with stereotyping and organizing the resulting 'types into relationships which highlight opposition'" (O'Regan, 1996, again quoting Morris, p. 225). With regard to *Oranges and Sunshine*, it could be argued that Len (David Wenham), the main Aussie character, does – to a certain extent – represent the rather one-dimensional "essential Australian" described by Russell Ward as

> male, working-class, sardonic, laconic, loyal to his mates, unimpressed by rank, an improviser, non-conformist and so on. These virtues are defined and refined under the hard conditions of the bush, workplace, war or sport, in which women, and the feminine qualities, are considered to be beside the point. (quoted in Rayner, 2000, p. 95)

However, even he is shown as desperate to trace his mother, having spent large amounts of money on private investigations; though a tough, brash and sometimes abrasive personality, a self-made entrepreneur, Margaret picks up on his well-hidden lack of self-worth and need for approval:

> Len: Well, no-one can say I owe them anything.

26 These apologies can be found at: http://pmrudd.archive.dpmc.gov.au/node/6321 and http://www.parliament.uk/business/news/2010/02/prime-ministers-statement-child-migration/ (accessed 27.12.11)

27 http://www.femail.com.au/jim-loach-oranges-and-sunshine-crew-interviews.htm

Margaret: No, I don't think you do. But maybe that's the monster living in your head. I don't like the idea of you walking around with a monster like that in your head. (0:54:06-0:54:25)

Thus even the 'stereotypical' characters are portrayed as being fully-rounded with a sometimes uncomfortable psychological development. Far from a fairytale happy-ever-after where he wins the girl over (as quintessential Australian hillbilly *Crocodile Dundee* does in uptown New York), Len's only concern is to make Margaret understand, and to persuade her to find his mother. And even when she does, their reunion is not marked by tears and hugs and teddy bears (as some of the others are). In fact, it is not shown at all, and the camera cuts back to Margaret as Len enters his mother's house for the first time (1:04:46). The lead-in to the credits informs the viewers that he is "still trying to build a relationship with his mother" (1:36:31). The other main male character, Jack (Hugo Weaving), is almost a foil to the "essential Australian" in many ways: though not at all effeminate, he is gentle, shy and sensitive, and it is in fact he who sets the ball rolling by contacting his long-lost sister, who attends Margaret's adoptee therapy group, through the Salvation Army.

Curiously, Hugo Weaving himself grew up between Australia and Britain (although not as an adoptee or a child migrant). In an interview with the Sydney Morning Herald in 2006, he said:

> I'm 'of the world'. There was a time when I thought, 'Oh, I must go back to England. I feel English.' Then I went and the longer I was away, the more Australian I felt. Now, I've come back here and I don't feel entirely Australian. But I certainly feel like this is my country.[28]

Otherwise, the cast is largely either 'authentically' English – sometimes even from Nottingham itself (such as Aisling Loftus, who plays a minor character called Susie) – or Australian. Of the latter, some are quite renowned for being part of Australia's film heritage (Tara Morice, for example, played the female protagonist "Fran" in Baz Luhrmann's first hit movie *Strictly Ballroom*), and in both countries, the actors come mainly from television and even soap operas, which, as already seen above, has an equally if not stronger cultural identity in the country of origin than film. Emily Watson, of course, is one of Britain's finest independent actresses, twice nominated for an Oscar (for her performances in *Breaking the Waves* and *Hilary and Jackie*) and top of Loach's "fantasy cast" (DVD Extras, Interview for BFI, 0:09:37).

"A Genuinely 50/50 Co-Production"

The (true) story behind *Oranges and Sunshine* is an extraordinary one, spanning thousands of miles and several decades. The film itself is no less extraordinary, with its mix of drama and truth, new and experienced personnel – including some of both Britain and Australia's finest feature actors as well as lesser-known television

28 http://www.smh.com.au/news/film/quiet-achiever/2006/04/02/1143916400860.html?page=5

actors – creative talent from the UK and Australia, and an enormous amount of funding from a wide variety of sources.

While official co-productions in Britain and Australia are generally substantially outnumbered by films made with inward investment – particularly from the US – they represent a similar contribution to their respective economies to domestic productions. The UK-Australia co-production treaty signed in 1990 was an early contribution to the encouragement of official international involvement and governmental support for this.

Taking advantage of the terms of this treaty, which allow production companies to benefit from local funding and tax rebates, *Oranges and Sunshine* is not only an official co-production in terms of funding but, as Sherman claims, a "genuinely 50/50 co-production in terms of its creative heart". As well as using locations, cast and crew from both countries, it can be argued that there is a convergence of cinematographic styles such as the superimposition of individualistic psychological characters on the landscape. It is true that the original child migrants, now adult, are torn between the country that took them in but did not adopt them, and the country they consider home but which they no longer know. By portraying the deep psychological divide these men feel, the filmmakers of *Oranges and Sunshine* have created a model of cinematographic co-operation.

More information about The Child Migrants Trust can be found at www.childmigrantstrust.com.

BIBLIOGRAPHY

BFI [British Film Institute]. *Film Production in the UK, first half year (H1) 2011*. BFI Research and Statistics Unit (2011), URL: http://www.bfi.org.uk/filmtvinfo/stats/H1-2011-Production-Report.pdf (05.01.2012).

Brabazon, T. "A Pig in Space? Babe and the Problem of Landscape". In: Craven, I. (ed.). *Australian Cinema in the 1990s*. London/Portland: Frank Cass,2011, p. 149-158.

French, L. "Patterns of Production and Policy: The Australian Film Industry in the 1990s." In: Craven, I. (ed.). *Australian Cinema in the 1990s*. London/Portland: Frank Cass, 2011, p. 15-36.

Geraghty, C. "Social issues and realist soaps: A study of British soaps in the 1980s/1990s". In: Allen, R. C. (ed.). *To be continued... Soap operas around the world*. London/New York: Routledge, 1995, p. 66-80.

Gibson, R. "Landscape". In: MacFarlane, B. / Mayer, G. / Bertrand, I. (eds.). *The Oxford Companion to Australian Film*. Oxford: Oxford University Press, 1999, p. 254-256.

Goldsmith, B. "Introduction: Australian Cinema". In: Goldsmith, B. / Lealand, G. (eds.). *Directory of World Cinema: Australia and New Zealand*. Bristol/Chicago: Intellect Books, 2010, p. 9-22.

Humphreys, M. *Empty Cradles*. London: Corgi, 2011.

Humphreys, P. *Mass media and media policy in Western Europe*. Manchester: Manchester University Press, 1996.

Leigh, J. *The Cinema of Ken Loach: art in the service of the people*. London/New York: Wallflower Press, 2002.

MacFarlane, B. / Mayer, G. / Bertrand, I. (eds.). *The Oxford Companion to Australian Film*. Oxford: Oxford University Press, 1999.
Moran, A. / Vieth, E. *Film in Australia: An Introduction*. Cambridge: CUP. 2006.
O'Regan, T. *Australian National Cinema*. London/New York: Routledge, 1996.
Pejkovic, M. "An interview with *Oranges and Sunshine* director Jim Loach". Matt's Movie Reviews (n.d.), URL: http://www.mattsmoviereviews.net/spotlight-interview-oranges-and-sunshine.html (05.01.2012).
Rayner, J. *Contemporary Australian cinema: An introduction*. Manchester: Manchester University Press, 2000.
Routt, W. D. "Story of the Kelly Gang, The". In: MacFarlane, B. / Mayer, G. / Bertrand, I. (eds.). *The Oxford Companion to Australian Film*. Oxford: Oxford University Press, 1999, p. 473.
Russo, A. *Oranges and Sunshine: Production Notes*. Cinema: International Rome Film Festival Competition (2011), URL: http://press2010.romacinemafest.org/FOTO%20E%20PRESSBOOK%20ITA/SELEZIONE%20UFFICIALE/CONCORSO/ORANGES%20AND%20SUNSHINE/PRESSBOOK/Pressbook_EN.pdf (14.01.2012).
Screen Australia. *The Drama Report 10/11. Production of Feature Films and TV Drama in Australia*. Screen Australia (2011), URL: http://www.screenaustralia.gov.au/documents/SA_publications/DramaReport.pdf (05.01.2012).
Street, S. *British National Cinema*. London/New York: Routledge 1997.
UK/Australia Co-Production Treaty Films co-production agreement between the government of Australia and the government of the United Kingdom of Great Britain and Northern Ireland. Canberra (1991). URL:
http://www.ukfilmcouncil.org.uk/media/pdf/8/9/UK-Australia_1990.pdf
http://www.sa-minihost.com/coproductions/copro-documents/Treaty_UK.pdf (05.01.2012).

FILMOGRAPHY

Australia (2008). Dir. Baz Luhrmann. Australia/USA/UK.
Breaking the Waves (1996). Dir. Lars von Trier. Denmark.
Crocodile Dundee (1986). Dir. Peter Faiman. Australia.
Hilary and Jackie (1998). Dir. Anand Tucker. UK.
Kes (1969). Dir. Ken Loach. UK.
Ladybird, Ladybird (1994). Dir. Ken Loach. UK.
Land and Freedom (1995). Dir. Ken Loach. UK/Spain.
Moulin Rouge! (2001). Dir. Baz Luhrmann. USA/Australia.
Oranges and Sunshine (2011). Dir. Jim Loach. Australia/UK.
Rabbit-Proof Fence (2002). Dir. Philip Noyce. Australia.
Strictly Ballroom (1992). Dir. Baz Luhrmann. Australia.
The History of the Kelly Gang (1906). Dir. Charles Tait. Australia.
The Leaving of Liverpool (1992). Miniseries. Dir. Michael Jenkins. Australia/UK.
William Shakespeare's Romeo + Juliet (1996). Dir. Baz Luhrmann. USA.

CANADIAN CINEMA AND EUROPEAN CULTURE: *THE RED VIOLIN* (FRANÇOIS GIRARD, 1998)

Jörg Türschmann

In the following lines, I will try to characterize *The Red Violin* referring to its paradoxical transnational appeal. Indeed, it is its specificity that has turned the film into an esteemed masterpiece of Canadian cinema, incorporating different countries, époques, and characters. Mainly European culture represented by Italian's 17th century handcraft has provoked the reception of the film as a promising example for Canadian film production. In summary, my concern correlates to the question if a national cinematography could be founded on transnational spheres.

Higbee and Lim (2010, p. 9) ask "if the term 'transnational' is entirely necessary in the above cases. For example, could we instead speak respectively of a supranational Chinese [or Canadian] cinema, a regional cinema or a pan-European cinema? This returns us to the question of what exactly is the critical purchase of the term 'transnational'". According to the narrative complexity of *The Red Violin*, any critical approach seems to be illusive or to go astray. The story of the violin depicts several scenes showing different "intratextual" audiences all over the world where the violin is in action (McIlroy, 2002, p. 191): "[…] *The Red Violin* creates specific intratextual audiences with historically contingent viewing formations. In the end, Girard's films are poststructuralist-influenced works that essentially aspire to make extratextual academic audience studies redundant." Related to this conception, the work seems already to be done. All is *within* the film and nothing *beyond*. At least, audience analysis seems to be obsolete, because audience variety forms part of the film itself. It should be asked if this conviction compasses a fundamental misleading confusion of the object and its investigation, a blending of audiences in concert halls and film theatres. Apart from the existing diverging studies on the structure and ideological functions of *The Red Violin*, Higbee and Lim state concerning audience analysis (2010, p. 18):

> It [the concept of 'transnational' cinema] may also wish to pay attention to the largely neglected question of the audience and to examine the capacity of local, global and diasporic audiences to decode films as they circulate transnationally (not only in cinema theatres but also on DVD and online), constructing a variety of meanings ranging from adaptation and assimilation to more challenging or subversive readings of these transnational films.

There are only very few strongly critical studies and reviews on *The Red Violin* (Gajan, 1998; Jones, 2002; Longfellow, 2001; Malvinni, 2003). In the majority of cases, the analysis of the brilliant music and the excellence of camera and sound technique replace the examination of "all forms of cross-border film-making activities" and should be revised (Higbee and Lim, 2010, p. 18).[1]

Distinguishing Marks of *The Red Violin*

The Red Violin, directed and co-written by François Girard, is an international co-production, released in 1998. The producer Niv Fichman from the Canadian Rhombus Media allied various production companies, among them the Italian Mikado Production and the English Channel Four Films.[2] In summary, the Canadian companies contributed to only twenty-five percent of the film's funding, as Fichman stated: "That is important as we move toward making bigger and better films in this country" (cit. by Longfellow, 2001, p. 7).

Director Girard is Québecois, *The Red Violin* was shot in American and British English, Italian, French, German, and Mandarin. The director called his feature film a "biography" of the violin (cit. by Malvinni, 2003, p. 59). The movie depicts a violin's journey from the 17th century to an auction in today's Montreal, and the instrument travels through many countries, from Cremona to Vienna, from Oxford to Shanghai. The creator of the violin is Nicolò Bussotti (Carlo Cecchi), Antonio Stradivari's alter ego (1644/1648-1737). One of its later owners, Frederick Pope (Jason Flemyng), represents a kind of English 'Paganini' (1782-1840). According to the plot, an impressive number of famous actors starred in the film. In addition to Cecchi and Flemyng, Samuel L. Jackson plays the assessor Charles Morritz in Montreal, Jean-Luc Bideau is the child prodigy's impresario Georges Poussin in Vienna, Greta Scacchi represents Pope's muse Victoria Byrd in Oxford, and Sylvia Chang in the Shanghai episode portrayed the Maoist Xiang Pei, influenced by bourgeois culture by her mother, who played the famous violin before the Red Guards assumed power.

Prior to the film shooting, the renowned John Corigliano composed the music, while the star soloist Joshua Bell played the violin part and contributed his personal ideas to the future film project with regard to the musical composition. Corigliano won an Oscar for Best Music in 2000, when the music was also nominated for a Grammy and, respectively, *The Red Violin* for a Golden Globe Award.[3]

---

1 Higbee and Lim precise their conception of the transnational in the field of film studies as follows (2010, p. 17-18): "In this regard, transnational film studies parallel the trajectories and power dynamics of transnational cinema: while border-crossing is the raison d'être of both transnational cinema and its studies, borders continue to be heavily policed and entry often comes with a price tag which can sometimes be waived if in possession of the right papers. If transnational subjects can be grouped into 'those who 'circulate capital' and those 'whom capital circulates'' (Žižek), transnational cinematic flow is also, 'contrary to the metaphor the word invokes', not 'a spontaneous force of nature, but shaped and produced by various social, economic and cultural forces' (Berry and Pang)."

2 Moreover, New Line International Releasing, Canada Television and Cable Production Fund, Telefilm Canada – Equity Investment Programm, CityTV, Bravo! New Style Arts Channel, Sony Classical, and with the assistance of the Canadian Film and Video Tax Credit (cf. Walz, 2002, p. 345).

3 The music was published on CD (Corigliano et al., 1999), commentated by the composer (Taxton, 1999), and scientifically analyzed (Deall, 2008).

Musical Structure

Anthology films have the following traits (Lommel, 2005; Treber, 2005, p. 113-119): successive simultaneity ("implosion of the episodic difference"), heterotopias, heterochronias, coincidence and necessity, as well as in the case of *The Red Violin*, the coalescence of human being and object, so that the impression is created that not only do the musicians play the instrument, but that the instrument plays with its players. As said, the following will deal with some aspects of the "all forms of cross-border film-making activities". These are to be searched for in *The Red Violin* in its international co-production, as well as in the plot, which binds the film together.[4] Though the distances between the different countries are becoming bigger and bigger corresponding to the new means of transportation, the intervals are becoming shorter and shorter: 100 to 110 years, then 65, then 30. Girard explains that this was not intended from the beginning, it only came about during the writing process (Girard and Fourlanty, 1999, p. 18-19). So, indeed there exists an "implosion of episodic difference", which in the end provides for a suspense-packed showdown.

Though *The Red Violin* cannot be assigned to one distinct genre, the music which can be heard is a significant trait of Girard's movie, be it, that it resounds from an offscreen voice and is a conventional *mood score*, be it, that the sound sources are to be classed among the visible or insinuated image space. Instrumental music and singing without lyrics are frequently considered to be uniting people of different nations, because there are no language barriers that need to be broken through. "This film can be considered a 'natural co-production' – all the more perhaps in respect of its focus on music with its cross-cultural appeal" (Baltruschat, 2003, p. 162). However, it is so that the composition and musical genre are of course anchored in a local culture. *The Red Violin* deals with 'classical' music of European master composers from the 17th to the 20th century, and in one sequence, with music of Romani tradition.

The prominence of European art music has encouraged academic film studies to also interpret the narrative structure of *The Red Violin* as a musical one. "Making film is making music", director Girard was quoted as saying, which is why he chose the violin to be the protagonist of his film (Cohen, 2002, p. 220-221). It is according to Cohen like the fundamental tone of a musical piece and forms the central reference. When it is spoken about the violin in the film, this can, in the musical sense, be considered a 'suspension'. Regarding *The Red Violin*, Cohen distinguishes between the "Large-scale form" and the "small-scale structure"[5] (Cohen, 2002, p. 223-227): concerning the "Large-scale form", according to his opinion, the film is akin to a rondo. For this reason, she structures the film as follows: "The structure of the film then resembles a musical rondo of the form ABACADAEAFA with the refrain A (auction) and episodes B (Italy), C (Austria), D (Oxford), E (China), and

4 *The Red Violin* is not a compilation movie like *Ten Minutes Older (The Trumpet)* and *Ten Minutes Older (The Cello)* (2002) dealing with the topic of time, for which the producer Nicolas McClintock had short films shot by renowned directors.

5 The term 'small-scale structure' indicates repetitions of motifs as in music. In *The Red Violin*, such motifs are stairways and mirrors with their metaphorical function.

F (Montréal)" (Cohen, 2002, p. 225). However, by this means, the film's structure is described in a very simplified manner, which Cohen justifies with the fact that she searches for the cognitive function of "Large-scale form" and "small-scale structure" and that these respectively are defined by their cognitive function. In this sense, she refers to a transnational, transgressive dimension, as long as the reception takes place in a cultural sphere in which the form of the rondo is counted among musical experience.

The director Girard composed his film from start to finish as a compact piece of work (Girard and Fourlanty, 1999, p. 18-21). The structure is that of a film which consists of five episodes,[6] while his previous Glenn Gould movie consists of thirty-two. The cohesion results from the different narrators: one looks into the future, the other into the past. They combine five roles of the violin: stillborn child, highly gifted child, excessively sexually indulgent adult, mature socially competent woman and the era of the master, when the character Morritz refers back to Bussotti. Overall, there exists a circular structure.

Girard regards this composition as the attempt to animate the violin in the form of a biography.[7] This is why he also considers himself an archeologist, who draws his conclusions of the existing remains and depends on these. Unlike Cohen suggests, the film is far more complex despite its compact form. In particular, the significant role of the maid should be mentioned, who, as Bussoni's wife who is soon to die, foretells the future with the aid of tarot cards. Furthermore, one should mention the sequence during which the Roma bring the violin to England on their journey from Austria. Taking account of Cohen's suggestion, there exist the following units: A (auction), B (Italy), C (Austria), D (Oxford), E (China), F (Montréal), G (gypsies), H (tarot). The structure then is as follows: B,A,H,B,A,C,H,G,A,D,A,E,A,H,E,F,B,F,A,H. Viewed in this light, the auction is no longer clearly recognizable as a 'refrain'. However, it should be acknowledged that the film lends varying degrees of substance to the settings, because Italy is particularly closely connected with the tarot card game, and the auction with the scenes in Montreal, and these are periods of the film that last rather long.[8] The movie's plot leads into in a conventional narrative without leaps in time and ends in Montreal with a view on the USA. Still, there is no pronounced hierarchy between episodes and 'refrain', because in the tarot game, the future is already present in the form of its prediction. And this is why the tarot cards are also still shown after Morritz's departure in the film's final images.

6 See Baltruschat (2003, p. 163).

7 Scenes in Egypt, India and France during the Second World War were envisaged. But since they had nothing to do with the violin, they were omitted (Girard and Fourlanty, 1999, p. 18).

8 That several plot and time levels are brought together in a final countdown is more typical of genre films, such as in the international co-production *Spy Game* (USA/Japan/Germany/France, Tony Scott, 2001), whose plot is set in different countries. However, the difference to *The Red Violin* is that the main characters continuously appear. If the change of protagonists is considered a requirement for an anthology film (Lommel, 2005, p. 132), then *Spy Game* is not an anthology film. Though in *The Red Violin*, the violin is always the center of attention, Lommel considers the film as an anthology film due to its 'heterochronia' (Lommel, 2005, p. 132).

The Red Violin and Folk Music

The transgressive culture of the Western world stands under the sign of the US-American entertainment industry, which is to a considerable degree influenced by cinema. At a first glance it may seem that *The Red Violin* is an example of *art house* cinema due to its complex structure of time and space, the sophisticated music and the artistic ambience. However, the appealing visual aesthetic, the quality of the music, the suspense and eccentricity of the plot point into another direction. *The Red Violin* is a film which approaches the popular mainstream without becoming absorbed by it:

> *The Red Violin* is our example of a mass-audience film, a major release by a major studio [...]. [...] I do not hesitate to caution, however, that even as a box-office success, this film does not speak to a true majority of the American population, as say a Spielberg mega-release does. Nor is it calculated as such. *The Red Violin* is rather a perfect example of the transposition of art film values into the arena of mass release. (Malvinni, 2003, p. 53)[9]

Therefore, the movie's marketing employed strategies of public cinema. As Malvinni notes (2003, p. 59-63), the fact that the instrument maker Bussotti painted the violin with the blood of his late wife is declared a "dark secret" and withheld. In the film itself, the music loses its autonomy, because it becomes subordinate to the picture and the anecdotal and is exploited. Still more: The music is reduced to stereotypes, just as the people who appear as musicians.

> However, according to the musicological stand of "authenticity", the source music (so-called "diagetic" [sic] music), by contrast, is a catastrophe. The divide in Corigliano's score between source and non-source music exhibits the difficulties and paradoxes involved in source integration for historical scenes. (Malvinni, 2003, p. 60)

This, according to Malvinni, especially applies to the sequence during which the Roma as a traveling people bring the violin from Austria to England. They are marked by a series of stereotypical attributes – "lust, energy, rebirth, traveling through time and space" (Malvinni, 2003, p. 61). More objectionable, according to Malvinni's opinion, however, is that Corigliano composed pseudo gypsy music which between on and off accompanies the images of the journey to England, while the performers do not speak a word. As they arrive in England, the master violinist Pope takes the violin off their hands, for which in return they are permitted to camp on his land and attend his concert. So while the gypsies stole the violin in the first place, now the land owner Pope is the thief. When the Roma woman, who played the violin during the journey, hears Pope playing during the concert, she ungrudgingly acknowledges that the instrument belongs in Pope's hands and ultimately, she applauds. This scene is remarkable, for it came about because the body of the actor portraying Pope, Jason Flemyng, complemented the hands and arms of violinist Joshua Bell and yet another musician in such a way that the others were standing behind him, so all three seemed like one person (Baldassarre, 2003, p. 66). Thus, the authenticity is lost in multiple ways: the music is neither on nor off, it does not

9 See Girard and Fourlanty, 1999, p. 25.

derive from any folk-like tradition, and it was not recorded using direct sound, where the integrity of the musician's body should have been respected.

One episode of the film is, as mentioned, set in China. The violin is brought there by Pope's servant and, indirectly, is acquired by a violinist. When Mao comes to power, the violinist's daughter saves the instrument, since it is a symbol for bourgeois culture and must be burned. In a tribunal, a party member explains that China prefers folk music from its own country, which is why all Western influences must be extinguished. It seems as if this episode of *The Red Violin* justifies the previous betrayal of Roma culture, as the radical effacement of Western musical culture is undoubtedly criticized here, whereby the violin becomes the symbol for the Western world and its precedence. "Socialism, as it is represented in the film by the violent and reactionary fanaticism of the Red Guard, is discredited as an historic aberration whose real crime consists of its inability to appreciate the transcendent values of the Western classical canon" (Longfellow, 2001, p. 15).

Authenticity and Commodity Character of the Violin

The China episode is, for some critics, the most expressive, because the violin as protagonist attains its highest degree of maturity (McIlroy, 2002, p. 190). From this perspective, the violin in this frame of the film is an independent actor who in quick succession travels through time as in none of the other episodes. If director Girard claims that he wants to relate the biography of the instrument, then he most assuredly does not intend to historically document the story of a single specimen. Instead, he invents an ideal type which embodies all characteristics of violins of the famous Italian luthier tradition. However, the violin is distinguished for its color and thereby should possess a unique character, even if this is fictitious. And the film does not stay loyal to this fiction, so as a result, the violin is not the protagonist after all, but only a pretext, with the purpose of introducing the characters to each other (Gajan, 1998). This criticism aims to demonstrate that the violin has no personality. In the case of the China episode, just about any violin could be concerned, since ultimately, it ends up in the attic with many others of its kind, and its own story is pushed into the background in favor of the characters. Thereby, also for the audience, it cannot become a cult object.

Indeed also the director's comments point into this direction and contradict the intention to relate a violin's biography, for the historical facts are of secondary importance, as Girard explains (Baldassarre, 2003, p. 64). Though the script writer Don McKellar and Girard studied the stories of many violins, they are only in the background of the plot. The story of the characters was more important, most notably that Bussotti built the violin for his child. Therefore, the Viennese boy is a real violinist, Jason Flemyng on the other hand, who personifies the alter ego of Paganini, is an actor. Consequently, the child can truly play the violin. The violin was meant for a child, and in the end, Morritz gives it to his daughter.

For Girard it seems to have been necessary to be authentic in the relationship between instrument and musician, more specifically in the way how the actors hold the instrument: "Some of the actors, for example, had to learn how to hold it, how to turn it, how to look at it. It was very complicated. So there was the workshop scene in Cremona where the violinmakers are working, and they were real violinmakers. They offered authenticity without too much effort" (Baldassarre, 2003, p. 65). Thus, the young Viennese master violinist Christoph Koncz transforms into an actor, whereas Jason Flemyng, portraying Pope, does not quite succeed at transforming into the violinist. Therefore, when it comes to close-ups, Girard uses images of Joshua Bell's left hand and of the elbow of another violinist, who wields the bow. "So these players had to be in perfect sync. I called that the octopus" (Baldassarre, 2003, p. 65). Thus, in all these cases, authenticity signifies making the physical contact between instrument and player believable. For this, musicians had to learn how to be actors, and actors how to portray musicians. The only real musician with a leading part in *The Red Violin* is a child.

Girard understands authenticity as detached from time and space. It is the mysterious moment of encounter between human being and object, in which both merge into a higher entity and in which culture obtains its highest level of maturity. "*The Red Violin* follows not a person or a coat, but an idea: the idea that humans in all times and places are powerfully moved, or threatened, by the possibility that with our hands and minds we can create something that is perfect" (Ebert, 1999)[10]. The mastership in instrument making and musical play are combined into a cultural peak performance. However, it is right here where Marxist criticism sees a weak point:

> What the film really poses as the antidote to the vulgar and ostentatious circuit of exchange mediated by money, are the higher spiritual values of bourgeois romantic aesthetics. Within this latter context, Art is given as the realm of timeless truth and authenticity. Like religion, it is the medium through which the individual transcends the material limitations of time, place, class or gender in order to connect to the ineffable mysteries of life. From a very different vantage point, of course, these are also the ideological values of the commodity: "mystical," Marx writes, "theological and metaphysical." (Longfellow, 2001, p. 15)

As a foundation for this mystification, Longfellow assumes the violin's commodity character, which objectifies the human relationships:

> Now the attribution of mystical and transcendental powers to a thing is precisely the formula that Marx uses to describe commodity fetishism, where fetishism refers to that process under capitalism where social relations – the division of labour, for example – takes the form of relations between things. One of the axioms of globalization theory is that this reification of social relations has intensified in the period of late, transnational capitalism to the point where even the private realms of bodily pleasures and pains, spiritual enlightenment or aesthetic contemplation are subject to complete and utter colonization by the market. (Longfellow, 2001, p. 14)

10 Richard Alleva (1999) takes an entirely different view. In his opinion, the violin is neither a symbol nor an animated being, nor does it merge into a hybrid with its player or possessor. Instead, it stands solely for itself, independent of the differing understanding of its users and owners: "The instrument can, of course, be regarded as a symbol of art itself, and the uses of it by its different owners display the various attitudes toward art through the ages-aristocratic pleasure, enemy of ideology, etc. But the double-headed surprise ending makes you realize that the red violin, finally, cannot be a symbol, since a symbol stands for something and serves a meaning, while the violin's ultimate destiny is simply to be and not to serve anyone's view of what art signifies."

The commodity fetishism should at this time be interpreted as a transnational phenomenon in the capitalist countries of the West. The same applies to its side effects: the reification of human relationships and the concealment of power. Thus, finally, the ending of the film, when the violin is brought into the core country of Western capitalism, the USA, can be interpreted as a completion of this tendency.

Eluned Jones, who mentions, but does not comment on Longfellow's main theses (Jones, 2002, p. 349), gives an example of an interpretation which gainfully takes account of this reification of human relationships. Jones compares the violin's fate with Frankenstein's story. The blood-painted violin should enable the deceased child in the instrument to survive and 'personifies' a being which must not die. Thus, the Viennese child prodigy Kaspar is an exception, because he dies at the feet of the prince before he can play the first note, and his death is the violin's true performance. The violin is mother and child simultaneously, because it consists of the mother's blood and was intended for her child. So, the violin never finds itself. Playing it is also no authentic expression of love and affection for the children, because they do not understand the rendering's purpose. If a child listens to the mother's violin playing, the relationship between musician and instrument achieves a special effect even then when the performance is not a musical master stroke. But the child does not recognize the affection the mother wishes to express by the means of her playing. In the China episode, the master violinist's daughter takes the violin out of its hiding place and amateurishly plays the film's musical theme to her son in order to convey to him the love she has for the instrument as well as for him:

> Pope's performances, for all their virtuosity, never achieve the resonance of Xiang Peis's quiet performance for her son. [...] In Xiang Pei's playing for her son, one senses the weight of another hiding-place, the place where love is kept secret, revealing itself tentatively in the playing of the violin. [...] "Worthiness" is therefore conceived of in the movie as being the ability to find that hidden beauty. (Jones, 2002, p. 360)

Although the son should not say anything about the violin, he does betray his mother to the father who is loyal to the system and has the apartment scoured for the instrument. At the end of the film, the hidden beauty plays a role once again. While Morritz departs with the real violin towards his daughter, the Russian master violinist purchases merely a replica by auction without anticipating it. Just as the violin was put into Kaspar's grave and concealed in a dark box in China, Morritz carries the violin to its grave through the forgery.

> If forgetting can be equated with death, as a figurative movement underground, replacing the violin with a false version of itself consigns the violin to an obscure gave. [...] By figuratively killing the violin, Morritz returns it to Bussotti's child, and the loving gift is once more placed securely in the child's hands. (Jones, 2002, p. 361)

The form of existence for the violin, of which the film holds out the prospect, is quite sad, because ultimately, in this interpretation, the violin is buried alive and only in this way can find itself. Jones mentions that for Morritz, the violin was, in the end, the perfect child, the coveted collectible for which he has always searched, and that the notion has something frightening, that we unnoticeably can be replaced by a copy in the public sphere. Jones's interpretation is indeed ingenious, for she formulates with the elements of bourgeois Romanticism the criticism of the reification of the individual and his/her relationships with others, and indirectly draws on the

Marxist reception of Freud, which Herbert Marcuse propounded in 1955 in *Eros and Civilization*.

Criticism of *The Red Violin*

The reason why *The Red Violin* is hailed as a national success in Canada is twofold: first, the film deals with the relation between art and commerce. "Girard establishes the tension between the cool mechanics of business and the genuine ardour of the passionate" (Yacowar, 2000). By this means, the film also expresses the economic pressures exercised on the native film industry due to the proximity of the US-American film market. Second, the response to this competition is to approach Europe, its history and its culture. "Establishing historical Europe before our Montreal reminds us that we live in the context of the historic" (Yacowar, 2000). The film positions itself between mainstream and art house cinema:

> *The Red Violin*, however, distinguishes itself from the run-of-the-mill Hollywood imitation precisely in its overt modeling of itself as European or, more particularly, as a Euro art cinema knock-off. Just at a time, in other words, when Europe, as Jameson puts it, "more wealthy and culturally elegant than ever, a glittering museum to a remarkable past," is confronting its own cultural marginalization and its failure to "generate its own forms of mass cultural production," *The Red Violin* is produced as a tribute to Europe's glorious and irretrievably past cultural hegemony. (Longfellow, 2001, p. 11)

However, *The Red Violin* is not entirely independent of US film. Don McKellar, who wrote the script together with Girard, belongs to the Toronto Group (Walz, 2002, p. XXXI), which was modeled on US independent cinema and was considered a Canadian manifestation of the French New Wave. In this regard, *The Red Violin* is the most ambitious Canadian film of all times, and, after *Porky's* (Bob Clark, USA/Canada, 1982), the second most successful at that time (Walz, 2002, p. XXXII). In its earnestness and orientation towards history, it considered typically Canadian. But other than that, the film is without locus. This is not changed by the fact that the auction takes place in Montreal. "That in itself signals a new direction in Canadian film; it cannot only hold its own on the global marketplace, but it can participate in filmic dialogues that transcend the merely nationalistic" (Jones, 2002, p. 348). The production company Rhombus had the option to have the film produced by US majors. In that case, it would have had to forgo the use of several languages, on which director Girard placed value. Because of this, for the production in Italy, Mikado, and the English Channel 4 were engaged (Acheson and Maule, 2001, p. 125). The American rights were able to be sold beforehand without changing the film's concept. Rhombus reserved further markets for itself. The company had experiences with TV productions of documentaries which were produced with European broadcasters such as ZDF and Arte (Longfellow, 2001, p. 12). For the production of *The Red Violin*, 75% of the costs were taken over by foreign companies (Longfellow, 2001, p. 7).

On the one hand, the success traces back to specifics such as the trick with the octopus method, which attracted reviewers' attention (Jones, 2002, p. 348). On the other hand, there was a fascination for the technical perfection which the music, images and expensive equipment displayed. Through its glossy surface, *The Red Violin* was even discussed in art magazines (Katz, 2009). However, not always was this perfection received well by critics; the film was said to be so good on a technical level that it leaves no room for interpretations (Royer, 1999). Indeed, one scene shows the discussion between Morritz and an acoustics technician, who is only intrigued by the construction of the red violin and does not perceive the aura surrounding the instrument. Technique and art go hand in hand, as Morritz subsequently explains that the violin is not merely a "perfect acoustic machine". But even if only the beautiful images and the good music find recognition, the complexity of the plot, changing locations and times as well as the disparate stock of characters prevent the film from truly carrying its audience. Thereby, the film has something fake, cold and calculated, demonstrates a cosmopolitanism and universalism, which however leaves one unmoved (Lahaye, 1999). The coldness and perfection that *The Red Violin* exudes are also traced back to the internationality of its production, which at least provided it with the necessary attention (Gajan, 1998).

The positive scores regarding the film's composition point exactly into the other direction. Here, it is the perfection which is considered an expression of passion. Yacowar (2000) believes that the film advocates passion. Not only money matters, and perfect art as well as crafts are a cure in a completely profane and material world. Thus, in his opinion, the various episodes depict aspects of Bussotti's original passion. From this perspective, death is read entirely differently: the red violin has a Lazarus soul, as it is also written on Kaspar's grave. For its survival, even other violins in the film are sacrificed, in Bussotti's studio, in China, or at the auction. Though, according to Yacowar, there are several characters who are not just interested in money: Kaspar's instructor Poussin, the Russian violinist Ruselsky at the auction and the pawnbroker in Shanghai. But the violin is an object admired for its perfection, and this perfection is also the key to the success of the film itself:

> But in *The Red Violin* and *Sunshine* [István Szabó, Austria/Canada/Germany/Hungary, 1999] the internationalism derives from strength not insecurity, from the passion of a compelling vision, not commercial expediency. In their post-colonized position the films transcend their national particularity instead of hiding it. The telling difference is between [commercial] project and passion. […] The scope and complexity of both films also speak for the passionate commitment of their respective filmmakers. Neither of these international epics is an expression – or symptom – of that Canadian bugbear, national self-disinterest. Neither pretends to swim in the American commercial mainstream. Rather, both espouse global themes and arenas that suspend the topical concerns of being Canadian for the wider worries of the vanishing human. (Yacowar, 2000, p. 86)

In spite of all the differences, or rather, with the aid of all differences, *The Red Violin* acquires a transnational character. Thus, the perfection indicates Girard's passion for his project and allows for several eras, continents and languages to be combined. André Lavoie even states that the film could be a model for European co-productions, which often only rely on the English language. But he also bears in mind the special relation between Canada and the USA, between French, which is spoken in Montreal, and American English, which Samuel L. Jackson speaks in the film:

> De plus, même s'il faut souligner la farouche détermination de Girard d'adopter la langue du pays où se situe l'action – une belle leçon à donner aux producteurs européens qui ne jurent que par l'anglais, peu importe que le film se déroule dans l'Espagne de Franco, la France occupée ou l'Italie de la Renaissance – l'épisode montréalais n'est pas sans contradictions ni ironie. Samuel L. Jackson débarque à Montréal avec toute son arrogance typiquement américaine, éclipsant les autres, dont sa complice effacée, Madame Leroux (Monique Mercure), forçant tout un chacun à ne parler qu'en anglais. Le Montréal de François Girard ressemble à celui de ces cinéastes américains pour qui le caractère français de la ville demeure au mieux folklorique. Et l'on ne peut s'empêcher de souligner l'ironie autour du vol du violon qui échouera dans peu de temps à New York... Un 'clin d'œil' à la faiblesse de notre dollar? (Lavoie, 1998, p. 9)[11]

It is interesting that a Canadian critic read so many things out of the film and its plot, whereas in Europe, the film is, at most, regarded as Canadian due to its nature of being a co-production; for small national cinematography often bases itself on this strategy in order to find an audience also outside the own nation. In the case of *The Red Violin*, from a European perspective exactly the strength of Canadian cinema is lost, namely the director's personal touch and the depiction of current social problems. "The only remaining attributes of the production thus were the Canadian passports of the director and of some other members of his production team" (Pospíšil, 2011, p. 23).

The Red Violin has the character of a résumé, a search for old values. It conducts itself as in Girard's art installation "La Paresse", which is about laziness concerning a forgotten ideal similar to "slowness, Carpe Diem, the apparently useless and mundane" (Décarie, 1999): His film is the search for the real and true. But this does not work out. Whoever attempts to grasp the dichotomous criticism of the film sees themselves exposed to the dilemma cited at the beginning, to which the "intratextual audiences" point: the possibility of a multitude of readings of the film itself. In this sense, *The Red Violin* can be considered an example for postmodern arbitrariness, which has often shaped 1990s cinema. However, the idea of authenticity is not abandoned. The red violin should be unique, both its construction and its sound. Though, because no film is able to convey the impression of authenticity, but only stage it, the high quality of the images and music remains superficial. Therefore it does not matter that the movie audience is, several times, shown the violin at its vendue in the auction hall, and only learns in the end that it is merely a replica. The fact that this scene is always shown from the perspective of a different participant should have warned the viewer: it all depends on the point of view. But

11 "But even if one takes Girard's wild determination into account to choose the language of the country in which the story is set – a nice lesson for the European producers, who only swear by English, no matter whether the film is set in Franco's Spain, in France during the occupation or in Italy during the Renaissance – the episode in Montreal is not free from contradictions and irony. Samuel L. Jackson in Montreal disembarks with his entire, typically American arrogance, dismisses the others, among them his diffident accomplice Madame Leroux (Monique Mercure), and forces everyone to speak only English. François Girard's Montreal is similar to that of those American film makers for whom the city's French character lives on in folklore at best. And one is not able to avoid emphasizing the irony in light of the theft of the violin, which fails shortly thereafter in New York… A 'wink' towards the weakness of our dollar?" Joshua Bell acquired a Stradivarius in 2001, which was stolen in 1936 and not found until the thief's death in 1985 (Anonymous, 2013).

this epistemological game only becomes viewing enjoyment in the form of the plot's ordinary suspense and does not – as in *eXistenZ* (1999) by the Canadian director David Cronenberg[12] – awaken curiosity concerning the conflicting nature of every insight.

Canadian film criticism sees the eclecticism of *The Red Violin* as a way to dissociate from US cinema and to place Canadian cinema into the international market. The European heritage, from this perspective, seems like a collection of eras and cultures, which is marked by native craftsmanship and musical virtuosity. From a European viewpoint, however, the film's episodes are fraught with perfectly staged stereotypes which can only stem from North America, whereas Canada remains invisible.

BIBLIOGRAPHY

Acheson, A.L.K. / Maule, C.J. *Much Ado about Culture: North American Trade Disputes*. Ann Arbor: University of Michigan Press, 2001.

Alleva, R. "Virtuosi: *The Red Violin & Election*". *Commonweal* 126.19 (1999).

Anonymous. "Joshua Bell". Wikipedia, 2013.

Baldassarre, A. *Reel Canadians: Interviews from the Canadian Film World*. Toronto: Guernica Editions, 2003.

Baltruschat, D. "International Film and TV Co-Productions: A Canadian Case Study". In: Cottle, S. (ed.). *Media Organization and Production*. London: Sage, 2003, p. 149-169.

Cohen, A.J. "Music Cognition and the Cognitive Psychology of Film Structure". *Can. Psychol.* 43 (2002), p. 215-232.

Corigliano, J. (composer) / Bell, J. (violin, vocal, and instrumental) / Salonen, E.-P. (conductor). The Red Violin: *Original Motion Picture Soundtrack*. New York: Sony Classical, 1999.

Deall, M.D. *The Role of Style in John Corigliano's Film Score* The Red Violin *(1999)*. Dissertation (part I). Gainesville: University of Florida, 2008.

Décarie, I. "La Paresse: Installation de François Girard." *Séquences* 205 (1999), p. 5.

Ebert, R. "*The Red Violin*: Movie Review & Film Summary" (1999), URL: http://www.rogerebert.com/reviews/the-red-violin-1999 (08.27.2013).

Gajan, P. "Un violon sans âme. *Le violon rouge* de François Girard". *24 Images* 48 (1998).

Girard, F. / Fourlanty, É. *Le violon rouge*. Saint-Laurent: Les Editions Fides, 1999.

Higbee, W. / Lim, S.H. "Concepts of Transnational Cinema: Towards a Critical Transnationalism in Film Studies". *Transnational Cinemas* 1 (2010), p. 7-21.

Jones, E. "Reconstructing the Past: Memory's Enchantment in *The Red Violin*". In: Walz, E.P. (ed.). *Canada's Best Features: Critical Essays on 15 Canadian Films*. Amsterdam: Rodopi, 2002, p. 347-362.

Katz, B. "*Le Violon rouge* (*The Red Violin*), François Girard (1998)". *Design and Culture* 1 (2009), p. 212-214.

12 The reference to Cronenberg proves the view of script writer McKellar "that a Canadian filmmaker need not to be straitjacketed by some preconception of 'Canadian' experience. Projects of MacKellar's that reflect this aspect of Cronenbergian influence include *The Red Violin*, and even more specifically *Childstar*, where McKellar casts Jennifer Jason Leigh, who he had worked with in *eXistenZ*" (Salmon, 2007, p. 378).

Lahaye, C. "*Le Violon Rouge*: Un Brillant Exercise De Style". *Québec français* 113 (1999), p. 89-90.

Lavoie, A. "'Moi, mon violon ont beaucoup voyagé'. *Le Violon rouge* de François Girard". *Ciné-Bulles* 17.3 (1998), p. 4-5.

Lommel, M. "Überlegungen zur Aktualität des Episodenfilms". In: Schnell, R. / Stanitzek, G. (eds.). *Ephemeres: Mediale Innovationen 1900/2000*. Bielefeld: Transcript, 2005, p. 123-137.

Longfellow, B. "*The Red Violin*, Commodity Fetishism, and Globalization". *Canadian Journal of Film Studies / Revue Canadiennes d'Etudes Cinématographiques* 10 (2001), p. 6-20.

Malvinni, D. "Gypsy Music as Film Music: Spectacle and Act". *European Meetings in Ethnomusicology* 10 (2003), p. 45-76.

McIlroy, B. "The Tuxedoed Fallacy: Intratextual Audiences in Two Films by François Girard". In: Beard, W. / White, J. / Feldman, S. (eds.). *North of Everything: English-Canadian Cinema Since 1980*. Edmonton: University of Alberta Press, 2002, p. 184-191.

Pospíšil, T. "Going Down the Road for *The Red Violin*: A Certain Tendency in Recent Canadian Cinema". *Central European Journal of Canadian Studies* 7 (2011), p. 17-24.

Royer, G. "*Le Violon Rouge* (*The Red Violin*)". *Séquences* 200 (1999), p. 38-39.

Salmon, P. "Don McKellar: Artistic Polymath". In: Melnyk, G. (ed.). *Great Canadian Film Directors*. Edmonton: University of Alberta Press, 2007, p. 363-384.

Taxton, F.A. "John Corigliano on Scoring *The Red Violin*". *Soundtrack* 18 (1999).

Treber, K. *Auf Abwegen: Episodisches Erzählen im Film*. Remscheid: Gardez!, 2005.

Walz, E.P. *Canada's Best Features: Critical Essays on 15 Canadian Films*. Amsterdam: Rodopi, 2002.

Yacowar, M. "Canadian Epics of Passion: *The Red Violin* and *Sunshine*". *Queens Q.* 107 (2000), p. 86-100.

CONTRIBUTORS

Doris Baltruschat is a Research Fellow in the Department of Theatre and Film/Centre for Cinema Studies at the University of British Columbia. Her research foci include globalization and culture, co-productions, media ecologies, digital/interactive and alternative media, and social movements. Her research has been featured in academic journals and books published in Canada, the U.S., England, Australia and China, as well as in her books titled *Global Media Ecologies: Networked Production in Film and Television* (Routledge, 2010), and *Independent Filmmaking around the Globe* (University of Toronto Press, 2014), co-edited with M. Erickson.

Sagrario Beceiro is Assistant Lecturer at the Carlos III University of Madrid, where she is a member of the research group TECMERIN. She has written extensively about media industry, political economy and culture industries in Spain and Latin America. She is a researcher in the Project "Cinema and TV in Post-Transition Spain".

Verena Berger teaches Hispanic Studies at the University of Vienna/Austria. Currently she is a Fellowship Holder at the Netherlands Institute for Advanced Study in the Humanities and Social Sciences (NIAS). She is the author of numerous articles on Spanish and Latin American cinema and culture, as well as the co-author, amongst others, of *América Latina: Identidades y fronteras en el cine y la televisión en la era de la globalización* (2013). Her main areas of research include Cultural Theory, Transnationality in Cinema, Television and Media, and Travel Studies in literature and film.

Ib Bondebjerg is Professor of Film and Media, Department of Media, Cognition and Communication, University of Copenhagen. He is a specialist in documentary film and television and European culture and film and media. Currently, he is co-directing (with Andrew Higson and Caroline Pauwels) the comparative HERA research project *Mediating Cultural Encounters Through European Screens* (2013-2016). His most recent books are: *Engaging with Reality. Documentary and Globalization* (2014), *A Small Region in a Global World. Patterns in Scandinavian Film and Television Culture* (2011, with Eva Redvall) and *Media, Democracy and European Culture* (2008, co-ed.).

Concepción Cascajosa is Senior Lecturer of Television Studies at the Carlos III University of Madrid, where she is a member of the research group TECMERIN. She has written three books and more than twenty essays about television fiction and media history and currently is the director of the MFA Program in Screenwriting for Cinema and TV at Carlos III. She is a researcher in the project "Cinema and TV in Post-Transition Spain".

Carmen Ciller is Senior Lecturer of Film Production at the Carlos III University of Madrid, where she is a member of the research group TECMERIN. She has published articles on film and television production in the framework of the European audiovisual policy. She has participated in the Group of Specialists in Media Diversity in the Council of Europe. She is a researcher in the Project "Cinema and TV in Post-Transition Spain".

Alberto Elena is currently Professor of Media Studies at the Carlos III University of Madrid. His publications include *Los cines periféricos (Africa, Oriente Medio, India)* (Barcelona, 1999), *The Cinema of Latin America* (London / New York, 2003; with Marina Díaz López), *The Cinema of Abbas Kiarostami* (London, 2005) and *La llamada de África. Estudios sobre el cine colonial español* (Barcelona, 2010), as well as various contributions to specialized journals.

Camille Gendrault is Assistant Professor of Film Studies at the University of Bordeaux 3, France. After her thesis at the University of Paris I on *Depictions, Images and Imaginations of Naples in Italian Films* (to be published by Editions L'Harmattan), she has published mainly on Italian cinema and her research is more specifically dedicated to the relationships between urban space, collective identity and film aesthetics. She is currently focusing her attention on intercultural issues.

Matthias Hausmann is Assistant Professor of French and Spanish Literature and Media at the University of Vienna. His research interests focus on Latin American cinema, 19th and 20th century French, Latin American and Spanish literature, and the relations between narrative literature and other media forms (film, visual arts and comic). His publications include *Die Ausbildung der Anti-Utopie im Frankreich des 19. Jahrhunderts* (2009), *Visionen des Urbanen* (2012, co-edited with Kurt Hahn) and *ErzählMacht. Narrative Politiken des Imaginären* (2013, co-edited with Kurt Hahn and Christian Wehr).

Juan Carlos Ibáñez is Senior Lecturer of Spanish Media History at the Universidad Carlos III de Madrid, where he is a member of the research group TECMERIN. He has written extensively about the history of cinema and television in Spain, including articles in the international journals *Memoria i Ricerca*, *Journal of Spanish Cultural Studies* and *Média Morphoses*. He was the co-editor (with Francesca Anania) of the book *Memoria histórica e identidad en cine y televisión* (2009). He is a researcher in the Project "Cinema and TV in Post-Transition Spain".

Miya Komori-Glatz is working on her PhD in intercultural communication at WU Vienna University of Economics and Business. She is co-editor of *Polyglot Cinema: Migration and Transnational Narration in France, Italy, Portugal and Spain* (Berger/Komori, 2010, LIT Verlag) and her research interests focus primarily on language and culture contact in Spanish-, German- and English-speaking contexts.

Manuel Palacio is Professor of Television and Film History at Carlos III University of Madrid, where he is also the Dean of the School of Humanities, Communication and Library Science. He has written eight books and more than one hundred contributions to books, journals and conferences. He is the director of the research group TECMERIN (TV-Cinema: Memory, Representation and Industry) and the leading researcher of the project "Cinema and TV in Post-Transition Spain", funded by the Government of Spain.

Eva Novrup Redvall is Assistant Professor in the Department of Film and Media Studies at the University of Copenhagen, where she is head of the Research Priority Area on Creative Media Industries together with Ib Bondebjerg. She holds a PhD on screenwriting as a creative process and has published a number of articles on Nordic film and television in books and journals. Her latest book is *Writing and Producing Television Drama in Denmark: From The Kingdom to The Killing* (Palgrave Macmillan, 2013).

Irini Stathi is an Associate Professor at the Department of Cultural Technology and Communication of the University of the Aegean (Greece). She is interested in film theory and history, film semiotics and cinema archives and audiovisual memory. She published several books, among which are *Film Theories* (Athens, Egokeros, 2002) and *Signs and Symbols in film Language* (Athens, Egokeros, 2011), and articles such as "The film as archive, the archive as film" (*Cinema and Cie*, 2011).

Jörg Türschmann is Professor for French and Spanish Literature and Media at the Department of Romance Studies, University of Vienna. His research interests are television series, film music, popular culture and transnational relations between Argentine, French, German and Spanish literature and cinema. He has published books on transnationality in cinema and television (*Miradas glocales: Cine español en el cambio de milenio*, with B. Pohl, 2007; *TV global*, 2011, with B. Wagner). His publications include various contributions to manuals, books, conferences and specialized journals dealing with historical contexts of film and television fiction. He has worked as film distributor and as organizer and jury member for film festivals in Germany, France and Switzerland.

Beiträge zur europäischen Theater-, Film- und Medienwissenschaft

hrsg. von Verena Berger, Andrea B. Braidt und Daniel Winkler

Verena Berger; Miya Komori (Eds.)
Polyglot Cinema
Migration and Transcultural Narration in France, Italy, Portugal and Spain

Polyglot Cinema brings together a diverse group of scholars from Europe, Canada and the USA, resulting in a dynamic account of plurilingual migrant narratives in contemporary films from France, Italy, Portugal and Spain.
In addition to the close analysis of key films, the essays cover theories of translation and language use as well as central paradigms of cultural studies, especially those of locality, globality and post-colonialism. The volume marks a transdisciplinary contribution to the question of cultural representation within film studies.
Verena Berger teaches Spanish and Latin American Studies at the University of Vienna. Her main research field is Film Studies and she recently co-published with Mercè Saumell Escenarios compartidos: *Cine y teatro en España en el umbral del siglo XXI* (2009).
Miya Komori is a lecturer at the WU Vienna University of Economics and Business. Her main research interests include semiotics, language and culture contact in Hispanic studies.
Bd. 2, 2010, 248 S., 24,90 €, br., ISBN 978-3-643-50226-1

Daniel Tödt
Vom Planeten Mars – Rap in Marseille und das Imaginäre der Stadt

Alltag im Ghetto, Gewalt auf der Straße, aber ein ungebrochener Stolz auf die sta"dtische Herkunft: Weltweit berichtet Rap-Musik von den verrufenen Ecken der Stadt. Am Beispiel von Marseille diskutiert der vorliegende Band popkulturelle Repräsentationen des Urbanen. Auf der Grundlage von Liedtexten, Musikvideos und Medienberichten zeigt der Autor, dass Rap in und aus Marseille mehr ist als eine lokale Kopie des US-amerikanischen HipHop. Die Musik vermittelt vielmehr Besonderheiten der Mittelmeermetropole, wie sie seit langer Zeit in verschiedenen Feldern der Kultur zum Ausdruck kommen.
Bd. 3, 2. Aufl. 2013, 128 S., 19,90 €, br., ISBN 978-3-643-50360-2

LIT Verlag Berlin – Münster – Wien – Zürich – London

Auslieferung Deutschland / Österreich / Schweiz: siehe Impressumsseite